A Collector's Guide to

Royal Copenhagen Porcelain

Caroline & Nick Pope

4880 Lower Valley Road, Atglen, PA 19310 USA

To
Rev. Tom

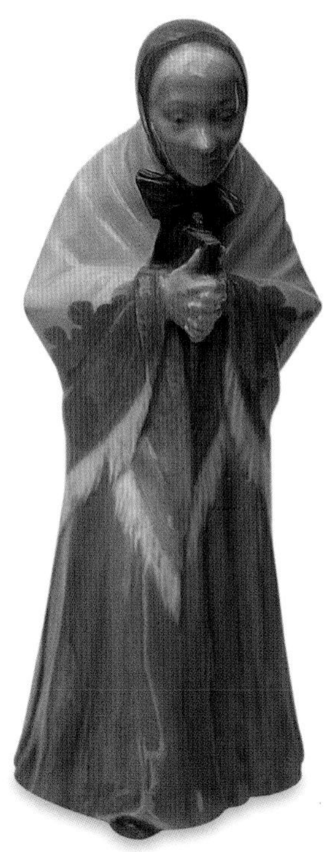

Library of Congress Cataloging-in-Publication Data

Pope, Caroline.
a collectors guide to Royal Copenhagen porcelain / Caroline & NIck Pope.
p. cm.
ISBN 0-7643-1386-X
1. Copenhagen porcelain--Collectors and collecting--Catalogs. 2. Porcelain figures--Collectors and collecting--Catalogs. I. Pope, Nick. II. Title.
NK4399.C6 P66 2001
738.8'2'0948913075-dc1
2001001545

Designed by Bonnie M. Hensley
Cover design by Bruce M. Waters; Cover concept by Charlotte Pope
Cover photographs by St. John Pope
Type set in Zapf Chancery Bd BT/Zapf Humanist BT

ISBN: 0-7643-1386-X
Printed in China
1 2 3 4

Published by Schiffer Publishing Ltd.
4880 Lower Valley Road
Atglen, PA 19310
Phone: (610) 593-1777; Fax: (610) 593-2002
E-mail: Schifferbk@aol.com
Please visit our web site catalog at **www.schifferbooks.com**
We are always looking for people to write books on new and related subjects. If you have an idea for a book please contact us at the above address.

This book may be purchased from the publisher.
Include $3.95 for shipping.
Please try your bookstore first.
You may write for a free catalog.

In Europe, Schiffer books are distributed by
Bushwood Books
6 Marksbury Ave.
Kew Gardens
Surrey TW9 4JF England
Phone: 44 (0) 20 8392-8585; Fax: 44 (0) 20 8392-9876
E-mail: Bushwd@aol.com
Free postage in the U.K., Europe; air mail at cost.

Contents

Acknowledgments

With thanks to:
Margaret, Dave, Rebecca, and Charlotte.
Chris Allen, Melissa Delson, Beatrix Forbes Fine Porcelain, 'Teddies', Wombat, Lee Rosbach, Betty, Joyce, Malcolm & Joan Floyde, M. Potterton, Jane, Colleen, and the many other dealers and collectors from around the world who have helped us along the way. Dreweatt Neate Auctioneers supplied photographs of #544 and #1404.

The Royal Copenhagen Porcelain Manufactory did not authorize this book nor furnish or approve any of the information contained therein. This book is derived from the authors' independent research.

Introduction

This book is intended to give both collectors and dealers an insight into the various and numerous figurines produced by Royal Copenhagen. It is impossible to give a fully comprehensive guide to the figurines produced but the reader will find listed well over 1300 different underglaze and overglaze figurines.

We have attempted to give as much information as possible about each piece but this is limited by the reference material available.

Until 1997 virtually no information was easily available on Royal Copenhagen figurines. The publication of Robert J. Heritage's book *Royal Copenhagen Porcelain Animals and Figurines* gave an insight into the diversity of the factory's output, particularly so far as underglaze models are concerned. This book is also a must for collectors in that it gives much more detailed descriptions of many of the more easily obtainable pieces.

Short History of Royal Copenhagen

The Royal Copenhagen Porcelain Manufactory was founded in 1775 by Frantz Henrich Muller. It is alleged that the Queen Dowager Julian Marie suggested the three wavy blue lines symbolizing Denmark's three ancient water-ways from the Cattegat to the Baltic – the Sound, the Great Belt, and the Little Belt.

Philip Schou took over the porcelain factory in 1884 and moved it from its original position in Kobmagergade to Frederiksberg, the site of the 'Aluminia' faience factory which he had run and partly owned since 1868. Here the factory had far more space at its disposal and, being situated beside the historic Frederiksberg Gardens and adjacent to the Zoological Gardens, the sculptors and decorators had easy access to inspiration both for animal subjects and flora and fauna decoration for vases, plates, and other wares.

Schou designed and built new, larger machines and also introduced new equipment.

In 1885 Schou appointed a young architect called Arnold Krog as art director. Krog had spent the previous five years restoring the Frederiksborg Castle, prior to that studying the making of majolica in Italy.

The first piece of underglaze — a vase by Arnold Krog — was bought by the Duke of Sutherland in 1885 only six months after Krog had made his first experiment with underglaze. The Royal Copenhagen Porcelain Manufactory exhibited a small collection of its new underglaze pieces at both the Northern Exhibition in Copenhagen in 1888 and The Paris Exhibition in 1889. Despite the modest proportions of the display, it caused great international sensation. One of the leading sculptors and painters in the early days was C. F. Liisberg who, in association with F. Aug. Hallin, mastered the underglaze technique particularly on vases and plates. It was Erik Nielsen who was the first to produce an underglaze painted figure of an animal (a dog). Hallin later joined Bing & Grondahl, where he introduced the underglaze technique.

Arnold Krog, who was given the honorary title of Professor, was Artistic Director from 1895 – 1915 when he took on the role of artistic adviser until his death in 1931. He reintroduced overglaze painting at the factory at the beginning of the twentieth century. At this time, overglaze and some plain white porcelain became known as the 'Juliane Marie Porcelain' and was marked with a crown in addition to the three wavy lines to avoid confusion with the original overglaze work of the eighteenth century.

A notable part of the development of overglaze was played by Carl Martin-Hansen, who modeled a series of figures in Danish national costume – still highly sought after today.

Whilst each item produced by the factory was given a number and for the most part numbers on figurines seem to be unique, a few early numbers have been used more than once (for instance we know of at least eight marked '1'). In addition, different sized vases of the same shape had the same number with a suffix (i.e. 45a, 45b, 45c, etc.). Some of the dinnerware also has a slightly different marking system in that parts which go together may have a decimal number if available separately and thus the Weeping faun on stand is 1188, the faun alone is 1188.1 and the stand 1188.2. This applies to a much greater extent to dinner ware such as cups and saucers or dishes and lids. Christian Thomsen alone produced at least 250 pieces, including figurines, plates, bowls, and vases.

In 1987 Royal Copenhagen amalgamated with Bing & Grondahl. At the same time production of many pieces was halted and a number of Bing & Grondahl pieces were produced under the Royal Copenhagen name. Initially pieces were produced with the Bing & Grondahl number but the Royal Copenhagen stamp, and subsequently these were re-numbered using old Royal Copenhagen numbers. It is therefore common to find the same piece numbered in two different ways or two pieces with the same number. Where possible, original Bing & Grondahl pieces have been identified in the comments and a list is provided in the Appendix.

To further confuse identification, many of the Royal Copenhagen pieces still in production have a modern number which bears little or no relation to the number assigned when first produced. Once again, a list is given in the Appendix though this may not be comprehensive.

Materials and techniques

Listed below are some of the types of wares and decorative finishes produced by the factory with brief descriptions to aid identification.

Porcelain

Hard paste porcelain originated in China but it was not until the middle of the eighteenth century that European chemists were able to duplicate the quality which the Chinese had been producing for hundreds of years. The particular feature is the high temperature at which the porcelain is fired (around 900°C for first firing and 1440°C during glazing).

Faience

The temperature at which faience is first fired is higher (1250°C) but after glazing is lower and so a wider range of colors can be used under the glaze. It appears that the factory also continued to use slip, i.e. using colored clays for decoration before firing. Faience was marketed by the factory under the trade name Aluminia (trade mark below).

Stoneware

Stoneware is basically the same constituents as faience, though gray clay is used in place of white. Firing temperatures are 900°C and 1300°C respectively.

Underglaze Decoration

The porcelain is allowed to dry after casting and then decorated by hand. After painting, the piece is covered with an opaque layer which melts in the final firing to become clear. The pigments used only show their color after firing and decorators have to be extremely skilled as they cannot see shades of color, which depend on the thickness of the pigment. Originally only blue was used but then red and green were added followed by gray and brown. It will be seen that an extraordinary range of colors and effects can be achieved. As all the figurines are hand painted there can be considerable variations in finish. Generally, the stronger colors seem to be in most demand.

Blanc de Chine

A porcelain with a special glaze which is pure white.

Overglaze Decoration

In this case a wide range of colors are applied on top of a white glaze. The figures are fired at least twice at 800°C. This technique of lower temperature firing allows for a wider range of colors and the plate pictured was apparently used as a palette by a decorator at the factory and has 70 discrete colors. Gold and silver are added before the final firing and are polished by hand.

Cracquelé

First produced in 1910 and perfected about 1920 by C. F. Ludvigsen, it is produced by allowing for different rates of shrinkage during the second firing resulting in a network of cracks being formed during cooling. Then color is applied into the cracks and a further protective glaze applied.

There are a number of other finishes, though these are less common, i.e. parian, gray porcelain (see #1864), sang de boeuf, 'sung' glaze, 'olivin', crystalline, and oeil de chat.

Chapter 1.
Factory Marks, Dating, and Sculptors

Prior to 1894 Royal Copenhagen porcelain was identified only by three wavy blue lines and between 1894 and 1935 three different factory stamps were used. Between 1935 and 1968 a more accurate annual system was introduced, after which marks identified a five year period.

On pieces with large bases it was possible to put the full factory mark but we have found from experience that even the largest of pieces sometimes lack the factory mark; however, the three blue lines are always present.

On smaller pieces where there is not the space for the full mark there are, in addition to the three wavy lines, a piece number and painter's number, with either the word Denmark and a crown or just Denmark.

In the vast majority of cases on underglaze pieces, the factory stamp and model number are in green and the painter's number or initials are in blue.

1894 – 1897

1898-1923

1923 – 1935

Painter's numbers were dropped in favor of lower case initials around 1928, so the photos that follow show pieces produced 1923 – 1928 and 1928 - 1935.

1923 – 1928

1928 – 1935

From 1935 onwards the date was indicated by a bar above or below one of the letters in the factory mark. The full list of date marks will be found below.

Mark for 1938

Small mark with crown.

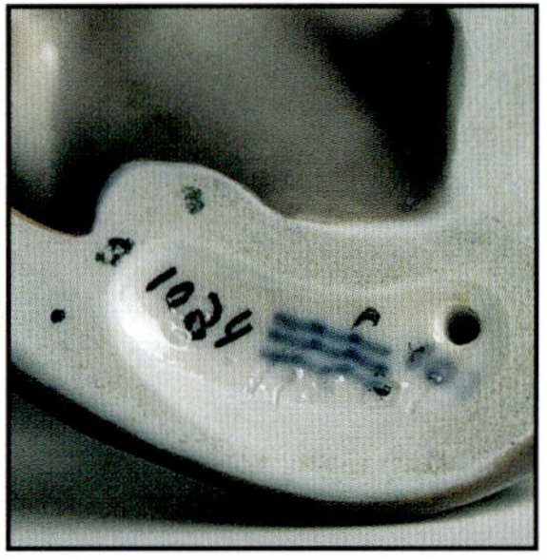

The smallest mark: three wavy lines, piece number, and painter's mark.

Where pieces were produced in different color variations a fractional number was used. The top number is always the color and the bottom one is the model. 0 is the most common and indicates a predominantly white piece.

Some pieces carry the 'PRIVAT' together with a name as well as the usual factory mark. Our information is that when decorators made pieces for themselves they were able to mark them appropriately.

Very occasionally marks are visible on the piece itself as opposed to the base.

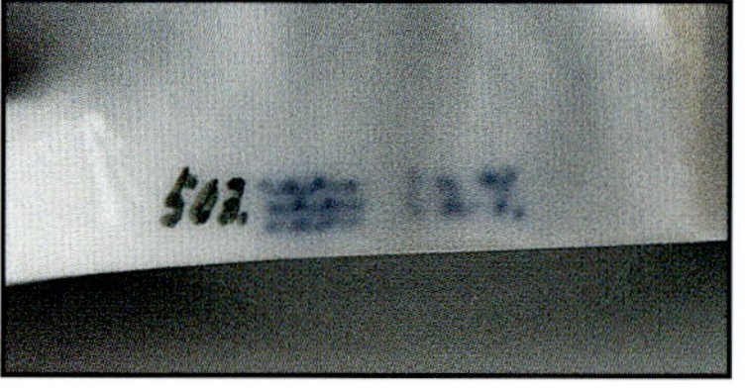

Overglaze and some white pieces produced from 1900 onwards are usually stamped with the 'Juliane Marie' mark.

Sometimes overglaze pieces by Gerhard Henning did not have the 'Juliane Marie' mark.

Dating Codes

On the full mark with Royal Copenhagen Denmark encircling the crown, a small bar (-) is painted above or below one of the letters, indicating a specific year. After 1969, the bar indicated a five year period.

Bar over

1935	1936	1937	1938	1939
R	O	Y	A	L

1940	1941	1942	1943	1944	1945	1946	1947	1948	1949
C	O	P	E	N	H	A	G	E	N

Bar below

R	O	Y	A	L
1950	1951	1952	1953	1954

D	E	N	M	A	R	K
1955	1956	1957	1958	1959	1960	1961

C	O	P	E	N	H	A	G	E	N
1962	1963	1964	1965	1966	1967	1968	69/74	75/79	80/84

From 1985, the bar was above two letters, also indicating a five year period.

85/89	90/94	95/99	00/04
RO	RY	RA	RL

On the smaller marks, the dating scheme is more difficult to confirm but according various sources we believe the system to be:

A strike (l) above

1935	1936	1937	1938	1939	1940	1941
D	E	N	M	A	R	K

A strike (l) below

D	E	N	M	A	R	K
1942	1943	1944	1945	1946	1947	1948

A (u) above

1949	1950	1951	1952	1953	1954	1955
D	K	E	R	N	A	M

A (u) below

D	K	E	R	N	A	M
1956	1957	1958	1959	1960	1961	1962

A (.) over

1963	1964	1965	1966	1967	1968	1969
D	K	E	R	N	A	M

A (.) below for 5 year periods

D	K	E	R	N	A	M
75/79	80/84	85/89	90/94	95/99	00/04	05/09

Overglaze dating

The system used is similar to the that used on the small mark but with a (.) only. However, as this date mark appears to have been added by hand, the mark varies considerably.

Mark under Denmark

K	R	A	M	N	E	D
1935	1936	1937	1938	1939	1940	1941

Mark over Denmark

1942	1943	1944	1945	1946	1947	1948
K	R	A	M	N	E	D

Mark under Copenhagen

N	E	G	A	H	N	E	P	O	C
1949	1950	1951	1952	1953	1954	1955	1956	1957	1958

Mark over Copenhagen

1959	1960	1961	1962	1963	1964	1965	1966	1967	1968
N	E	G	A	H	N	E	P	O	C

Mark in five year periods

69/73	74/78	79/83	84/88	89/93
L	A	Y	O	R

We are reasonably happy with the accuracy of the dating system for underglaze decorated pieces with a full mark but for those with small marks and overglaze pieces we cannot vouch for it.

Seconds (or worse)

Sometimes the factory failed to produce perfection and pieces were marked as 'seconds'. This was done by scratching through the 3 wavy blue lines either with a diamond cutter or a wheel. There are also thirds, fourths, etc. From our experience in looking at many seconds, beauty is in the eye of the beholder. The reasons why some pieces are seconds are sometimes unclear, ranging from minor color variations from the norm to obvious blemishes.

We have also found that with the older pieces (pre-1935), production techniques/quality controls were not as stringent as today. Some early pieces were not marked as seconds even though there are glazing or color defects.

In essence if a piece is rare, attractive, or unusual, the fact that it is a second should not dissuade a collector from buying. In our opinion, if the piece is rare enough and the blemish does not detract, it is worth buying.

Whether to buy a second is a personal matter and some collectors will not tolerate seconds (we have a number of seconds, thirds, and fourths).

Pontil marks

Some of the larger pieces require additional support during firing, resulting in small circular marks beneath the supported area. It is not always possible to eliminate the color variation caused, thus leaving a pontil mark which, in our opinion, does not detract from attractiveness or value.

Glazing flaws

Porcelain is fired at very high temperatures and dark glazes on older pieces tend to be prone to firing defects, particularly to eyes. We feel small glazing flaws are to be expected on pieces over 80 years old.

Damage/Restoration

As restoration techniques are improving all the time, it is more and more difficult to detect restoration to high glaze porcelain pieces. Use of black (ultra violet) light can help but we have been deceived and feel that the best method of detection is touch.

There is no reason to refuse to buy a restored piece provided the price is right and you like it.

Painter's Marks

The table below sets out the numbers and dates of painters and a few of their names up to 1928 when initials were introduced. In some circumstances combining the dates of a painter with the other dating information can date a piece more accurately.

When initials were introduced only two were used for each painter with the addition of 'x' at the end which is similar to *fecit* – painted by.

#	Date/s	Painters Name
12	1897-1931	E Benzon
14	1893-98	
15	1911-1927	Ingeborg Thorup
18	1897-1903	Z Hansen
19	1893-98	
21	1893-95	
26	1897-1931	E Oland
27	1889	Anna Smidth
35	1893-1918	A Nicolaisen
43	1897-1923	A Christensen
47	1897-1931	M Hansen
49	1893-95	
50	1893-1931	L Boll
51	1893-97	
52	1893-1931	
53	1893-1931	E Gad
54	1893-1915	J M Lorenz
55	1893-97	
56	1893-1900	B Mortensen
57	1893-1931	
58	1893-1931	Frl A Richter
59	1893-1908	D S Ost
60	1894-1900	
61	1894-	
62	1895-1931	
63	1895-97	
64	1896-1931	Frl Schacke-Andersen
65	1896-1921	K Kabell
66	1896-1931	Frl I Heine
67	1896-97	
68	1896-99	
69	1896-1901	R Martin
70	1897-1931	J Engelstoft
71	1897-1924	G Klausen
72	1897-1931	
73	1897-1904	A Utke
74	1897-1926	W Amesen
75	1898-1931	
76	1898-1909	C G Jorgling
78	1898-1908	K Braestrup
79	1898-1927	K Rower
81	1898-99	
82	1898-1902	
83	1898-1931	
84	1899-1910	
85	1899-1920	
86	1900-1931	
87	1901-31	
88	1901-10	
89	1902-26	A Christensen
90	1902-31	E Linck
91	1902-20	
92	1902-05	
93	1902-08	

#	Date/s	Painters Name
94	1902-31	
95	1901-31	J Debois
96	1903-24	M Hershind
97	1903-14	K Holm verh Barfoed
98	1903-06	
99	1903-22	Ch Manicus-Hansen
100	1904-11	H Hansen
101	1903-08	
102	1903-13	M Hansen
103	1903-08	
104	1903-08	G Appel
105	1903-	
106	1904-06	
107	1904-06	
108	1904-06	
109	1904-31	E Hassager
110	1904-31	
111	1904-31	J Hanschell
112	1904-19	A Thusen
113	1904-08	E Welding
114	1904-16	Frl E Tychsen
115	1904-05	
116	1904-08	
117	1904	Frl Orsted
118	1904	
119	1904-05	
120	1905-06	
121	1905-12	E Momme
122	1907-10	
123	1907-23	
124	1907-31	
125	1907-14	
126	1907-19	
127	1908-14	
128	1908-31	
129	1908-31	
130	1909-12	
133	1909-17	
134	1909-31	
135	1909-31	
136	1909-31	
137	1909-13	
139	1909-14	
140	1910-20	
141	1910-18	
142	1910-17	D Wright
143	1910-13	
144	1911	
145	1910-12	
146	1910-21	
147	1910-11	
148	1910-14	
149	1910-25	

#	Date/s	Painters Name
150	1910-20	
151	1911	
152	1911-14	
153	1911	K Thomsen
154	1911-27	
155	1911-12	
156	1911-31	
157	1911-14	
158	1911-31	
159	1911-31	
160	1911-12	
161	1911-31	
162	1911-24	T Bruun
163	1912-31	Lund
164	1912	
165	1912-17	
166	1912-18	
167	1912-14	
168	1912-23	H Henrichsen
169	1912	
170	1913-31	
171	1913-19	Kjaer
172	1913-31	
173	1913-31	
174	1913-23	
175	1913-21	
177	1913-23	
178	1914	
179	1914-20	
180	1917-22	
181	1917-19	
182	1919-22	
183	1919-21	
185	1919-20	
186	1919-31	
188	1919-23	
189	1919-28	
192	1920-23	
193	1920-31	
194	1920-31	
195	1920	
197	1920-22	
197	1920-26	
203	1910-18	Astrid Nielsen
211	1917-20	
213	1917-21	

The Sculptors and Their Work

Set out below are the sculptors, their marks, and available information about their work.

Agergaard, Merete (MEA)
535 Polar bear cub standing
536 Polar bear cub feet up
537 Polar bear cub on back
538 Polar bear cub on back

Ahlmann, Michaela (MA)
408 'Good morning' (Girl in nightdress)
427 'Two friends' (child with dog)
468 'Happy trio'

Andresen ? (AND)
0371 Scorpion Fish (Gurnard)

Balslov, Jorgen (JOB)
3131 Dish - crab
3498 Dish - lobster

Benter, Lotte (LB)
1911 - 1914 Modeled 14 figurines (13 listed below) depicting girls in peasant costumes.

Benter Lotte Benter Benter Lotte Benter

1251 Amager girl
1252 Little girl
1314 Girl knitting
1315 Amager girl
1316 Amager girls (shopping)
1317 Woman knitting
1323 Girl from Bornholm
1324 Fanoe Woman
1374 Ballet dancer
1382 Girl with sled
1395 Girls - pair
1398 Greenland girl
1654 Eskimo

Bisen (BI)
1021 Mother holding child

Bonfils, Adda (AB) (1883 – 1943)
Worked 1915 – 1941

AB. AB Adda Bonfils

1739 Child, crawling
1938 Girl with doll
3468 Boy with teddy bear
3476 Terrier with slipper
3539 Girl with doll standing
3556 Boy with umbrella
3647 Drummer
3667 Child with accordion
3677 Girl with pot-cover
3689 Boy with horn
4027 Girl on stone

Bonnesen , Carl Johan (CJB) (1868 – 1933)

C.J.B

320 Polar bear walking
321 Polar bear feeding
330 Clown & 2 dancing bears
471 Percheron
1269 Hippos - pair

Borlwiych, Jessie (JB)
1622 Collie dog lying
1623 Male lion

Bovenschulte, Mogens (MB)
4645 Butcher

Brunoe, Soren (SB)
532 Boy with raincoat

Bussenius (BU)
1096 Marmot

Christensen, Holger (HC) (1890 - 1966)
Most notable 'The Girl with the Horn of Gold'

HC

2604 Boy with pillows
3034 Mother & child
3049 'Henrik & Else'
3070 Sailor boy on plinth
3171 'Knight & Maiden'
3457 Mother with child
3634 Boxer dog standing
3635 Boxer dog lying
3650 Great dane - harlequin
3655 Giraffe
3661 Ashtray
3664 Tray
3665 Tray
4075 Ballet girl (OG)
4187 'Agnete & the Merman'
4374 'Thumbelina'
4503 Schoolgirl
12242 'Girl with the Horn of Gold'

Erhardt, Aage (AE)

ERH

3250 Boy with broom
3272 Boy with sailing boat
3321 Mermaid
3519 Boy with bucket & spade
3542 Boy with ball
4438 'Little Matchgirl'

Eriksen, Edvard (EE) (1876 – 1959)
Best known for 'The Little Mermaid'

Edvard Eriksen

4431 'The Little Mermaid'
5689 'The Little Mermaid'

Fischer, Vilhelm Theodor (VTF) (1857-1928)
2033 Golden eagle (Blue)

Galster, John (JOG)

4631 Girl with cat
4642 Ballet dancer
4648 Girl dressing hair
4649 Teenagers with books
4669 Child on back
4670 Children reading
4680 Boy eating apple
4703 Nude girl turning
4704 Nude girl lying
4727 Plumber
4989 Footballer

Grut, Jeanne (JG) (1927-)
Worked at factory from 1959.

JG

4562 Stoat
4572 Weasels - pair
4593 Corgi
4609 Shetland pony
4611 Shetland pony sitting
4616 Basset hound
4638 Poodle
4643 Tiger
4647 Baboon & baby
4652 Guinea-pig crouching
4653 Foal standing
4654 Mink
4659 Jaguar cub
4676 Rabbit
4678 Jersey cow standing
4682 Budgie on gourd
4683 Jersey cow sitting
4687 Tiger & cubs
4698 Mare & foal
4705 Rabbit
4726 Goat
4744 Goat with kid
4746 Hoopoe
4752 Lippizzanner
4753 Polar bear
4757 Poodle
4760 Kid on rock
4762 Chowchow
4780 Polar bear & cubs
4783 Puma cub
4784 Turkey
4787 Pigeon
4852 Danish bird dog
4882 Horse
4917 Scottie
4918 West Highland White terrier
4952 Old English sheepdog
5136 Golden retriever
5154 Kangaroo
5423 Llasa Apso dog
5690 Mare
5691 Foal

22653 Rabbit
22685 Rabbit
22690 Rabbit
22740 Elephant
22741 Elephant

Hansen, Hans H (HHH) (1894 – 1965)

1997 'Adam & Eve'
2051 Deer on green base
2053 'Leda & the Swan'
2064 Dove
2111 Girl with fawn
2188 Girl & sheep with dove on back
2189 Girl & sheep
2201 Monkeys - pair
2856 'Spring'
2857 'Summer'
2858 'Autumn'
2859 'Winter'
3231 Dish - mermaid
3658 Madonna (OG)
4216 Hans Christian Andersen (OG)
4523 'January' - girl skater
4524 'February' - boy juggler
4525 'March' - girl with posy
4526 'April' - boy with umbrella
4527 'May' - girl with flowers
4528 'June' - boy with briefcase
4529 'July' - girl bathing
4530 'August' - boy with piglet
4531 'September' - girl with satchel
4532 'October' - boy with fruit
4533 'November' - girl in riding habit
4534 'December' - boy with sack
4639 'Helena' - girl with mirror

Hasted, Martha (MH) (1888-1992)

Worked from 1911-1920
1232 Marabou storks
1289 Night heron
2108 Parrot

Hedegaard, Johannes (JH)

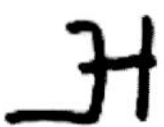

4359 Woman with water jug
4367 'Emperor & The Nightingale'
4377 Bricklayer
4382 'Emperor & Nightingale'
4418 Woman with eggs
4424 Girl plaiting hair
21427 Woman in blue dress

Henning, Gerhard (GH) (1880 – 1967)

1010 Cross legged woman on pedestal
1119 Nymph & faun
1188 Weeping faun on stand
1188.1 Weeping faun
1188.2 Stand for weeping faun
1238 'Princess & The Pea'
1244 Girl with mirror
1476 Fairy Tale I
1586 Fairy Tale II
1646 'Grief'
1664 Fairy Tale III
1796 Man & woman
2109 'The Kiss on the Hand'
2162 Chinese couple
2274 'Ali & Peribanu'
2409 'The Nightingale'
2413 'Moon Girl'
2417 'Venus'
2423 'Susanna'
2428 Girl bathing

Hermissen? (HE)
345 Bear sitting

Herold, Peter (PH) (1879 – 1920)

1034 Coati Mundi
1086 Guinea-fowl
1189 Finches - pair
1204 Bassett puppy
1209 Badger
1281 Guinea-pig
1329 Lynx
1331 Owl long eared
1402 Wolverine
1430 Fox
1440 Lynx
1468 Seagull
1482 Mountain lion
1493 Lark
1504 Wren
1505 Bluetit
1506 Crested tit
1507 Wagtails - pair
1509 Sole
1516 Robin
1600 Partridge - pair
1652 Hound standing
1661 Falcon
1679 Great Dane
1684 Poodle sitting
1688 German Shepherd sitting
1691 Rabbit
1701 Collie
1719 Poodle
1769 Kingfishers
1771 Elephant
1772 Pekingese sitting
1775 Easter egg
1776 Pekingese
1787 Raccoons - pair
1788 Vixen with cubs
1798 Belgian Shepherd reclining
1829 Snowy owl
1830 Boy with bricks
1846 Basket - herons
1859 Dog
1860 Pekingese puppy
1863 Mandarin ducks
1878 Boy with sailing boat
1882 Huskies - pair
1920 Borzoi
1924 Duck - tufted
1925 Duck
1926 Eider duck
1933 Duck - drake
1934 Mallard
1941 Duck - tufted
1951 Pheasants on base
2005 Lady with bird
2065 Tiger gnawing a bone
2068 Geese
2084 Finch
2125 Guinea-fowl
2126 Cat looking back
2127 Seal scratching head
2152 Baboon
2166 Rabbit
2175 Lion cub
2180 Bison
2181 Sitting dog
2202 Stag jumping a mound
2232 Jay on perch
2257 Kingfisher holding fish
2261 Partridge
2387 Husky
2394 Pheasant

Heuch, Jacob Aall (JAH) (1862 – 1913)

4 Walking stick handle - mice
8 Walking stick handle - mice
144 Vase
176 Vase - snake around rim
467 Snowy owl
487 Pen tray - bat
503 Guinea-pig
504 Rabbit begging
509 Curled snake
602 Ashtray
1486 Donkeys - pair
2451 Dish - frog
2452 Bowl - fish
2480 Snail on blotter

Hoffman, Anker (AH)
2970 Mother & child

Howitz (HO)
469 Kangaroo turning

Jacobsen, J (JJ)

C L Jacobsen

0115 Vase
0125 Vase
0186 Vase
0234a Vase
0237a Vase

0247 Vase
0352 Vase
0354 Vase
0730 Vase
0763 Vase
0767 Vase
0873 Vase
0886 Vase

Jahn, Adolf (AJ)
1413 'Nathan the Wise'

Jensen, Dahl (DJ) (1874-1960)

Dahl Jensen

405 Pig
407 Kingfisher
409 Polar bear sitting
410 Titmouse - 'Optimist'
411 Titmouse - 'Pessimist'
415 'Protection' - 3 birds
419 Mouse white
420 Black grouse
423 Cuckoo
428 Gull with fish
429 Gull crying
430 Gull

Jensen, Edinger (EJ)
1479 Cockatoo

Jensen, Lauritz (LJ) (1859 – 1935)

L Jensen

444 Pointer
446 Cow
451 Sealyham
714 Tiger
753 Terrier sitting
804 Lioness
805 Leopardess licking foot
856 Dachshund
1205 Bull (head down)
1268 Lion yawning
1310 Cow - brown
1322 Bloodhound - female
1341 Bloodhound sniffing - male
1343 Leopard
1362 Horse
1465 French bulldog standing
1466 French bulldog sitting
1634 Pointer (head down)
1635 Pointer (head up)

Jensen, Oluf (OJ) (1871-1934)
2208 Sparrow on base

Jespersen, Svend (SJ0)
448 Calf
449 Trout (brown)
450 Cocker spaniel
457 Budgerigar - blue
458 Polar bear sitting
459 Polar bear
474 Robin
478 Up to mom (girl - pick me up!)
489 Old fisherman
491 Nurse

Jonzen, Karin (KJ)
5207 Girl with teddy

Kelsey, Sterrett (SK)
5268 Ballet dancer
5269 Ballet dancer
5271 Ballet dancer
5273 Girl with crown
5605 'Lucy'
5651 Boy on rocking horse
5652 Boy with teddy
5653 Girl with rabbit
5654 Girl praying
5655 Girl with teddy
5656 Girl with snowball
5657 Footballer
5658 Snowman
5659 Girl on toboggan
5660 Boy with dog

Kjaer (K)
370 Seagull spread wings

Krog, Arnold (AK) (1856-1931)
Artistic Director 1895-1916, Artistic Adviser until 1931.

AKrog AK AK

12 Vase
29 Vase
32 Vase
33 Vase
35 Vase
42 Vase
47 Vase
51 Vase
52 Vase
53 Vase
61 Vase
63 Vase
65 Vase
66 Vase
68 Vase
69 Vase
70 Vase
74 Vase
75 Vase
78 Vase
88 Vase
88 Lamp
90 Vase
100 Vase
101 Vase
108 Vase
110 Vase
113 Vase
118 Vase
124 Cachepot
131 Vase
132 Vase
134 Vase
135 Vase
136 Vase
139 Vase
142 Vase
178 Vase
184 Vase
185 Vase
187 Vase
189 Vase
204 Vase
209 Vase
212 Vase
218 Vase
228 Vase
230 Vase
231 Vase
232 Vase
238 Vase
244 Vase
283 Owls - pair
292 Vase
293 Vase
294 Vase
474 Dwarf clock case
505 Duck
518 Rabbits - pair
521 Mice - pair
522 Mice - pair heads apart
563 Mice on ashtray
618 Fish on ashtray
619 Fish on ashtray
711 Jardiniere
712 Jardiniere
751 Peacock on globe base
1438 Vase - faun with kid on lid
2481 Inkstand
5808 Vase

Kyhn, Knud (KK) (1880-1969)
Worked at factory 1903-67

KnudKyhn K

432 Calf
433 Polar bear (large)
706 Calf
721 Orangutans - pair
729 Polar bear cub
756 Stag
757 Bear lying
758 Cat looking up for food
773 Polecats - pair
774 Cat - white grooming
775 Stoat with duck
776 Otter biting tail
778 English bulldog sitting
780 Seal pup
781 Dachshund asleep
800 Cow with calf
801 English bulldog
802 Elephants - pair
825 Polar bear looking up
826 Camel
829 Duck
830 Goat
940 Monkeys - trio
956 French bulldog

957 French bulldogs - fused
976 Faun backwards on bear
1036 Faun with cat
1037 Bears (3) & tree stump
1061 Faun crying
1072 Calf
1078 Gnome with cat
1107 Polar bears cubs playing
1108 Polar bear & seal
1124 Bear
1137 Polar bear standing
1195 Bull
1199 Monkey & baby
1201 Monkeys
1804 Faun pulling bear's ear
1849 Child sitting on cow
1880 Faun on tortoise
2317 Polar bears
2318 Faun & bear wrestling
2326 Bulldogs playing
2330 Cuckoo being fed
2337 Mermaid riding seal with fish
2345 Otter with fish
2360 Bear
2365 Wolves fighting
2367 Otter & duck
2373 King Charles spaniel
2402 Faun & bear
2424 Faun with parrot
2425 Husky
2439 Gazelle with baby gazelle on back
2487 Lynx
2496 Faun with 2 monkeys
2507 Chimpanzee
2512 Wild cat grooming
2532 Siamese cat
2549 Snowy owl
2555 Panther
2565 Pekingese snarling
2573 2 Fauns with grapes
2589 Monkey
2590 Faun with puppy
2595 Cow & calf
2596 Lion cub
2607 Wild cat
2608 Dalmatian puppy
2609 Fawn
2621 Terrier sitting
2622 Bulldog turning
2623 Squirrel
2624 Horse biting rear
2625 Weasel/ferret
2636 Fawn head up
2638 Cat turning
2644 Dormouse
2648 Fawn head down
2649 Fawn asleep
2667 Scottish terrier
2668 Terrier head up
2668 Scottish terrier
2686 Lamb - standing
2697 Pekingese - snarling
2701 Setter lying
2703 Donkey
2720 Lamb - sitting
2734 Lion cubs playing
2735 Lamb - standing
2741 Cat
2743 Peewit
2751 Seagull
2753 West Highland terrier sitting
2755 Wire Haired terrier
2761 Dog
2768 Fox
2769 Lambs - pair
2786 Terrier turning, head down
2802 English bulldog sitting
2803 German Shepherd
2805 Spaniels - pair
2806 Mastiff
2811 Owl
2813 Elk
2822 Faun with bear
2823 Faun with goose?
2830 Dog
2841 Bear walking
2842 Bear with paw raised
2852 Faun with lion cub
2853 Terrier standing
2863 English bulldog
2868 Faun with brown bear
2871 Schnauzer
2940 German Shepherd
2941 Scottie
2942 Dog
2969 Spitz
2989 Snowy owl
2991 Bears - pair
2993 Goat
2997 Pekingese looking up
2998 Elephant
3000 Great Dane
3005 Elephant
3014 Bear cub eating
3015 Bear squatting
3082 Faun on tortoise
3083 Faun fighting a cockerel
20220 Elephant
21432 Bear
21433 Bear sitting
21434 Bear
21435 Bear
21519 Bear standing
21520 Bear lying
22745 Bear
22746 Bear
22747 Bear
22748 Bear

Liisberg C.F. (CFL) (1860-1909)
Worked at factory 1885-1909

Liisberg

388 Cat crawling
412 Drake & duck
457 Codfish
458 Cod - mouth open wide
462 Conger eel
463 Eel pout
464 Catfish
465 Common eel
470 Stoat snarling
472 Crawling panther
473 Cat crawling
502 Polar bear
1162 Conger eel
1350 Leopard - crawling
2272 Terrier begging
2284 Cat on back
2322 Cat? licking

Liisberg, Hugo (HL) (1896-1958)
2336 Serval

Lindhardt, Svend (SL)
453 'Headache' (white)
454 'Toothache' (white)
455 'Tummyache' (white)
456 'Earache' (white)

Locher, Axel (AL) (1879 – 1941)

AXEL LOCHER

443 Dairy maid
452 Girl with milkcan
460 Smith
465 Fish market
568 Woman on a stone seat
673 Thoughtful woman in chair
894 Woman sitting on chair
1372 Elephant
1373 Elephant
1375 Woman with collie
1376 Elephant
1451 'Fashionable pair'
1521 Minister
1522 Man leaning on walking stick
1523 Actor
1524 Woman with lapdog
1663 Sultan
3668 Fisherman

Lundberg, Theodor (TL) (1852-1926)
1132 'Wave & Rock'

Madsen, Sveistrup (SM)
431 Penguin

Madsen, Theodor (TM) (1880-1965)
Worked at factory 1896-1935

245 Vase
265 Sea lion
302 Bonbon dish
317 Bonbon dish
323 Jardinière - dragonfly handles
325 Bowl
367 Barn owl - small
373 Card tray - finches
376 Bird with long tail on ashtray
402 Lovebirds
417 Penguin
417 Penguins - pair
417 Penguins - triple
447 Elephant
501 Elephant

532 Heron
598 Lemming?
599 Elephant calf
606 Swan
607 Donkey with baskets
615 Beaver on ashtray
628 Rabbit on ashtray
632 Dish - beaver?
649 Parrots on branches
834 Owls - pair
1441 Sea lion
1738 Faun on stump
1741 Owl
1742 Owl asleep
2475 Flower bowl
2862 Siamese cat
2872 Siamese cat playing
2918 Penguins
2965 Cat creeping
2975 Penguin
2999 Owl
3002 Heron
3003 Penguin
3007 Boy with spaniel
3009 'Rosebud'
3063 Terrier
3085 Sealyham standing
3086 Sealyham squatting
3087 Sealyham turning
3116 Cocker spaniel
3139 Airedale terrier
3140 Dachshund (sitting)
3142 Spitz
3161 Scottish terrier standing
3162 Scottish terrier sitting
3165 Wire haired terrier
3169 Pug puppy
3170 Wire haired terrier
3235 Cairn terrier
3251 Scottie on side
3252 Irish setter
3261 German Shepherd
3280 Bull terrier
3281 Siamese cat
3501 Dalmatian
3510 Pigeon
3660 Ashtray

Malinowski, Arno (AM) (1899 – 1976)

1929 Cherub
1930 Cherub
2195 Cherub drinking
2196 Cherub squatting
2217 Woman - nude
2218 Cherub standing on a ball
2228 Cherub with dolphin
2230 Cherub riding a dolphin
2244 Cherub
2248 Cherub drinking (no base)
2249 Wood spirit
2268 Cherub, toe in mouth
2279 Cherub sitting (no base)
2342 Opium smoker
3330 Satyr & woman
4161 Maiden on seahorse
12237 Cherub with wings
12238 Bali dancer
12428 Crucifix
12454 Susanna
12456 'Market Girl'
12458 Child arms raised ? Buddha
12459 Mermaid
12460 Flora
12461 Huguenot girl
12463 Iceland
12466 'Diana'
12469 Woman sitting on dog
12470 Bowl
12471 Man kneeling with jackal cape
12473 Vase
12475 'Seventeen Years'
12477 Cupid on scooter
12480 Girl sitting
12481 Dish - mermaid
12485 'Europe'
12486 'Asia'
12487 'Africa'
12488 'Australasia'
12489 'America'
12756 Woman with piglets

Marie, Prinsesse (PM) (1865 – 1909)

309 Pigmy hippopotamus
426 Pigmy hippopotamus on rock
809 Ashtray

Martin-Hansen, Carl (CMH) (1877-1941)
Best known for his overglaze figurines in National Costume

1879 Girl with teddy
12100 Amager man's church-going costume
12101 Amager woman's church-going costume
12102 Amager woman's market costume
12103 Amager man's market costume
12104 Amager cook's costume
12105 Amager boy's & girl's costume
12106 Amager boy's & girl's costume
12107 Amager woman's mourning costume
12138 Blavandshuk
12162 Hacdrup
12163 Hedebo
12164 Iceland
12165 Laesoe
12166 Refsnaes
12171 Skovshoved, woman
12172 Skovshoved, man & woman
12210 Ringe
12211 Ringkobing
12213 Roemoe
12214 The Skaw
12215 Langeland
12216 Falster
12217 Bornholm
12218 Fanoe
12219 Samsoe
12220 Als
12221 Faroe Islands woman
12222 Faroe Islands man
12223 North Slesvig
12224 Greenland woman
12225 Greenland man
12226 Denmark, Jutland, Funen, Sealand
12227 Frederiksborg
12228 Randers
12229 Lolland
12230 Horne
12231 Mors
12412 Amager girl
12413 Fanoe girl
12414 Amager boy
12415 Greenland girl
12416 Faroe Islands girl
12417 Slesvig girl
12418 Sealand girl
12419 Greenland boy
12420 Funen girl
12421 Jutland girl

Mathiesen, Olaf (OM) (1878 – 1953)

672 Bonbon dish - insect handles
1157 Barn owls - trio
1192 Duck
1208 Faun on tree stump with rope
1407 Dachshund (lying on back)
1408 Dachshund (chasing tail)
2119 Dachshunds - pair
2120 Dachshunds - pair
2122 Drake
2128 Drake & duck
2131 Vase
2177 Inkstand - barn owls
2190 Inkstand - penguins

Moller, Knud (KM)

441 Gyrfalcon
1450 Dachshund
1457 Boston terrier
1533 Setter with pheasant
1558 Terrier sitting
1602 Trout (small)
1653 Peahen
1678 Birds - pair
1690 Jay

Mortensen, Carl (CM) (1861-1945)

214 Vase

Nielsen, Erik (EN) (1857-1947)
Worked at factory 1887-1926

11 Mouse on ashtray
12 Vase
14 Lobster on ashtray
19 Snake crushing frog
259 Pointer puppy
260 Pointer puppies - pair
282 Plaice
284 Cat curled
307 Cat
312 Inkstand
322 Cat lying - white
332 Cat lying
340 Cat
351 Bear chewing toe
366 Bear cubs playing
369 Rainbow trout
375 Rabbit
378 Rabbit scratching
414 Pig
419 Pig lying down
422 Cat
422 Cat - tabby
437 Fox large barking
438 Fox curled
442 Pekingese
445 Pekingese puppy
448 Pekingese puppy
453 Pointer puppies playing
460 Lumpsucker fish
480 Card tray - cod
481 Card tray - cod
482 Card tray - fish
483 Card tray - crab
484 Card tray - crayfish
485 Card tray - lobster
491 Jardinière
492 Jardinière - mouse peeping over edge
493 Jardinière
507 Frog on stone
510 Mouse on sugar
511 Mouse on chestnut
512 Mouse on corn cob
513 Mouse on fish head
515 Duck
516 Ducklings
517 Duckling
530 Musk ox
546 Fox on hollow mound
547 Cats playing
667 Cat yawning
668 Chicken with frog on base
683 Pigs - pair
691 Piglets - pair
693 Dog looking in basket
709 Seals - pair
750 Hound puppies
755 Swan
824 Bears standing
850 Dachshund
1311 Pointer puppy
1399 Pig on wheat sheaf
1400 Pig
1475 Fox
1662 Pekingese reclining
1752 Cats playing
2450 Jardinière
2461 Bonbon Dish - monkey on lid
2465 Card tray - Crab
2474 Flower bowl
2477 Frog on ashtray
2482 Inkstand - snake crushing frog
2483 Inkstand - fly
2484 Inkstand
2539 Rabbits (3) fused
3277 Card tray - crayfish

Nielsen, Ingeborg (IN)

609 Geese
1088 Goose
1182 Perch - group of 4
1185 Turkey chick
1235 Redwing
1303 Cockerel

Nielsen, Niels (NN) (1872 – 1921)

Niels Nielsen

417 Polar bear sniffing
425 Polar bear walking
434 Rabbits
436 Kingfisher
437 Goose (small)
438 Bullfinch
439 St. Bernard
442 Polar bear
1444 Monkey

Nissen, J M (JMN)

JMN

4502 Blacksmith
4507 Nurse
4535 Carpenter
4539 Boy with gourd
4502 Blacksmith
4507 Nurse
4535 Carpenter
4539 Boy with gourd

Oppenheim, Ville (VO)(1886-1949)
1495 Girl with butterfly

Pedersen, A (Nielsen) (AN/AP)(1872 – 1936)

266 Turkey chick
287 Lizard on ashtray
288 Veil-tail (fish)
308 Lizard on ashtray
313 Grasshopper
344 Mouse with nut
357 Axolotl
372 Tench
411 Fantail pigeon
431 Monkey holding its tail
432 Monkey scratching back
605 Chicken squatting
671 Jardinière - dragonfly handles
674 Jardinière - swallows
692 Monkey on ashtray
695 Mice on ashtray
715 Fish - pair
727 Cat playing
862 Pheasants
879 Eels - pair on ashtray
930 Skink
931 Fantail fish on ashtray
953 Pigs on ashtray
977 Spitz/Husky
981 Squirrel on ashtray
982 Squirrel with nut
1022 Pigs - pair
1023 Angel fish
1040 Finch
1041 Finch preening
1045 Finch group
1081 Sparrow tail up
1100 Card tray - lizard
1103 Magpie
1138 Perch
1139 Eel on ashtray
1304 Tawny owl
1309 Sparrows - pair
1443 Musk ox
1519 Sparrow
1778 Bonbon dish - turkey chick
1803 Cat, plain gray
1881 Pheasant
2214 Lizards (triple) on ashtray
2466 Card tray - lizard
2467 Card tray - lizards
2468 Card tray - lizard

Pedersen, Michael (MP) (1882-1918)
2082 Boy with golden hair
2083 Boy on a chair

Petersen, Arman (ARP)
503 Blue Ara

Platen-Hallermundt, Francis Valdemar (PL.H)
(1875 – 1965)

PH

1982 Woman kneeling on pot base
1983 Woman kneeling on pot lid
2036 Mouse on base
2133 Pied flycatcher
2138 Wagtail
2144 Flycatcher
2165 Duck
2169* Mouse
2178 Falcon on rock
2198 Squirrel
2215 Duck - flying
2216 Woodpecker
2220 Cat
2224 Cat playing with ball
2227 Woman
2238 Robin
2242 Duck - flying on ashtray
2258 Nuthatch?
2259 Tit

2260 Warbler?
2262 Robin squatting
2264 Thrush on base
2265 Bunting on base
2266 Robin
2270 Puppies playing
2286 Sparrow
2288 Arctic fox
2301 Squirrel
2309 Turkey
2310 Cockerels fighting?
2319 Raccoon
2335 Duck
2366 Warbler?
2374 Swallow
2384 Mink
2414 Crucian carp
2427 Pike
2449 Bream
2494 Roach
2524 Bird - long tailed
2545 Fish curled
2553 Perch
2562 Gull?
2564 Vole
2674 Fish
2675 Roach
2676 Trout (rainbow)
2738 Fish - pair
2756 Grayling (fish)
2837 Shark
2838 Fish
2851 Fish - pair (trout?)
2869 Fish
2870 Minnows
2962 Wrasse
2967 Wirehaired terrier
3020 Wirehaired terrier (male)
3050 Flying fish
3064 Fantail
3084 Angel fish
3164 Sunfish
3194 Grebe with young
3234 Kingfisher
3263 Grebe
3270 Starling fledgling

Plockross-Irminger, Ingeborg (IP)
(1872-1962)

IPI

400 Little girl
401 Mother & child
402 Reading children
403 Playing children
404 'Else'
406 'Love refused'
412 'Dickie' (boy crouching)
413 'Dickie's Mama'
414 'Grethe' (girl on packing case)
416 Woman with guitar
418 'Victor' (boy on stool)
421 'Only one drop' (girl with cat)
422 'Ole' (boy with puppy)
424 'Little Mother' (girl with cat)
435 Cat sitting
440 Boy with dog
561 'Mary' (spotted dress)

Sandholt, Else (ES)
473 'Ida's flowers'
486 Pierrot
487 Harlequin
488 Columbine
502 Salmon trout
1517 Child sitting
1518 Crawling child

Schou, Helen (HS)
4558 Boar
4559 Sow
4561 Boar feeding

Seidelin, Henning (HES)
445 Hans Christian Andersen

Spies, Sophie (SS) (1858 – 1934)

1286 Mole

Storch (ST) – we are unhappy with attribution on his sole piece as this is the monogram.

2171 Faun kneeling with grapes

Strand, George K (GKS) (1895 – 1930)

G.Strand G

2014 Chihuahua
2039 Cat grooming
2167 Seagull
2519 Two sea-lions
2574 Toucan
2834 Greenland girl

Therkelsen, Allan (AT) (1960-)
Worked at factory since 1990
301 Cat sitting
302 Kitten lying
303 Kittens lying
304 Kittens (3) lying
305 Kitten standing
306 Cat sneaking
359 Swan male
360 Swan with cygnets
361 Cygnet stretching
362 Cygnet
363 Cygnets
364 Cygnet with raised wing
662 Panda eating
663 Panda sitting
664 Panda climbing
665 Panda sleeping
666 Panda with cubs
667 Panda playing

Thomsen, Christian (CT) (1860-1921)
Worked at factory 1898-1920

Th Chr.Th. Chr.Th. Chr.Thomsen. Thr

20 Oil lamp
249 Vase
250 Vase - frog in relief
251 Vase
253 Vase
263 Icelandic falcon
273 Barn owl
274 Flower holder - barn owls
275 Flower holder - bat
280 Card tray - insect
286 Catfish open mouth
318 Labrador puppy 'Bob'
319 Desert foxes - pair
326 Vase - snakes
335 Belt buckle
347 Paperweight - snake with frog
348 Insect handles on ashtray
349 Woman crying on chair
358 Card tray -ducklings
365 Crow
415 Monkeys - pair
416 Squirrels - pair
429 Black-headed gull
430 Candlestick
433 Faun with lizard
435 Woman sitting, thinking
439 Faun with rabbit
446 Cockerel & hen
450 Owl & mice on base
456 Faun with squirrel
461 Carp
466 Goat
468 Guillemot
495 Dish
498 Faun with goat
524 Inkstand - cockerels
527 Goose-girl
528 Goose-girl
531 Candlestick
544 Sisters (1 on plinth)
557 Fox on small base
566 Cockerel on clock case
567 Cockerel on base
580 Chicken on base
600 Hen with chicks raised base
601 Bowl - otters
608 Woman
610 Owl & 3 mice on ashtray
620 Shepherd boy
627 Farmer with sheep
629 Little girl
634 Sheep & lamb
635 Common gull
648 Faun with bear
655 Harvest girl
665 Goat & kid
685 Man with scythe
694 Girl with goats
704 Dog chewing bone
707 Children with dog
719 Otters playing
737 Faun on goat
752 Faun with parrot

772 Boy with calf
779 Girl with calf
782 Shepherd with dog
784 Old woman with bonnet
813 Man with rake
815 Peasant girl with lunch
827 Tern squatting
832 Cat lying with ball of wool
848 Swineherd
857 Faun on tortoise & rope
858 Faun on tortoise
865 Boy at lunch
866 Blue parrot on column
878 Rabbit on ashtray
892 Churchgoer
899 Milkmaid
903 Girl with hay & rake
905 Boy cutting stick
908 Girl with sheaf
922 Girl with book
939 Girls with doll
955 Sailor girl with book
963 Sailor boy sitting
975 Cat playing with ball of wool
990 Children sitting with doll
1001 Old man, hands in pocket
1012 Woman feeding cat
1019 Rabbit
1024 Hen
1025 Cock
1043 Woman with washing
1065 Turkey
1087 Hunter with dog
1094 Cock & hen
1112 'The Soldier & Witch'
1114 'Princess & Swineherd'
1126 Cock head up
1127 Cock head down
1129 'The Sandman'
1145 'The Sandman'
1156 'Soldier & Dog'
1180 'Soldier & Princess'
1210 Mermaid on ice rock
1212 Paperweight - mermaid in water
1228 'Hans Clodhopper'
1229 Girl bathing
1276 'Shepherdess & Chimneysweep'
1288 'Emperor's New Clothes'
1300 Harvest group
1307 Boy with tree
1319 'The Gossips'
1326 Peasant couple dancing
1327 Desert fox
1352 Harvest group
1383 Victorian man
1385 Victorian lady
1404 Mother & child
1473 Princess & Hans Clodhopper
1478 King
1494 Queen
1528 Woman with hoe
1549 Woman collecting potatoes
1593 Victorian couple
1648 Boy Scout at tree stump
1649 Boy Scout with staff
1659 Boy on rock
1660 Man
1680 'The Proposal'
1712 Faun with snake
1713 Faun with frog
1736 Faun playing pipes
1737 Children walking
1744 Boy seated eating apple
1761 'Flight to America'
1762 Girl plucking a duck
1770 Lady
1783 'Hans & Trine'
1785 Lady holding roses
1786 Boy bathing
1818 Girl with baby
1828 Boy
1833 Boy with flowers
1847 'The Nightingale'
1848 Hans Christian Anderson
1858 Boy with calves
1891 Girl and two soldiers
1905 Old men
1922 Faun & Squirrel clock case
1969 'Lady & Beau'
2030 Hairdresser
2046 'The Kiss'
2071 Girl with trumpet
2072 Girl with musical instrument
2078 Man holding lamb?
2107 Faun with owl
2113 Faun with crow
2123 Woman
2139 'Goose-thief'
2140 Boy with terrier
2146 Owl with 2 fauns
2157 Girl with musical instrument
2158 Girl with jar
2168 Man & woman on bench
2211 Harlequin & Columbine
2460 Bonbon dish - mouse on lid
2462 Dish - swan?
2463 Bonbon dish - lizard on lid
2469 Card tray - woman
2470 Card tray - woman
2824 'Lady & Beau' clock case

Thylstrup, Georg (GT) (1884 – 1930)

Thylstrup GT GT

Thymann, Vita (VT)

VT

477 Girl with puppy (kneeling)
479 'Birgitte'

Timyn, William (WT)

W.T

5298 Giant panda
5401 Raccoon
5402 Koala

Trapp, Anna (ANT)(1877 – 1943)

aT

1008 Pigeon
1044 Ptarmigan
1071 Eider duck
1190 Penguins - pair
1283 Penguin
1284 Penguins - trio

Varming, Hanne (HV)
4793 Girl sitting
4794 Child in carnival dress
4795 Girl with butterfly
4796 Girl with trumpet
5194 Girl with pram
5195 Girl with teddy
5196 Boy with rocking horse
5245 Hans Christian Andersen
5284 Girl with flute
5460 'See no evil'
5461 'Hear no evil'
5462 'Speak no evil'

Wagner, Siegfried (SW) (1874-1952)
1535 Chess piece - King - Saracen
1536 Chess piece - Queen - Saracen
1537 Chess piece - Castle - Saracen
1538 Chess piece - Knight - Saracen
1539 Chess piece - Bishop - Saracen
1540 Chess piece - Pawn - Saracen
1541 Chess piece - King - Crusaders
1542 Chess piece - Queen - Crusaders
1543 Chess piece - Castle - Crusaders
1544 Chess piece - Knight - Crusaders
1545 Chess piece - Bishop - Crusaders
1546 Chess piece - Pawn - Crusaders
5166 Chess Board

Waldorff, Vilhelm (VW) (1877 – 1935)

VW

2285 Bear squatting
2298 Faun with small girl
2299 Faun with mermaid
2313 Mermaid
2323 Child with grapes
2332 Girl holding duck
2333 Otter with fish
2334 Fox
2347 Boy Neptune riding fish
2348 Mermaid with fish
2361 Faun with grapes
2412 Mermaid sitting on rock
2444 Dancing girl
2445 Boy with cockerel
2537 Girl sitting with puppy
2561 Girl with doll

Weiss, Claire (CW)
447 'Youthful boldness'
466 'Spilt milk'
467 'First book' (girl reading)
490 'Pardon me'
492 Dancing couple

Willumsen, Bode (BW)

4047 Fishwife
4050 Sailor with anchor
4065 Woman hands on hips
4066 Man standing
4070 Woman with basket
4071 Man with sack (white)
4082 Man with cartwheel
4083 Woman with pail
4087 Woman arms crossed at wrists
4091 Hunter
4092 Man carrying painting?
4093 Woman with urn
4097 Woman
4100 Man with violin
4102 Woman holding bowl?
4109 Man
4111 Blacksmith?
4112 Woman with baby
4113 Woman with cage
4122 Old man reading
4125 Man with child
4131 Woman leaning on style
4132 Man with saw
4136 Man with wood
4137 Woman with shopping
4183 Woman with sickle
4189 Old man

Chapter 2
Numerical List with Descriptions

As far as possible we have allocated relevant descriptions to piece numbers, some of which have been used more than once.

1	Bowl	
1	Leaf dish with dragonfly	
1	Dish	
1	Tray	
1	Dish	
1	Walking stick handle	
2	Dish	
2	Bonbon dish - snail on lid	
2	Egg shaped	
2	Walking stick handle	
2	Tray	
3	Walking stick handle	
3	Dish	
3	Curled snake on base	
3	Egg	
3	Bowl	
4	Dish	
4	Walking stick handle - mice	JAH
4	Walking stick handle	
4	Crab	
4	Jug	
4	Bowl	
5	Bowl	
5	Dish	
5	Paperweight - snail	
6	Bowl hanging - snake ? handles	
6	Crab	
6	Basket	
6	Cup	
6	Vase	
7	Walking stick handle - cockerel	
7	Bowl	
7	Dish - flower	
7	Dish - lizard	
7	Dish	
7	Cup	
8	Walking stick handle - mice	JAH
8	Magnolia flower	
8	Dish with lid	
8	Dish - woman	
8	Cup	
8	Dish with lid	
9	Bowl	
9	Dish with lid	
9	Walking stick handle - snail	
9	Cup	
10	Bowl	
10	Box	
10	Ashtray	
11	Vase	
11	Bonbon dish - monkey on lid	
11	Walking stick handle	
11	Mouse on ashtray	EN
12	Vase	AK
12	Dish - snakes on lid	
12	Vase	EN
12	Dish - frog	
13	Vase	
13a	Vase	
13	Dish	
14	Lobster on ashtray	EN
14	Bonbon dish - crab lid	
14	Walking stick handle	
15	Dragonfly on ashtray	
15	Frog	
16	Moth on ashtray	
16	Stag beetle	
17	Dish	
17a	Dish	
18	Insect	
18	Vase	
19	Dish - woman lying on back	
19	Snake crushing frog	EN
19	Pot	
20	Inkstand	
20	Oil lamp	CT
21	Dish - peacock	
22	Inkstand	
22	Dish	
22	Bonbon dish	
23	Vase	
23	Bonbon dish - lizard on lid	
24	Dish - merman	
24	Dish - spider on lid	
25	Bonbon dish - lizard	
26	Dish - lizards (3)	
26	Bonbon dish - marmots ? handles	
27	Vase	
28	Bowl	
29a	Vase	AK
29b	Vase	AK
29c	Vase	AK
29	Lamp	
30	Vase	
30	Dish - woman	
32	Vase	AK
33	Vase	AK
33a	Vase	AK
33b	Vase	AK
34	Vase	
35	Vase	AK

35a	Vase	AK
35b	Vase	AK
36	Vase	
38	Vase	
39	Vase	
42	Vase	AK
42a	Vase	AK
42b	Vase	AK
42c	Vase	AK
43	Vase	
43a	Vase	
43b	Vase	
43c	Vase	
44	Vase	
45a	Vase	
47	Vase	
47a	Vase	AK
47b	Vase	AK
47c	Vase	AK
47d	Vase	AK
47e	Vase	
51	Vase	AK
52	Vase	AK
53	Vase	AK
54a	Vase	
55	Vase	
56	Vase	
57	Vase	
58	Flask	
59	Vase	
60	Vase	
60a	Vase	
61	Vase	AK
63	Vase	AK
65	Vase	AK
65a	Vase	AK
65b	Vase	AK
66	Vase	AK
66a	Vase	
67	Vase	
68	Vase	AK
68a	Vase	AK
69	Vase	AK
70	Vase	AK
74	Vase	AK
75	Vase	AK
78	Vase	AK
84	Bowl	
88	Vase	AK
88	Lamp	AK
89	Vase	
90	Vase	AK
91	Vase	
92	Vase	
95	Vase	
96	Vase	
100	Vase	AK
101	Vase	AK
104	Vase	
105	Vase	
106	Vase	
107	Vase	
108	Vase	AK
109	Vase	
110	Vase	AK
112	Vase	
113	Vase	AK
114	Vase	
115	Vase	JJ
116	Vase	
118	Vase	AK
121	Vase	
124	Cachepot	AK
125	Vase	JJ
128	Vase	
129	Vase	
130	Vase - cockerel head lid	
131	Vase	AK
132	Vase	AK
134a	Vase	AK
134b	Vase	AK
134c	Vase	
134d	Vase	
134e	Vase	
135	Vase	AK
136	Vase	AK
137	Vase	
138	Vase	
139	Vase	AK
140	Vase	
142	Vase	AK
142a	Vase	AK
143	Vase - snake wrapped around	
144	Vase	JAH
149	Vase	
150	Vase	
152	Vase	
153	Vase	
154	Vase	
155	Vase	
156	Vase	
157	Vase	
158	Vase	
159	Bowl	
160	Lamp	
162	Vase	
166	Scent bottle	
167	Vase	
168	Vase	
171	Vase	
172	Vase	
176	Vase - snake around rim	JAH
177	Vase	
178	Vase	AK
180	Vase	
181	Vase	
182	Vase	
184	Vase	AK
185	Vase	AK
186	Vase	JJ
187	Vase	AK
189	Vase	AK
192	Vase	
193	Vase	
197	Vase	
198	Vase	
199	Vase	
200	Vase	
201	Vase	
202	Vase	
203	Vase	
204	Vase	AK
206	Vase	
207	Vase	
208	Vase	
209	Vase	AK?

209a	Vase	
209b	Vase	
212	Vase	AK
214	Vase	CM
215	Vase	
218	Vase	AK
219	Vase	
220	Vase	
222	Vase	
223	Vase	
224	Vase	
225	Vase	
227	Vase	
228	Vase	AK
229	Vase	
230	Vase	AK
231	Vase	AK
232	Vase	AK
232	Bear on side	
233	Vase	
233	Bear sitting arm up	
234	Bear on back	
234	Vase	JJ
235	Vase	
235	Bear upright	
236	Vase - peacock heads at waist	
237	Bear standing	
237	Vase	JJ
238	Vase	AK
238	Bear sitting	
239	Vase	
240	Vase	
241	Vase	
243	Vase	
244	Vase	AK
245	Vase	TM
246	Vase	
247	Vase	JJ
249	Rabbit (looking left)	
249	Vase	CT
250	Vase - frog in relief	CT
251	Vase	CT
252	Dish with lid	
253	Vase	CT
254	Bonbon dish -grasshopper on lid	
255	Vase	
256	Vase	
257	Vase	
258	Inkstand	
259	Pointer puppy	EN
260	Pointer puppies - pair	EN
263	Icelandic falcon	CT
265	Sealion	TM
266	Turkey chick	AN (AP)
267	Dragonfly	
268	Bee	
270	Moth	
271	Vase	
272	Moth	
273	Barn owl	CT
274	Flower holder - barn owls	CT or AK
275	Flower holder - bat	CT
278	Vase	
280	Card tray - insect	CT
282	Plaice	EN
283	Owls - pair	AK
284	Cat curled	EN
286	Catfish open mouth	CT
287	Lizard on ashtray	AP (AN)
288	Veil-tail (fish)	AP (AN)
292	Vase	AK
293	Vase	AK
294	Vase	AK
295	Vase	
296	Bonbon dish - mouse on lid	
297	Place marker	
299	Bonbon dish	
299	Box	
301	Cat sitting (white)	AT
301	Bonbon dish	
301	Box	
301	Cat sitting	AT
302	Kitten lying	AT
302	Kitten lying (white)	AT
302	Egg	
302	Bonbon dish	TM
303	Place marker	
303	Kittens lying (white)	AT
303	Kittens lying	AT
304	Kittens (3) lying (white)	AT
304	Place marker	
304	Kittens (3) lying	AT
305	Kitten standing (white)	AT
305	Kitten standing	AT
306	Cat sneaking (white)	AT
306	Vase - bird handles	
306	Cat sneaking	AT
307	Cat	EN
308	Lizard on ashtray	AP (AN)
309	Pigmy hippopotamus	PM
310	Dish	
312	Inkstand	EN
313	Grasshopper	AN (AP)
317	Bonbon dish	TM
317	Starfish on stone	
318	Labrador puppy 'Bob'	CT
319	Desert foxes - pair	CT
320	Polar bear walking	CJB
321	Polar bear feeding	CJB
322	Cat lying - white	EN
323	Jardiniere - dragonfly handles	TM
324	Cat seated	
325	Bowl	TM
326	Vase - snakes	CT
327	Bonbon dish - cat lid	
328	Vase - butterfly wings	
329	Dish - octopus	
330	Clown & 2 dancing bears	CJB
332	Cat lying	EN
333	Belt buckle	
334	Belt buckle	
335	Belt buckle	CT
336	Belt buckle	
337	Belt buckle	
338	Belt buckle	
340	Cat	EN
341	Flower bowl	
343	Dish - butterfly	
344	Mouse with nut	AP (AN)
345	Bear - sitting	HE
347	Paperweight - snake with frog	CT
348	Insect handles on ashtray	CT
349	Woman crying on chair	CT
351	Bear chewing toe	EN
352	Vase	JJ
354	Vase	JJ

355	Vase	
357	Axolotl	AP (AN)
358	Card tray -ducklings	CT
359	Swan male	AT
360	Swan with cygnets	AT
361	Cygnet stretching	AT
362	Cygnet	AT
363	Vase	
363	Cygnets	AT
364	Cygnet with raised wing	AT
365	Crow	CT
366	Bear cubs playing	EN
367	Barn owl - small	TM
368	Bonbon dish - pigeon on lid	
369	Rainbow trout	EN
369	Gnome with lamp	
370	Gnome with porridge	
370	Seagull wings spread	K
371	Scorpion fish (Gurnard)	AND
372	Tench	AP (AN)
373	Card tray - finches	TM
375	Rabbit	EN
376	Bird with long tail on ashtray	TM
377	Fruit stand - monkeys to base	
378	Rabbit scratching	EN
382	Bonbon dish - fox on lid	
382	Bonbon dish - insect? on lid	
388	Cat crawling	CFL
389	Vase	
390	Vase	
392	Vase	
393	Vase	
394	Vase	
395	Vase	
396	Vase	
400	Bonbon dish	
400	Little girl	IP
401	Dish - snails	
401	Mother & child	IP
402	Lovebirds	TM
402	Reading children	IP
403	Vase	
403	Playing children	IP
404	'Else'	IP
405	Vase	
405	Pig	DJ
406	'Love refused'	IP
407	Kingfisher	DJ
408	Candelabra	
408	'Good morning' (girl in nightdress)	MA
409	Polar bear sitting	DJ
410	Vase	
410	Titmouse - 'Optimist'	DJ
411	Fantail pigeon	AP (AN)
411	Titmouse - 'Pessimist'	DJ
412	Drake & duck	CFL
412	'Dickie' (boy crouching)	IP
413	'Dickie's Mama'	IP
414	Pig	EN
414	'Grethe' (girl on packing case)	IP
415	Monkeys - pair	CT
415	'Protection' - 3 birds	DJ
416	Squirrels - pair	CT
416	Woman with guitar	IP
417	Penguin	TM
417	Polar bear sniffing	NN
417a	Penguins - pair	TM
417b	Penguins - triple	TM
418	'Victor' (boy on stool)	IP
419	Pig lying down	EN
419	Mouse white	DJ
420	Black grouse	DJ
421	Vase	
421	'Only one drop' (girl with cat)	IP
422	Cat	EN
422	'Ole' (boy with puppy)	IP
422	Cat - tabby	EN
423	Vase	
423	Cuckoo	DJ
424	Bonbon dish	
424	'Little Mother' (girl with cat)	IP
425	Polar bear walking	NN
426	Pigmy hippopotamus on rock	PM
426	Mason	
427	Walking stick handle - duck	
427	'Two friends' (child with dog)	MA
428	Walking stick handle - gull	
428	Gull with fish	DJ
429	Blackheaded gull	CT
429	Gull crying	DJ
430	Candlestick	CT
430	Gull	DJ
431	Monkey holding its tail	AP (AN)
431	Penguin	SM
432	Monkey scratching back	AP (AN)
432	Calf	KK
433	Faun with lizard	CT
433	Polar bear (large)	KK
434	Rabbits	NN
435	Woman sitting, thinking	CT
435	Cat sitting	IP
436	Easter egg	
436	Kingfisher	NN
437	Fox large barking	EN
437	Goose (small)	NN
438	Fox curled	EN
438	Bullfinch	NN
439	Faun with rabbit	CT
439	St. Bernard	NN
440	Boy with dog	IP
441	Gerfalcon	KM
442	Pekingese	EN
442	Polar bear	NN
443	Dairy maid	AL
444	Pointer	LJ
445	Pekingese puppy	EN
445	Hans Christian Andersen	HES
446	Cockerel & hen	CT
446	Cow	LJ
447	Elephant	TM
447	'Youthful boldness'	CW
448	Pekingese puppy	EN
448	Calf	SJ
449	Trout (brown)	SJ
450	Owl & mice on base	CT
450	Cocker spaniel	SJ
451	Sealyham	LJ
452	Girl with milkcan	AL
453	Pointer puppies playing	EN
453	'Headache' (white)	SL
454	'Toothache' (white)	SL
455	'Tummyache' (white)	SL
456	Faun with squirrel	CT
456	'Earache' (white)	SL
457	Codfish	CFL
457	Budgerigar - blue	SJ

458	Cod - mouth open wide	CFL
458	Polar bear sitting	SJ
459	Sardine	
459	Polar bear	SJ
460	Lumpsucker fish	EN
460	Blacksmith	AL
461	Carp	CT
462	Conger eel	CFL
463	Eel pout	CFL
464	Catfish	CFL
465	Common eel	CFL
465	Fish market	AL
466	Goat	CT
466	'Spilt milk'	CW
467	Snowy owl	JAH
467	'First book' (girl reading)	CW
468	Guillemot	CT
468	'Happy trio'	MA
469	Kangaroo turning	HO
470	Stoat snarling	CFL
471	Percheron	CJB
472	Crawling panther	CFL
473	Cat crawling	CFL
473	'Ida's flowers'	ES/SJ
474	Dwarf clock case	AK
474	Robin	SJ
475	Vase	
476	Bowl	
477	Girl with puppy (kneeling)	VT
478	Vase	
478	'Up to mom' (girl - pick me up!)	SJ
479	Mice on top of sack	
479	'Birgitte'	VT
480	Card tray - cod	EN
481	Card tray - cod	EN
481	Titmouse	
482	Card tray - fish	EN
482	Titmouse	
483	Card tray - crab	EN
483	Titmouse	
484	Card tray - crayfish	EN
484	Titmouse	
485	Card tray - lobster	EN
485	Titmouse	
486	Pierrot	ES/SJ
486a	Garniture - shell	
486b	Garniture - shell	
486c	Garniture - shell	
486d	Garniture - shell	
486e	Garniture - shell	
486f	Garniture - shell	
486g	Garniture - shell	
486h	Garniture - shell	
486i	Garniture - shell	
486k	Garniture - shell	
486l	Garniture - shell	
487	Pen tray - bat	JAH
487	Harlequin	ES/SJ
488	Vase	
488	Columbine	ES/SJ
489	Crab	
489	Old fisherman	SJ
490	Dish	
490	'Pardon me'	CW
491	Jardiniere	EN
491	Nurse	SJ
492	Jardiniere - mouse peeping over edge	EN
492	Dancing couple	CW

493	Jardiniere	EN
493	Turkey cock	
494	Dish	
494	Turkey hen	
495	Dish	CT
495	'Thirst' (thirsty man)	
496	Dish	
498	Faun with goat	CT
499	Cat white	
500	Cat grey	
501	Elephant	TM
502	Polar bear	CFL
502	Salmon trout	ES
503	Guinea-pig	JAH
503	Blue Ara	ARP
504	Rabbit begging	JAH
504	Kitten lying	
505	Duck	AK
505	Kitten sitting	
506	Kitten standing	
507	Frog on stone	EN
507	Kitten tail up	
508	Sea urchin?	
508	Clown	
509	Curled snake	JAH
509	Clown	
510	Mouse on sugar	EN
510	Clown	
511	Mouse on chestnut	EN
511	Clown	
512	Mouse on corn cob	EN
513	Mouse on fish head	EN
514	Mouse in skull	
514	Kitten lying	
515	Duck	EN
515	Kitten sitting	
516	Ducklings	EN
516	Kitten standing	
517	Duckling	EN
517	Kitten tail up	
518	Rabbits - pair	AK
521	Mice - pair	AK or AP
522	Mice - pair heads apart	AK or AP
524	Inkstand - cockerels	CT
525	'Tea Party'	
527	Goose-girl	CT
527	Cat	
528	Goose-girl	CT
530	Musk ox	EN
530	Lion cub	
531	Candlestick	CT
532	Heron	TM
532	Boy with raincoat	SB
533	Girl dressed up	
535	Bonbon dish	
535	Polar bear cub standing	MEA
536	Polar bear cub feet up	MEA
537	Polar bear cub on back	MEA
538	Polar bear cub on back	MEA
539	Pidgeon tail up	
540	Easter egg	
540	Pigeon tail down	
541	Vase	
541	Seal on front	
542	Seal on back	
543	Seal on back	
544	Sisters (1 on plinth)	CT
544	Boy dressed up	

546	Fox on hollow mound	EN
546	'The Little Gardener'	
547	Cats playing	EN
547	Spaniel white	
548	Gypsy girl	
549	Witch (girl dressed up)	
552	Tortoise	
557	Fox on small base	CT
558	Lamb sleeping	
560	Lamb	
561	'Mary' (spotted dress)	IP
562	Bream	
562	Lamb	
563	Mice on ashtray	AK
564	Beagle standing	
565	Beagle lying	
566	Cockerel on clock case	CT
567	Cockerel on base	CT
568	Woman on a stone seat	AL
569	Women	
573	Elephant	
575	Elephant	
576	Elephant	
580	Chicken on base	CT
582	Vase	
583	Bowl	
586	Bonbon dish	
587	Bonbon dish	
590	Vase	
591	Vase	
592	Vase	
593	Bowl	
597	Vase	
598	Lemming?	TM
599	Elephant calf	TM
600	Hen with chicks raised base	CT
601	Bowl - otters	CT
602	Ashtray	JAH
604	Bonbon dish - grasshopper on lid	
605	Chicken squatting	AN (AP)
606	Swan	TM
607	Donkey with baskets	TM
608	Woman	CT
609	Geese	IN
610	Owl & 3 mice on ashtray	CT
611	Vase	
615	Beaver on ashtray	TM
617	Bonbon dish - head	
618	Fish on ashtray	AK
619	Fish on ashtray	AK
620	Shepherd boy	CT
621	Fish on slab	
622	Bonbon dish	
623	Bonbon dish	
624	Bonbon dish	
625	Bonbon dish	
626	Bonbon dish	
627	Farmer with sheep	CT
628	Rabbit on ashtray	TM
629	Little girl	CT
632	Dish - beaver?	TM
634	Sheep & lamb	CT
635	Common gull	CT
638	Ashtray	
639	Ashtray	
640	Ashtray	
642	Ashtray	
643	Ashtray	
644	Dish	
645	Vase	
646	Ashtray	
647	Ashtray	
648	Faun with bear	CT
649	Parrots on branches	TM
650	Vase	
652	Bonbon dish - eagle spread wings	
653	Flask	
654	Flask	
655	Harvest girl	CT
658	Easter egg	
662	Panda eating	AT
663	Panda sitting	AT
664	Panda climbing	AT
665	Goat & kid	CT
665	Panda sleeping	AT
666	Panda with cubs	AT
667	Cat yawning	EN
667	Panda playing	AT
668	Chicken with frog on base	EN
670	Bonbon dish - mouse on lid	
671	Jardiniere - dragonfly handles	AP (AN)
672	Bonbon dish - insect handles	OM
673	Thoughtful woman in chair	AL
674	Jardiniere - swallow handles	AP (AN)
677	Vase	
679	Vase	
681	Bowl	
682	Vase	
683	Pigs - pair	EN
685	Man with scythe	CT
691	Piglets - pair	EN
692	Monkey on ashtray	AN (AP)
693	Dog looking in basket	EN
694	Girl with goats	CT
695	Mice on ashtray	AN (AP)
698	Bonbon dish	
699	Bonbon dish	
700	Bonbon dish	
701	Bonbon dish	
702	Bonbon dish	
703	Bowl - mouse on lid	
704	Dog chewing bone	CT
706	Calf	KK
707	Children with dog	CT
709	Seals - pairs	EN/KK?
711	Jardiniere	AK
712	Jardiniere	AK
713	Ashtray with flower handles	
714	Tiger	LJ
715	Fish - pair	AN (AP)
719	Otters playing	CT
721	Orangutans - pair	KK
727	Cat playing	AN (AP)
729	Polar bear cub	KK
730	Vase	JJ
733	Vase	
734	Vase	
735	Vase	
737	Faun on goat	CT
738	Dish	
741	Fly on rock	
743	Vase	
744	Dish - woman	
746	Butterfly	
747	Grasshopper on ashtray	
750	Hound puppies	EN

751	Peacock on globe base	AK
752	Faun with parrot	CT
753	Terrier sitting	LJ
755	Swan	EN
756	Stag	KK
757	Bear lying	KK
758	Cat looking up for food	KK
763	Vase	JJ
764	Vase	
767	Vase	JJ
770	Flower bowl	
771	Bowl	
772	Boy with calf	CT
773	Polecats - pair	KK
774	Cat - white grooming	KK
775	Stoat with duck	KK/PM
776	Otters biting tail	KK
777	Vase	
778	English bulldog sitting	KK
779	Girl with calf	CT
780	Seal pup	KK
781	Dachshund asleep	KK
782	Shepherd with dog	CT
784	Old woman with bonnet	CT
786	Fruitstand	
800	Cow with calf	KK
801	English bulldog	KK
802	Elephants - pair	KK
804	Lioness	LJ
805	Leopardess licking foot	LJ
806	Picture frame	
808	Ashtray	
809	Ashtray	PM
812	Ducks - trio	
813	Man with rake	CT
815	Peasant girl with lunch	CT
818	Vase	
822	Women	
824	Bears standing	EN
825	Polar bear looking up	KK
826	Camel	KK
827	Tern squatting	CT
829	Duck	KK
830	Goat	KK
832	Cat lying with ball of wool	CT
834	Owls - pair	TM
848	Swineherd	CT
850	Dachshund	EN
851	Ashtray	
852	Ashtray	
854	Ashtray	
855	Ashtray	
856	Dachshund	LJ
857	Faun on tortoise & rope	CT
858	Faun on tortoise	CT
860	Flying insect	
861	Ashtray	
862	Pheasants	AN (AP)
863	Vase	
865	Boy at lunch	CT
866	Blue parrot on column	CT
871	Vase	
873	Vase	JJ
876	Vase	
877	Easter egg	
878	Rabbit on ashtray	CT
879	Eels - pair on ashtray	AN (AP)
880	Frog on lily pad	

881	Frog on flat base	
882	Frog on dish	
883	Frog on rock	
884	Frog on rock	
886	Vase	JJ
887	Vase	
888	Vase	
890	Vase	
892	Churchgoer	CT
893	Woman with lute on pedestal	
894	Woman sitting on chair	AL
898	Bell	
899	Milkmaid	CT
901	Vase	
902	Vase	
903	Girl with hay & rake	CT
905	Boy cutting stick	CT
906	Bell with mouse on top	
908	Girl with sheaf	CT
922	Girl with book	CT
926	Blotter	
927	Fly	
928	Fly	
929	Fly	
930	Skink	AP (AN)
931	Fantail fish on ashtray	AN (AP)
932	Vase	
934	Vase	
935	Vase	
936	Ashtray	
938	Dish	
939	Girls with doll	CT
940	Monkeys - trio	KK
941	Tray	
942	Tray	
943	Tray	
944	Ashtray	
945	Ashtray	
946	Tray	
947	Tray	
948	Tray	
949	Tray	
950	Tray	
951	Ashtray	
952	Ashtray	
953	Pigs on ashtray	AN (AP)
955	Sailor girl with book	CT
956	French bulldog	KK
957	French bulldogs - fused	KK
960	Ashtray	
963	Sailor boy sitting	CT
964	Ashtray	
969	Ashtray	
970	Dish	
975	Cat playing with ball of wool	CT
976	Faun backwards on bear	KK
977	Spitz/Husky	AP (AN)
981	Squirrel on ashtray	AN (AP)
982	Squirrel with nut	AN (AP)
983	Vase	
984	Vase	
985	Ashtray	
986	Ashtray	
987	Ashtray	
989	Picture frame	
990	Children sitting with doll	CT
1001	Old man, hands in pocket	CT
1005	Ashtray	

1006	Ashtray	
1007	Ashtray	
1008	Pigeon	ANT
1010	Cross legged woman on pedestal	GH
1012	Woman feeding cat	CT
1019	Rabbit	CT
1020	Victorian woman - curtsying	
1021	Mother holding children	BI
1022	Pigs - pair	AP (AN)
1023	Angel fish	AP (AN)
1024	Hen	CT
1025	Cock	CT
1034	Coati Mundi	PH
1036	Faun with cat	KK
1037	Bears (3) & tree stump	KK
1039	Bonbon dish	
1040	Finch	AN (AP)
1041	Finch preening	AN (AP)
1042	Woman with baby?	
1043	Woman with washing	CT
1044	Ptarmigan	ANT
1045	Finch group	AN (AP)
1046	Ashtray	
1047	Ashtray	
1048	Vase	
1049	Vase	
1050	Vase	
1052	Wall plate	
1055	Smokers set	
1056	Smokers set	
1057	Smokers set	
1058	Smokers set	
1059	Smokers set	
1061	Faun crying	KK
1064	Old woman	
1065	Turkey	CT
1067	Tray	
1071	Eider duck	ANT
1072	Calf	KK
1078	Gnome with cat	KK
1081	Sparrow tail up	AN (AP)
1082	Vase	
1086	Guinea-fowl	PH
1087	Hunter with dog	CT
1088	Goose	IN
1094	Cock & hen	CT
1095	Easter egg	
1096	Marmot	BU
1099	Vase	
1100	Card tray - lizard	AP (AN)
1101	Owl on ball	
1103	Magpie	AP (AN)
1104	Inkstand	
1107	Polar bear cubs playing	KK
1108	Polar bear & seal	KK
1109	Ashtray	
1112	'The Soldier & Witch'	CT
1114	'Princess & Swineherd'	CT
1115	Wall plate	
1117	Wall plate	
1119	Nymph & faun	GH
1120	Wall plate	
1122	Wall plate	
1124	Bear	KK
1125	Wall plate	
1126	Cock head up	CT
1127	Cock head down	CT
1128	Wall plate	
1129	'The Sandman'	CT
1132	'Wave & Rock'	TL
1137	Polar bear standing	KK
1138	Perch	AN (AP)
1139	Eel on ashtray	AN (AP)
1141	Vase	
1145	'The Sandman'	CT
1148	Vase	
1156	'Soldier & Dog'	CT
1157	Barn owls - trio	OM
1159	Pot	
1161	Vase	
1162	Conger eel	CFL
1165	Vase	
1166	Lampshade	
1167	Picture frame	
1174	Vase	
1180	'Soldier & Princess'	CT
1182	Perch - group of 4	IN
1185	Turkey chick	IN
1188	Weeping faun on stand	GH
1188.1	Weeping faun	GH
1188.2	Stand for weeping faun	GH
1189	Finches - pair	PH
1190	Penguins - pair	ANT
1192	Duck	OM
1195	Bull	KK
1199	Monkey & baby	KK
1201	Monkeys	KK
1204	Bassett puppy	PH
1205	Bull (head down)	LJ
1208	Faun on tree stump with rope	OM
1209	Badger	PH
1210	Mermaid on ice rock	CT
1212	Paperweight - mermaid in water	CT
1215	Vase	
1216	Vase	
1217	Vase	
1218	Vase	
1223	Vase	
1224	Vase	
1227	Vase	
1228	'Hans Clodhopper'	CT
1229	Girl bathing	CT
1232	Marabou storks	MH
1235	Redwing	IN
1238	'Princess & The Pea'	GH
1241	Vase	
1242	Vase	
1244	Girl with mirror	GH
1251	Amager girl	LB
1252	Little girl	LB
1253	Bonbon dish - cats playing on lid	
1254	Bonbon dish - finches (3) on lid	
1257	Vase	
1258	Vase	
1259	Vase	
1260	Vase	
1261	Vase	
1262	Vase	
1268	Lion yawning	LJ
1269	Hippos - pair	CJB
1276	'Shepherdess & Chimneysweep'	CT
1281	Guinea-pig	PH
1283	Penguin	ANT
1284	Penguins - trio	ANT
1286	Mole	SS
1288	'Emperor's New Clothes'	CT

1289	Night heron	MH
1293	Vase	
1294	Vase	
1300	Harvest group	CT
1303	Cockerel	IN
1304	Tawny owl	AP (AN)
1307	Boy with tree	CT
1309	Sparrows - pair	AN (AP)
1310	Cow - brown	LJ
1311	Pointer puppy	EN
1313	Vase for car	
1314	Girl knitting	LB
1315	Amager girl	LB
1316	Amager girls (shopping)	LB
1317	Woman knitting	LB
1319	The Gossips	CT
1320	Ring tree	
1322	Bloodhound - female	LJ
1323	Girl from Bornholm	LB
1324	Fanoe woman	LB
1325	Bonbon dish	
1326	Peasant couple dancing	CT
1327	Desert fox	CT
1329	Lynx	PH
1331	Owl long eared	PH
1337	Bonbon dish - rabbit	
1338	Rabbit crouching	
1341	Bloodhound sniffing - male	LJ
1343	Leopard	LJ
1350	Leopard - crawling	CFL
1352	Harvest group	CT
1362	Horse	LJ
1372	Elephant	AL
1373	Elephant	AL
1374	Ballet dancer	LB
1375	Woman with collie	AL
1376	Elephant	AL
1382	Girl with sled	LB
1383	Victorian man	CT
1385	Victorian lady	CT
1395	Girls - pair	LB
1398	Greenland girl	LB
1399	Pig on wheatsheaf	EN
1400	Pig	EN
1402	Wolverine	PH
1404	Mother & child	CT
1407	Dachshund	OM
1408	Dachshund	OM
1409	Bonbon dish	
1411	Vase	
1413	'Nathan the Wise'	AJ
1414	Woman on plinth	
1427	Cat - wild	
1430	Fox	PH
1437	Bonbon dish - rabbit on lid	
1438	Vase - faun with kid on lid	AK
1440	Lynx	PH
1441	Sealion	TM
1443	Musk ox	AN (AP)
1444	Monkey	NN
1448	Bonbon dish - cockerel on lid	
1450	Dachshund	KM
1451	'Fashionable pair'	AL
1455	Bonbon dish - rabbits (2) on lid	
1457	Boston terrier	KM
1463	Bonbon dish - bird on lid	
1464	Bonbon dish - sparrow on lid	
1465	French bulldog standing	LJ

1466	French bulldog sitting	LJ
1468	Seagull	PH
1469	Jaguar	
1470	Bonbon dish - mouse on lid	
1473	Princess & Hans Clodhopper	CT
1475	Fox	EN
1476	Fairy Tale I	GH
1478	King	CT
1479	Cockatoo	EJ
1482	Mountain lion	PH
1486	Donkeys - pair	JAH
1493	Lark	PH
1494	Queen	CT
1495	Girl with butterfly	VO
1502	Vase	
1504	Wren	PH
1505	Bluetit	PH
1506	Crested tit	PH
1507	Wagtails - pair	PH
1508	Bonbon dish	
1509	Sole	PH
1516	Robin	PH
1517	Child sitting	ES
1518	Crawling child	ES
1519	Sparrow	AN (AP)
1521	Minister	AL
1522	Man leaning on walking stick	AL
1523	Actor	AL
1524	Woman with lapdog	AL
1528	Woman with hoe	CT
1530	Girl in red	
1531	Girl with deer	
1533	Setter with pheasant	KM
1535	Chess piece - King - Saracen	SW
1536	Chess piece - Queen - Saracen	SW
1537	Chess piece - Castle - Saracen	SW
1538	Chess piece - Knight - Saracen	SW
1539	Chess piece - Bishop - Saracen	SW
1540	Chess piece - Pawn - Saracen	SW
1541	Chess piece - King - Crusaders	SW
1542	Chess piece - Queen - Crusaders	SW
1543	Chess piece - Castle - Crusaders	SW
1544	Chess piece - Knight - Crusaders	SW
1545	Chess piece - Bishop - Crusaders	SW
1546	Chess piece - Pawn - Crusaders	SW
1548	Bonbon dish - mouse on lid	
1549	Woman collecting potatoes	CT
1551	Vase	
1554	Vase	
1555	Vase	
1557	Vase	
1558	Terrier sitting	KM
1586	Fairy Tale II	GH
1587	Vase	
1589	Vase	
1590	Vase	
1593	Victorian couple	CT
1595	Fisherman	GT
1596	Easter egg - rabbit	
1600	Partridge - pair	PH
1602	Trout (small)	KM
1613	Bonbon dish - pig on lid	
1622	Collie dog lying	JB
1623	Male lion	JB
1634	Pointer (head down)	LJ
1635	Pointer (head up)	LJ
1637	Woman standing	GT
1646	'Grief'	GH

1648	Boy Scout at tree stump	CT
1649	Boy Scout with staff	CT
1652	Hound standing	PH or LJ
1653	Peahen	KM
1654	Eskimo	LB
1659	Boy on rock	CT
1660	Man	CT
1661	Falcon	PH
1662	Pekingese reclining	EN
1663	Sultan	AL
1664	Fairy Tale III	GH
1670	Birds - triple	
1678	Bird - pair	KM
1679	Great Dane	PH
1680	'The Proposal'	CT
1684	Poodle sitting	PH
1688	German Shepherd sitting	PH
1690	Jay	KM
1691	Rabbit	PH
1695	Ashtray	
1697	Vase	
1699	Bonbon dish	
1701	Collie	PH
1703	Wall plate	
1707	Vase	
1712	Faun with snake	CT
1713	Faun with frog	CT
1715	Vase	
1716	Vase	
1719	Poodle	PH
1723	Ashtray	
1732	Vase	
1733	Vase	
1736	Faun playing pipes	CT
1737	Children walking	CT
1738	Faun on stump	TM
1739	Child, crawling	AB
1740	Vase	
1741	Owl	TM
1742	Owl asleep	TM
1744	Boy seated eating apple	CT
1752	Cats playing	EN
1756	Bonbon dish	
1760	Woman with maid servant	GT
1761	'Flight to America'	CT
1762	Girl plucking a duck	CT
1769	Kingfishers	PH
1770	Lady	CT
1771	Elephant	PH
1772	Pekingese sitting	PH
1775	Easter egg	PH
1776	Pekingese	PH
1777	Bonbon dish	
1778	Bonbon dish - turkey chick	AN (AP)
1779	Bowl	
1783	'Hans & Trine'	CT
1785	Lady holding roses	CT
1786	Boy bathing	CT
1787	Racoons - pair	PH
1788	Vixen with cubs	PH
1791	Vase	
1796	Man & woman	GH
1798	Belgian Shepherd reclining	PH
1803	Cat, plain grey	AN (AP)
1804	Faun pulling bear's ear	KK
1809	Vase	
1811	Vase	
1812	Vase	

1813	Vase	
1814	Vase	
1815	Vase	
1816	Vase	
1817	Vase	
1818	Girl with baby	CT
1819	Vase	
1827	Woman kneeling	
1828	Boy	CT
1829	Snowy owl	PH
1830	Boy with bricks	PH
1833	Boy with flowers	CT
1835	Vase	
1838	Woman kneeling	
1842	Vase	
1846	Basket - herons	PH
1847	'The Nightingale'	CT
1848	Hans Christian Anderson	CT
1849	Child sitting on cow	KK
1854	Vase	
1858	Boy with calves	CT
1859	Dog	PH
1860	Pekingese puppy	PH
1861	Bonbon dish	
1863	Mandarin ducks	PH
1864	Native woman kneeling	
1866	Woman kneeling	
1868	Bonbon dish	
1869	Wall plate	
1871	Woman kneeling	
1875	Woman kneeling with bird	
1878	Boy with sailing boat	PH
1879	Girl with teddy	CMH
1880	Faun on tortoise	KK
1881	Pheasant	AN (AP)
1882	Huskies - pair	PH
1891	Girl and two soldiers	CT
1899	Vase	
1905	Old men	CT
1906	Vase	
1907	Vase	
1908	Vase	
1912	Vase	
1920	Borzoi	PH
1922	Faun & Squirrel clock case	CT
1924	Duck - tufted	PH
1925	Duck	PH
1926	Eider duck	PH
1928	Robin	
1929	Cherub	AM
1930	Cherub	AM
1933	Duck - drake	PH
1934	Mallard	PH
1938	Girl with doll	AB
1941	Duck tufted	PH
1946	'Leda & the Swan'	
1951	Pheasants on base	PH
1958	Wall plate	
1969	Lady & Beau	CT
1975	Bonbon dish	
1976	Vase	
1982	Woman kneeling on pot base	PL.H
1983	Woman kneeling on pot lid	PL.H
1997	'Adam & Eve'	HHH
2005	Lady with bird	PH
2007	Vase	
2012	Vase	
2014	Chihuahua	G. K. Strand

2020	Lamp	
2030	Hairdresser	CT
2033	Golden eagle (Blue)	VTF
2036	Mouse on base	PL.H
2037	Vase	
2039	Cat grooming	G. K. Strand
2040	Vase	
2043	Blotter	
2046	'The Kiss'	CT
2051	Deer on green base	HHH
2053	'Leda & the Swan'	HHH
2061	Girl with basket	
2064	Dove	HHH
2065	Tiger gnawing a bone	PH
2067	Vase	
2068	Geese	PH
2071	Girl with trumpet	CT
2072	Girl with musical instrument	CT
2078	Man holding lamb?	CT
2082	Boy with golden hair	MP
2083	Boy on a chair	MP
2084	Finch	PH?
2085	Chinese man	GT
2086	Chinese woman	GT
2093	Flask	
2107	Faun with owl	CT
2108	Parrot	MH
2109	'The Kiss on the Hand'	GH
2111	Girl with fawn	HHH
2113	Faun with crow	CT
2119	Dachshunds - pair	OM
2120	Dachshunds - pair	OM
2122	Drake	OM
2123	Woman	CT
2125	Guinea fowl	PH
2126	Cat looking back	PH
2127	Seal scratching head	PH
2128	Drake & duck	OM
2129	Vase	
2130	Vase	
2131	Vase	OM
2133	Pied flycatcher	PL.H
2138	Wagtail	PL.H
2139	'Goose-thief'	CT
2140	Boy with terrier	CT
2144	Flycatcher	PL.H
2146	Owl with 2 fauns	CT
2152	Baboon	PH
2157	Girl with musical instrument	CT
2158	Girl with jar	CT
2160	Vase	
2162	Chinese couple	GH
2163	'Little Matchgirl'	
2165	Duck	PL.H
2166	Rabbit	PH/VW
2167	Seagull	GKS
2168	Man & woman on bench	CT
2169	Cocker spaniel	SJ
2169	Mouse	PL.H
2171	Faun kneeling with grapes	ST
2175	Lion cub	PH
2177	Inkstand - barn owls	OM
2178	Falcon on rock	PL.H
2180	Bison	PH
2181	Sitting dog	PH
2187	Marmot on base	
2188	Girl & sheep with dove on back	HHH
2189	Girl & sheep	HHH
2190	Inkstand - penguins	OM
2195	Cherub drinking	AM
2196	Cherub squatting	AM
2198	Squirrel	PL.H
2201	Monkeys - pair	HHH
2202	Stag jumping a mound	PH
2208	Sparrow on base	OJ
2211	Harlequin & Columbine	CT
2214	Lizards (triple) on ashtray	AN (AP)
2215	Duck - flying	PL.H
2216	Woodpecker	PL.H
2217	Woman - nude	AM
2218	Cherub standing on a ball	AM
2220	Cat	PL.H
2224	Cat playing with ball	PL.H
2227	Woman	PL.H
2228	Cherub with dolphin	AM
2230	Cherub riding a dolphin	AM
2232	Jay on perch	PH
2233	Vase	Christian Joachim
2234	Vase	
2237	Lamp	
2238	Robin	PL.H
2239	Woodpecker on ashtray	
2240	Sparrow on ashtray	
2242	Duck - flying on ashtray	PL.H
2244	Cherub	AM
2248	Cherub drinking (no base)	AM
2249	Wood spirit	AM
2250	Robin on ashtray	
2251	Cat on ashtray	
2257	Kingfisher holding fish	PH
2258	Nuthatch?	PL.H
2259	Tit	PL.H
2260	Warbler?	PL.H
2261	Partridge	PH
2262	Robin squatting	PL.H
2264	Thrush on base	PL.H
2265	Bunting on base	PL.H
2266	Robin	PL.H
2268	Cherub, toe in mouth	AM
2270	Puppies playing	PL.H
2272	Terrier begging	CFL
2274	'Ali & Peribanu'	GH
2279	Cherub sitting (no base)	AM
2284	Cat on back	CFL
2285	Bear squatting	VW
2286	Sparrow	PL.H
2288	Arctic Fox	PL.H
2289	Vase	
2290	Vase	
2298	Faun with small girl	VW
2299	Faun with mermaid	VW
2301	Squirrel	PL.H
2302	Vase	
2303	Lamp with child & grapes	
2304	Vase	
2305	Vase	
2306	Vase	
2308	Vase	
2309	Turkey	PL.H
2310	Cockerels fighting?	PL.H
2313	Mermaid	VW
2315	Vase	
2317	Polar bears	KK
2318	Faun & bear wrestling	KK
2319	Racoon	PL.H

2320	Lamp	
2322	Cat? licking	CFL
2323	Child with grapes	VW
2326	Bulldogs playing	KK
2327	Vase	
2330	Cuckoo being fed	KK
2332	Girl holding duck	VW
2333	Otter with fish	VW
2334	Fox	VW
2335	Duck	PL.H
2336	Servil	HL
2337	Mermaid riding seal with fish	KK
2342	Opium smoker	AM
2345	Otter with fish	KK
2347	Boy Neptune riding fish	VW
2348	Mermaid with fish	VW
2350	Vase	
2351	Vase	
2353	Vase	
2354	Bowl	
2355	Bowl	
2356	Bowl	
2357	Card tray	
2360	Bear	KK
2361	Faun with grapes	VW
2365	Wolves fighting	KK
2366	Warbler?	PL.H
2367	Otter & Duck	KK
2368	Vase	
2373	King Charles spaniel	KK
2374	Swallow	PL.H
2377	Tray	
2383	Dish	
2384	Mink	PL.H
2385	Vase	
2387	German Shepherd lying	PH
2388	Vase	
2390	Vase	
2391	Vase	
2392	Vase	
2393	Vase	
2394	Pheasant	PH
2399	Vase	
2402	Faun & bear	KK
2409	'The Nightingale'	GH
2411	Mountain lion attacking stag	
2412	Mermaid sitting on rock	VW
2413	'Moon Girl'	GH
2414	Crucian carp	PL.H
2417	'Venus'	GH
2420	Vase	
2422	Tray	
2423	'Susanna'	GH
2424	Faun with parrot	KK
2425	Husky	KK
2427	Pike	PL.H
2428	Girl bathing	GH
2435	Lamp	
2438	Lamp	
2439	Gazelle with baby gazelle on back	KK
2443	Rabbit on haunches	
2444	Dancing girl	VW
2445	Boy with cockerel	VW
2449	Bream	PL.H
2450	Jardiniere	EN
2451	Dish - frog	JAH
2452	Bowl - fish	JAH
2453	Bonbon dish	
2454	Bonbon dish	
2456	Bonbon dish	
2457	Bonbon dish	
2458	Bonbon dish	
2459	Bonbon dish	
2460	Bonbon dish - mouse on lid	CT
2461	Bonbon dish - monkey on lid	EN
2462	Dish - swan?	CT
2463	Bonbon dish - lizard on lid	CT
2464	Pen tray	
2465	Card tray - crab	EN
2466	Card tray - lizard	AP (AN)
2467	Card tray - lizards	AP (AN)
2468	Card tray - lizard	AP (AN)
2469	Card tray - woman	CT
2470	Card tray - woman	CT
2471	Ring tray	
2472	Ring tray	
2473	Ring tray	
2474	Flower bowl	EN
2475	Flower bowl	TM
2476	Match holder	
2477	Frog on ashtray	EN
2478	Snail on ashtray	
2479	Paperweight	
2480	Snail on blotter	JAH
2481	Inkstand	AK
2482	Inkstand - snake crushing frog	EN
2483	Inkstand - fly	EN
2484	Inkstand	EN
2485	Square	
2486	Tray	
2487	Lynx	KK
2494	Roach	PL.H
2496	Faun with 2 monkeys	KK
2506	Bulldog	
2507	Chimpanzee	KK
2512	Wild cat grooming	KK
2519	Sea-lions	GKS
2524	Bird - long tailed	PL.H
2528	Bowl	
2532	Wild dog?	KK
2535	Vase	
2537	Girl sitting with puppy	VW
2539	Rabbits (3) fused	EN
2543	Tray	
2545	Fish curled	PL.H
2549	Snowy owl	KK
2553	Perch	PL.H
2555	Panther	KK
2559	Tray	
2561	Girl with doll	VW
2562	Gull?	PL.H
2564	Vole	PL.H
2565	Pekingese snarling	KK
2573	2 Fauns with grapes	KK
2574	Toucan	GKS
2584	Vase	
2585	Vase	
2586	Vase	
2589	Monkey	KK
2590	Faun with puppy	KK
2594	Vase	
2595	Cow & calf	KK
2596	Lion cub	KK
2604	Boy with pillows	HC
2605	Vase	
2607	Wild cat	KK

2608	Dalmation puppy	KK
2609	Fawn	KK
2611	Dealer sign	
2618	Bowl	
2619	Bowl	
2621	Terrier sitting	KK
2622	Bulldog turning	KK
2623	Squirrel	KK
2624	Horse biting rear	KK
2625	Weasel/ferret	KK
2627	Chuhuahua	
2630	Bowl	
2636	Fawn head up	KK
2638	Cat turning	KK
2644	Dormouse	KK
2648	Fawn head down	KK
2649	Fawn asleep	KK
2650	Dish - monkey?	
2658	Vase	
2661	Vase	
2662	Vase	
2663	Vase	
2664	Vase	
2665	Vase	
2667	Scottish terrier	KK
2668	Terrier head up	KK
2668	Scottish terrier	KK
2674	Fish	PL.H
2675	Roach	PL.H
2676	Trout (rainbow)	PL.H
2686	Lamb - standing	KK
2697	Pekingese - snarling	KK
2701	Setter lying	KK
2703	Donkey	KK
2720	Lamb - sitting	KK
2725	Vase	
2726	Vase	
2734	Lion cubs playing	KK
2735	Lamb - standing	KK
2738	Fish - pair	PL.H
2741	Elephant (leg in trunk)	
2741	Cat	KK
2742	Cat	
2743	Peewit	KK
2746	Vase	
2747	Vase	
2748	Vase	
2749	Vase	
2750	Vase	
2751	Seagull	KK
2753	West Highland terrier sitting	KK
2755	Wire haired terrier	KK
2756	Grayling (fish)	PL.H
2761	Dog	KK?
2768	Fox	KK
2769	Lambs - pair	KK
2770	Vase	
2771	Vase	
2786	Terrier turning, head down	KK
2793	Vase	
2800	Tray	
2801	Tray	
2802	English bulldog sitting	KK
2803	German Shepherd	KK
2805	Spaniels - pair	KK
2806	Mastiff	KK
2811	Owl	KK
2813	Elk	KK
2822	Faun with bear	KK
2823	Faun with goose?	KK
2824	Lady & Beau clock case	CT
2830	Dog	KK
2834	Greenland girl	GKS
2837	Shark	PL.H
2838	Fish	PL.H
2841	Bear walking	KK
2842	Bear with paw raised	KK
2845	Vase	
2846	Vase	
2849	Vase	
2850	Dish	
2851	Fish - pair (trout?)	PL.H
2852	Faun with lion cub	KK
2853	Terrier standing	KK
2855	Hound scratching	
2856	'Spring'	HHH
2857	'Summer'	HHH
2858	'Autumn'	HHH
2859	'Winter'	HHH
2862	Siamese cat	TM
2863	English bulldog	KK
2864	Vase	
2866	Vase	
2868	Faun with brown bear	KK
2869	Fish	PL.H
2870	Minnows	PL.H
2871	Schnauzer	KK
2872	Siamese cat playing	TM
2911	Cat	
2913	Vase	
2918	Penguins	TM
2934	Vase	
2940	German Shepherd	KK
2941	Scottie	KK
2942	Dog	KK
2944	Vase	
2945	Vase	
2952	Dove - faience	
2959	Tray	
2960	Tray	
2961	Tray	
2962	Wrasse	PL.H
2965	Cat creeping	TM
2966	Vase	
2967	Wire haired terrier	PL.H
2969	Spitz	KK
2970	Mother & child	AH
2975	Penguin	TM
2977	Christmas candlestick	
2978	Tray	
2983	Vase	
2984	Vase	
2989	Snowy owl	KK
2991	Bears - pair	KK
2993	Goat	KK
2997	Peke looking up	KK
2998	Elephant	KK
2999	Owl	TM
3000	Great Dane?	KK
3002	Heron	TM
3003	Penguin	TM
3005	Elephant	KK
3007	Boy with spaniel	TM
3009	'Rosebud'	TM
3014	Bear cub eating	KK
3015	Bear squatting	KK

3018	Greyhound	
3020	Wire haired terrier (male)	PL.H
3030	Vase	
3034	Mother & child	HC
3035	Tray	
3038	Tray	
3041	Minnows	
3042	Fish - pair	
3043	Vase	
3044	Vase	
3049	'Henrik & Else'	HC
3050	Flying fish	PL.H
3062	Dog	
3063	Terrier	TM
3064	Fantail	PL.H
3070	Sailor boy on plinth	HC?
3082	Faun on tortoise	KK
3083	Faun fighting a cockerel	KK
3084	Angel fish	PL.H
3085	Sealyham standing	TM
3086	Sealyham squatting	TM
3087	Sealyham turning	TM
3088	Vase	
3110	Pointer	
3116	Cocker spaniel	TM
3118	Penguins - pair	
3128	French bulldog	
3131	Dish - crab	JOB
3139	Airedale terrier	TM
3140	Dachshund (sitting)	TM
3142	Spitz	TM
3161	Scottish terrier standing	TM
3162	Scottish terrier sitting	TM
3164	Sunfish	PL.H
3165	Wire haired terrier	TM
3167	Tray	
3169	Pug puppy	TM
3170	Wire haired terrier	TM
3171	'Knight & Maiden'	HC
3194	Grebe with young	PL.H
3205	Tray	
3206	Tray	
3216	Tray	
3219	Tray	
3231	Dish - mermaid	HHH
3234	Kingfisher	PL.H
3235	Cairn terrier	TM
3249	Terrier	
3250	Boy with broom	AE
3251	Scottie on side	TM
3252	Irish setter	TM
3261	German Shepherd	TM
3263	Grebe	PL.H
3270	Starling fledgling	PL.H
3272	Boy with sailing boat	AE
3277	Card tray - cray fish	EN
3280	Bull terrier	TM
3281	Siamese cat	TM
3287	Pot	
3299	Wall plate	
3300	Vase	
3302	Tray	
3309	Flask	
3310	Tray	
3314	Tray	
3315	Tray	
3321	Mermaid	AE
3326	Tray	
3330	Satyr & woman	AM?
3333	Tray	
3335	Candlestick	
3337	Tray	
3347	Tray	
3352	Tray	
3353	Tray	
3354	Tray	
3355	Vase	
3357	Tray	
3358	Tray	
3365	Tray	
3366	Tray	
3367	Vase	
3368	Tray	
3369	Tray	
3370	Tray	
3371	Tray	
3373	Tray	
3376	Tray	
3379	Tray	
3382	Tray	
3387	Tray	
3396	Tray	
3405	Tray	
3406	Tray	
3407	Lapland boy	
3408	Tray	
3415	Tray	
3421	Tray	
3423	Tray	
3424	Tray	
3426	Tray	
3430	Vase	
3432	Dish - girl & duck	
3438	Tray	
3439	Tray	
3441	Tray	
3442	Tray	
3444	Tray	
3449	Tray	
3453	Tray	
3454	Tray	
3457	Mother with child	HC
3458	Tray	
3460	Tray	
3463	Tray	
3464	Tray	
3465	Tray	
3466	Tray	
3467	Tray	
3468	Boy with teddy bear	AB
3476	Terrier with slipper	AB
3477	Tray	
3478	Tray	
3479	Tray	
3480	Tray	
3484	Tray	
3485	Tray	
3488	Tray	
3489	Tray	
3490	Vase	
3498	Dish - lobster	JOB
3501	Dalmation	TM
3502	Tray	
3509	Tray	
3510	Pigeon	TM
3514	Dish	

3519	Boy with bucket & spade	AE
3528	Tray	
3529	Tray	
3530	Tray	
3532	Tray	
3534	Tray	
3535	Tray	
3539	Girl with doll standing	AB
3540	Tray	
3542	Boy with ball	AE
3546	Tray	
3547	Vase	
3549	Vase	
3551	Vase	
3554	Tray	
3556	Boy with umbrella	AB
3558	Vase	
3559	Tray	
3560	Vase	
3572	Tray	
3582	Vase	
3588	Tray	
3595	Bowl	
3596	Bowl	
3597	Vase	
3598	Vase	
3604	Vase	
3605	Tray	
3606	Bowl	
3609	Tray	
3610	Tray	
3611	Tray	
3612	Tray	
3614	Tray	
3615	Tray	
3618	Tray	
3621	Dish	
3629	Tray	
3634	Boxer dog standing	HC
3635	Boxer dog lying	HC
3637	Tray	
3638	Tray	
3639	Tray	
3643	Tray	
3644	Vase	
3645	Tray	
3646	Tray	
3647	Drummer	AB
3650	Great Dane - harlequin	HC
3654	Tray	
3654	Cat - faience	
3655	Giraffe	HC
3657	Ashtray	
3658	Madonna	HHH
3660	Ashtray	
3661	Ashtray	HC
3662	Tray	
3663	Tray	
3664	Tray	HC
3665	Tray	HC
3667	Child with accordion	AB
3668	Fisherman	AL
3671	Tray	
3673	Tray	
3674	Tray	
3675	Tray	
3677	Girl with pot-cover	AB
3679	Nude female kneeling	
3686	Fisherman with fish	
3687	Ashtray	
3689	Boy with horn	AB
3690	Tray	
3703	Bowl	
3726	Tray	
3727	Tray	
3794	Lion Blanc de Chine	
3859	Plaque	
3864	Plaque	
3868	Plaque	
3872	Plaque	
3876	Plaque	
3880	Plaque	
4010	Flask	
4011	Dish with lid	
4012	Dish	
4015	Flask	
4016	Box	
4027	Girl on stone	AB
4044	Vase	
4047	Fishwife	BW
4050	Sailor with anchor	BW
4055	Vase	
4061	Tray	
4065	Woman hands on hips	BW
4066	Man standing	BW
4070	Woman with basket	BW
4071	Man with sack	BW
4074	Vase	
4075	Ballet girl	HC
4082	Man with cartwheel	BW
4083	Woman with pail	BW
4085	Basket	
4087	Woman arms crossed at wrists	BW
4090	Tray	
4091	Hunter	BW
4092	Man carrying painting?	BW
4093	Woman with urn	BW
4097	Woman	BW
4100	Man with violin	BW
4102	Woman holding bowl?	BW
4103	Vase	
4109	Man	BW
4111	Blacksmith?	BW
4112	Woman with baby	BW
4113	Woman with cage	BW
4117	Vase	
4118	Vase	
4119	Vase	
4121	Vase	
4122	Old man reading	BW
4125	Man with child	BW
4126	Woman	
4131	Woman leaning on style	BW
4132	Man with saw	BW
4136	Man with wood	BW
4137	Woman with shopping	BW
4138	Dish	
4142	Vase	
4144	Vase	
4161	Maiden on seahorse	AM?
4162	Vase	
4183	Woman with sickle	BW
4187	'Agnete & the Merman'	HC
4189	Old man	BW
4216	Hans Christian Andersen	HHH
4217	Vase	

4228	Tray	
4356	Tray	
4359	Woman with water jug	JH
4361	Ashtray	
4365	Ashtray	
4366	Ashtray	
4367	'Emperor & The Nightingale'	JH
4371	Ashtray	
4374	'Thumbelina'	HC
4377	Bricklayer	JH
4379	Tray	
4382	'Emperor & Nightingale'	JH
4384	Vase	
4385	Tray	
4414	Tray	
4418	Woman with eggs	JH
4424	Girl plaiting hair	JH
4431	'The Little Mermaid'	EE
4433	Tray	
4434	Tray	
4436	Tray	
4437	Box	
4438	'Little Matchgirl'	AE
4444	Tray	
4445	Tray	
4446	Tray	
4448	Tray	
4449	Tray	
4450	Tray	
4451	Tray	
4452	Tray	
4453	Tray	
4457	Tray	
4458	Tray	
4459	Tray	
4460	Tray	
4463	Vase	
4468	Vase	
4476	Tray	
4498	Tray	
4502	Blacksmith	JMN
4503	Schoolgirl	HC
4507	Nurse	JMN
4523	'January' - girl skater	HHH
4524	'February' - boy juggler	HHH
4525	'March' - girl with posy	HHH
4526	'April' - boy with umbrella	HHH
4527	'May' - girl with flowers	HHH
4528	'June' - boy with briefcase	HHH
4529	'July' - girl bathing	HHH
4530	'August' - boy with piglet	HHH
4531	'September' - girl with satchel	HHH
4532	'October' - boy with fruit	HHH
4533	'November' - girl in riding habet	HHH
4534	'December' - boy with sack	HHH
4535	Carpenter	JMN
4539	Boy with gourd	JMN
4544	Tray	
4545	Tray	
4546	Tray	
4547	Vase	
4548	Vase	
4549	Vase	
4552	Vase	
4557	Vase	
4558	Boar	HS
4559	Sow	HS
4561	Boar feeding	HS

4562	Stoat	JG
4563	Tray	
4564	Vase	
4565	Vase	
4566	Vase	
4567	Vase	
4568	Vase	
4569	Vase	
4570	Vase	
4571	Vase	
4572	Weasels - pair	JG
4576	Vase	
4584	Tray	
4585	Tray	
4587	Tray	
4588	Vase	
4593	Corgi	JG
4609	Shetland pony	JG
4611	Shetland pony sitting	JG
4614	Vase	
4615	Vase	
4616	Basset hound	JG
4631	Girl with cat	JOG
4638	Poodle	JG
4639	'Helena' - girl with mirror	HHH
4642	Ballet dancer	JOG
4643	Tiger	JG
4644	Vase	
4645	Butcher	MB
4646	Vase	
4647	Baboon & baby	JG
4648	Girl dressing hair	JOG
4649	Teenagers with books	JOG
4652	Guinea-pig crouching	JG
4653	Foal standing	JG
4654	Mink	JG
4659	Jaguar cub	JG
4661	Vase	
4669	Child on back	JOG
4670	Children reading	JOG
4672	Dish	
4676	Rabbit	JG
4678	Jersey cow standing	JG
4679	Wall plate	
4680	Boy eating apple	JOG
4682	Budgie on gourd	JG
4683	Jersey cow sitting	JG
4686	Vase	
4687	Tiger & cubs	JG
4698	Mare & foal	JG
4703	Nude girl turning	JOG
4704	Nude girl lying	JOG
4705	Rabbit	JG
4719	Vase	
4726	Goat	JG
4727	Plumber	JOG
4734	Dish	
4735	Vase	
4744	Goat with kid	JG
4746	Hoopoe	JG
4752	Lippizzanner	JG
4753	Polar bear	JG
4754	Wall plate	
4757	Poodle	JG
4760	Kid on rock	JG
4762	Chowchow	JG
4764	Vase	
4765	Vase	

4766	Vase	
4780	Polar bear & cubs	JG
4781	Vase	
4783	Puma cub	JG
4784	Turkey	JG
4787	Pigeon	JG
4793	Girl sitting	HV
4794	Child in carnival dress	HV
4795	Girl with butterfly	HV
4796	Girl with trumpet	HV
4830	Dish	
4844	Scotties - black & white	
4851	Tray	
4852	Danish bird dog	JG
4854	Tray	
4855	Tray	
4856	Tray	
4857	Tray	
4858	Tray	
4859	Tray	
4869	Ashtray	
4878	Vase	
4879	Vase	
4880	Vase	
4882	Horse	JG
4884	Dish	
4917	Scottie	JG
4918	West Highland white terrier	JG
4919	Dish	
4935	Dish	
4937	Dish	
4938	Vase	
4939	Dish	
4947	Dish	
4950	Vase	
4951	Dish	
4952	Old English Sheepdog	JG
4959	Vase	
4963	Dish	
4989	Footballer	JOG
5076	Dish	
5103	Vase	
5104	Vase	
5136	Golden retriever	JG
5154	Kangaroo	JG
5166	Chess board	SW
5172	Dish	
5173	Dish	
5194	Girl with pram	HV
5195	Girl with teddy	HV
5196	Boy with rocking horse	HV
5200	Vase	
5205	Dish	
5207	Girl with teddy	KJ
5209	Ashtray	
5242	Ashtray	
5243	Ashtray	
5245	Hans Christian Andersen	HV
5268	Ballet dancer	SK
5269	Ballet dancer	SK
5271	Ballet dancer	SK
5273	Girl with crown	SK
5284	Girl with flute	HV
5292	Dish	
5293	Dish	
5298	Giant panda	WT
5302	Dish	
5303	Dish	

5306	Dish	
5401	Racoon	WT
5402	Koala	WT
5423	Llasa Apso	JG
5456	Leaping salmon	
5460	'See no evil'	HV
5461	'Hear no evil'	HV
5462	'Speak no evil'	HV
5582	Vase	
5593	Vase	
5594	Vase	
5598	Girl with deer	GT
5599	Kneeling girl	GT
5605	'Lucy'	SK
5651	Boy on rocking horse	SK
5652	Boy with teddy	SK
5653	Girl with rabbit	SK
5654	Girl praying	SK
5655	Girl with teddy	SK
5656	Girl with snowball	SK
5657	Footballer	SK
5658	Snowman	SK
5659	Girl on toboggan	SK
5660	Boy with dog	SK
5689	'The Little Mermaid'	EE
5690	Mare	JG
5691	Foal	JG
5780	Vase	
5808	Vase	AK
9091	Eggcup	
9104	Tray	
9199	Dish	
9265	Tray	
9306	Dish with lid	
9527	Basket	
9528	Basket	
9875	Female	
9875	Male	
9932	Bowl	
12100	Amager man's church-going costume	CMH
12101	Amager woman's church-going costume	CMH
12102	Amager woman's market costume	CMH
12103	Amager man's market costume	CMH
12104	Amager cook's costume	CMH
12105	Amager boy's & girl's costume	CMH
12106	Amager boy's & girl's costume	CMH
12107	Amager woman's mourning costume	CMH
12110	'Asia'	
12114	'America'	
12118	'Africa'	
12127	Lady at a table	
12130	'Europe'	
12134	'Autumn'	
12136	Flute-player	
12138	Blavandshuk	CMH
12141	'Spring'	
12145	Sea horse	
12146	Sea horse	
12151	Hunter group	
12159	Mother with children	
12162	Hacdrup	CMH
12163	Hedebo	CMH
12164	Iceland	CMH
12165	Laesoe	CMH
12166	Refsnaes	CMH
12167	Woman beating baby	
12171	Skovshoved, woman	CMH

12172	Skovshoved, man & woman	CMH
12176	'Summer'	
12189	'Winter'	
12208	Man & woman	
12210	Ringe	CMH
12211	Ringkobing	CMH
12213	Roemoe	CMH
12214	The Skaw	CMH
12215	Langeland	CMH
12216	Falster	CMH
12217	Bornholm	CMH
12218	Fanoe	CMH
12219	Samsoe	CMH
12220	Als	CMH
12221	Faroe Islands woman	CMH
12222	Faroe Islands man	CMH
12223	North Slesvig	CMH
12224	Greenland woman	CMH
12225	Greenland man	CMH
12226	Denmark, Jutland, Funen, Sealand	CMH
12227	Frederiksborg	CMH
12228	Randers	CMH
12229	Lolland	CMH
12230	Horne	CMH
12231	Mors	CMH
12237	Cherub with wings	AM
12238	Bali dancer	AM
12242	'Girl with the Horn of Gold'	HC
12406	Stand for 10 children	CMH
12412	Amager girl	CMH
12413	Fanoe girl	CMH
12414	Amager boy	CMH
12415	Greenland girl	CMH
12416	Faroe Islands girl	CMH
12417	Slesvig girl	CMH
12418	Sealand girl	CMH
12419	Greenland boy	CMH
12420	Funen girl	CMH
12421	Jutland girl	CMH
12428	Crucifix	AM
12454	Susanna	AM
12456	'Market Girl'	AM
12458	Child arms raised ? Buddha	AM
12459	Mermaid	AM
12460	Flora	AM
12461	Huguenot girl	AM
12463	Iceland	AM
12466	'Diana'	AM
12469	Woman sitting on dog	AM
12470	Bowl	AM
12471	Man kneeling with jackal cape	AM
12473	Vase	AM
12475	'Seventeen Years'	AM
12477	Cupid on scooter	AM
12480	Girl sitting	AM
12481	Dish - mermaid	AM
12484	Dish	
12485	'Europe'	AM
12486	'Asia'	AM
12487	'Africa'	AM
12488	'Australasia'	AM
12489	'America'	AM
12756	Woman with piglets	AM
20138	Mammoth	
20140	Bear standing	
20155	Bear	
20179	Bear roaring	
20182	Hippopotamus	
20183	Fawn	
20187	Ape	
20188	Ape	
20193	Bear with cub	
20206	Bear sitting	
20207	Mammoth	
20217	Monkey	
20220	Elephant	KK
20223	Monkey	
20225	Elephants	
20230	Faun	
20231	Westies playing	
20239	Hippopotamus	
20240	Bears - pair	
20242	Bears fighting	
20244	Child with cat	
20262	Girl with cat	
20271	Bear lying on back	
20283	Panther	
20325	Mammoth	
20497	Vase	
20498	Flask	
20502	Man on horse	
20507	Stag	
20542	Pot - figurines on lid	
20569	Vase	
20570	Vase	
21152	Bear standing	
21400	Wild cat	
21406	Bear with cub	
21407	Falcon	
21410	Duck	
21427	Woman in blue dress	JH
21432	Bear	KK
21433	Bear sitting	KK
21434	Bear	KK
21435	Bear	KK
21436	Bear	
21449	Deer - pair	
21454	Bear	
21516	Horse	
21519	Bear standing	KK
21520	Bear lying	KK
21645	Bear standing	
21675	Bear sitting	
21737	Bear	
21818	Bear on back	
21819	Sparrows - pair	
21940	Bear lying	
22607	Fawn	
22653	Rabbit	JG
22663	Swan	
22685	Rabbit	JG
22690	Rabbit	JG
22692	Rabbit	
22693	Rabbit	
22714	Elephant	
22740	Elephant	JG
22741	Elephant	JG
22745	Bear	KK
22746	Bear	KK
22747	Bear	KK
22748	Bear	KK
22750	Badger	
22752	Fox	

Bear Family

232	Bear on side	
233	Bear sitting arm up	
234	Bear on back	
235	Bear upright	
237	Bear standing	
238	Bear sitting	
320	Polar bear walking	CJB
321	Polar bear feeding	CJB
345	Bear - sitting	HE?
351	Bear chewing toe	EN
366	Bear cubs playing	EN
409	Polar bear sitting	DJ
417	Polar bear sniffing	NN
425	Polar bear walking	NN
433	Polar bear (large)	KK
442	Polar bear	NN
458	Polar bear sitting	SJ
459	Polar bear	SJ
502	Polar bear	CFL
535	Polar bear cub standing	MEA
536	Polar bear cub feet up	MEA
537	Polar bear cub on back	MEA
538	Polar bear cub on back	MEA
729	Polar bear cub	KK
757	Bear lying	KK
824	Bears standing	EN
825	Polar bear looking up	KK
1107	Polar bear cubs playing	KK
1108	Polar bear & seal	KK
1124	Bear	KK
1137	Polar bear standing	KK
2285	Bear squatting	VW
2317	Polar bears	KK
2360	Bear	KK
2841	Bear walking	KK
2842	Bear with paw raised	KK
2991	Bears - pair	KK
3014	Bear cub eating	KK
3015	Bear squatting	KK
4753	Polar bear	JG
4780	Polar bear & cubs	JG
21433	Bear sitting	KK
21434	Bear	KK
21435	Bear	KK
21436	Bear	
21454	Bear	
21519	Bear standing	KK
21520	Bear lying	KK
21645	Bear standing	
21675	Bear sitting	
21737	Bear	
21818	Bear on back	
21940	Bear lying	
22745	Bear	KK
22746	Bear	KK
22747	Bear	KK
22748	Bear	KK

Birds

21	Dish - peacock	
107	Sparrow	
120	Duck	
236	Vase - peacock heads at waist	
263	Icelandic falcon	C T
273	Barn owl	CT
274	Flower holder - barn owls	CT or AK
283	Owls - pair	AK
306	Vase - bird handles	
358	Card tray - ducklings	CT
359	Swan male	AT
360	Swan with cygnets	AT
361	Cygnet stretching	AT
362	Cygnet	AT
363	Cygnets	AT
364	Cygnet with raised wing	AT
365	Crow	CT
367	Barn owl - small	TM
368	Bonbon dish - pigeon on lid	
370	Seagull wings spread	Kjae
373	Card tray - finches	TM
376	Bird with long tail on ashtray	TM
402	Lovebirds	TM
407	Kingfisher	DJ
410	Titmouse - 'Optimist'	DJ
411	Fantail pigeon	AP (AN)
411	Titmouse - 'Pessimist'	DJ
412	Drake & duck	CFL
415	'Protection' - 3 birds	DJ
417	Penguin	TM
420	Black grouse	DJ
423	Cuckoo	DJ
427	Walking stick handle – duck	
428	Walking stick handle - gull	
428	Gull with fish	DJ
429	Blackheaded gull	CT
429	Gull crying	DJ
430	Gull	DJ
431	Penguin	SM
436	Kingfisher	NN
437	Goose (small)	NN
438	Bullfinch	NN
441	Gerfalcon	KM
450	Owl & mice on base	CT
457	Budgerigar - blue	SJ
467	Snowy owl	JAH
468	Guillemot	CT
474	Robin	SJ
481	Titmouse	
482	Titmouse	
483	Titmouse	
484	Titmouse	
485	Titmouse	
503	Blue Ara	ARP
505	Duck	AK
515	Duck	EN
516	Ducklings	EN
517	Duckling	EN
532	Heron	TM
539	Pidgeon tail up	
566	Cockerel on clock case	CT
606	Swan	TM
609	Geese	IN
610	Owl & 3 mice on ashtray	CT
635	Common gull	CT
649	Parrots on branches	TM
652	Bonbon dish - eagle spread wings	
674	Jardiniere - swallows	AP (AN)
751	Peacock on globe base	AK
755	Swan	EN
812	Ducks – trio	
827	Tern squatting	CT
829	Duck	KK
834	Owls - pair	TM
862	Pheasants	AN (AP)
866	Blue parrot on column	CT

1008	Pigeon	ANT
1040	Finch	AN (AP)
1041	Finch preening	AN (AP)
1044	Ptarmingan	ANT
1045	Finch group	AN (AP)
1071	Eider duck	ANT
1081	Sparrow tail up	AN (AP)
1086	Guinea-fowl	PH
1088	Goose	IN
1101	Owl on ball	
1103	Magpie	AP (AN)
1157	Barn owls - trio	OM
1189	Finches - pair	PH
1190	Penguins - pair	ANT
1192	Duck	OM
1232	Marabou storks	MH
1235	Redwing	IN
1254	Bonbon dish - finches (3) on lid	
1283	Penguin	ANT
1284	Penguins - trio	ANT
1289	Night heron	MH
1304	Tawny owl	AP (AN)
1309	Sparrows - pair	AN (AP)
1331	Owl long eared	PH
1448	Bonbon dish - cockerel on lid	
1463	Bonbon dish - bird on lid	
1464	Bonbon dish - sparrow on lid	
1468	Seagull	PH
1479	Cockatoo	E J
1493	Lark	PH
1504	Wren	PH
1505	Bluetit	PH
1506	Crested tit	PH
1507	Wagtails - pair	PH
1516	Robin	PH
1519	Sparrow	AN (AP)
1600	Partridge - pair	PH
1653	Peahen	KM
1661	Falcon	PH
1670	Birds – triple	
1678	Bird - pair	KM
1690	Jay	KM
1741	Owl	TM
1742	Owl asleep	TM
1769	Kingfishers	PH
1778	Bonbon dish - turkey chick	AN (AP)
1829	Snowy owl	PH
1846	Basket - herons	PH
1863	Mandarin ducks	PH
1881	Pheasant	AN (AP)
1924	Duck - tufted	PH
1925	Duck	PH
1926	Eider duck	PH
1928	Robin	
1933	Duck - drake	PH
1934	Mallard	PH
1941	Duck tufted	PH
1951	Pheasants on base	PH
2033	Golden eagle (Blue)	VTF
2064	Dove	HHH
2068	Geese	PH
2084	Finch	PH?
2108	Parrot	MH
2122	Drake	OM
2125	Guinea-fowl	PH
2128	Drake & duck	OM
2133	Pied flycatcher	PL.H
2138	Wagtail	PL.H
2144	Flycatcher	PL.H
2165	Duck	PL.H
2167	Seagull	GKS
2177	Inkstand - barn owls	OM
2178	Falcon on rock	PL.H
2208	Sparrow on base	OJ
2215	Duck - flying	PL.H
2216	Woodpecker	PL.H
2232	Jay on perch	PH
2238	Robin	PL.H
2239	Woodpecker on ashtray	
2240	Sparrow on ashtray	
2242	Duck - flying on ashtray	PL.H
2250	Robin on ashtray	
2257	Kingfisher holding fish	PH
2258	Nuthatch?	PL.H
2259	Tit	PL.H
2260	Warbler?	PL.H
2261	Partridge	PH
2262	Robin squatting	PL.H
2264	Thrush on base	PL.H
2265	Bunting on base	PL.H
2266	Robin	PL.H
2286	Sparrow	PL.H
2310	Cockerels fighting?	PL.H
2330	Cuckoo being fed	KK
2335	Duck	PL.H
2366	Warbler?	PL.H
2374	Swallow	PL.H
2394	Pheasant	PH
2462	Dish - swan?	CT
2524	Bird - long tailed	PL.H
2549	Snowy owl	KK
2562	Gull?	PL.H
2574	Toucan	GKS
2592	Dove (faience)	
2743	Peewit	KK
2751	Seagull	KK
2811	Owl	KK
2918	Penguins	TM
2975	Penguin	TM
2989	Snowy owl	KK
2999	Owl	TM
3002	Heron	TM
3003	Penguin	TM
3194	Grebe with young	PL.H
3234	Kingfisher	PL.H
3263	Grebe	PL.H
3270	Starling fledgling	PL.H
3510	Pigeon	TM
4682	Budgie on gourd	JG
4746	Hoopoe	JG
4784	Turkey	JG
4787	Pigeon	JG
21407	Falcon	
21410	Duck	
21819	Sparrows – pair	
22663	Swan	

Cats

284	Cat curled	EN
301	Cat sitting (white)	AT
301	Cat sitting	AT
302	Kitten lying	AT
302	Kitten lying (white)	AT
303	Kittens lying (white)	AT
303	Kittens lying	AT

304	Kittens (3) lying (white)	AT
304	Kittens (3) lying	AT
305	Kitten standing (white)	AT
305	Kitten standing	AT
306	Cat sneaking (white)	AT
306	Cat sneaking	AT
307	Cat	EN
322	Cat lying - white	EN
324	Cat	
324	Cat seated	
327	Bonbon dish - Cat lid	
332	Cat lying	EN
340	Cat	EN
388	Cat crawling	CFL
422	Cat	EN
422	Cat - tabby	EN
435	Cat sitting	IP
473	Cat crawling	CFL
499	Cat white	
500	Cat grey	
504	Kitten lying	
505	Kitten sitting	
506	Kitten standing	
507	Kitten tail up	
514	Kitten lying	
515	Kitten sitting	
516	Kitten standing	
517	Kitten tail up	
527	Cat	
547	Cats playing	EN
667	Cat yawning	EN
727	Cat playing	AN (AP)
758	Cat looking up for food	KK
774	Cat - white grooming	KK
832	Cat lying with ball of wool	EN
975	Cat playing with ball of wool	CT
1752	Cats playing	EN
1803	Cat, plain grey	AN (AP)
2039	Cat grooming	GKS
2126	Cat looking back	PH
2220	Cat	PL.H
2224	Cat playing with ball	PL.H
2251	Cat on ashtray	
2284	Cat on back	CFL
2322	Cat? licking	CFL
2638	Cat turning	KK
2741*	Cat	KK
2742	Cat	
2862	Siamese cat	TM
2872	Siamese cat playing	TM
2911	Cat	
2965	Cat creeping	TM
3281	Siamese cat	TM
3654	Cat (faience)	

Dogs

259	Pointer puppy	EN
260	Pointer puppies - pair	EN
318	Labrador puppy 'Bob'	CT
439	St. Bernard	NN
442	Pekingese	EN
444	Pointer	LJ
445	Pekingese puppy	EN
448	Pekingese puppy	EN
450	Cocker spaniel	SJ
451	Sealyham	LJ
453	Pointer puppies playing	EN
547	Spaniel white	
564	Beagle standing	
565	Beagle lying	
693	Dog looking in basket	EN
704	Dog chewing bone	CT
750	Hound puppies	EN
753	Terrier sitting	LJ
778	English bulldog sitting	KK
781	Dachshund asleep	KK
801	English bulldog	KK
850	Dachshund	EN
856	Dachshund	LJ
956	French bulldog	KK
957	French bulldogs - fused	KK
977	Spitz/Husky	AP (AN)
1204	Bassett puppy	PH
1311	Pointer puppy	EN
1322	Bloodhound - female	LJ
1341	Bloodhound sniffing - male	LJ
1407	Dachshund (lying on back)	OM
1408	Dachshund (chasing tail)	OM
1450	Dachshund	KM
1457	Boston terrier	KM
1465	French bulldog standing	LJ
1466	French bulldog sitting	LJ
1533	Setter with pheasant	KM
1558	Terrier sitting	KM
1622	Collie dog lying	JB
1634	Pointer (head down)	LJ
1635	Pointer (head up)	LJ
1652	Hound standing	PH ? LJ
1662	Pekingese reclining	EN
1679	Great Dane	PH
1684	Poodle sitting	PH
1688	German Shepherd sitting	PH
1701	Collie	PH
1719	Poodle	PH
1772	Pekingese sitting	PH
1776	Pekingese	PH
1798	Belgian Shepherd reclining	PH
1859	Dog	PH
1860	Pekingese puppy	PH
1882	Huskies - pair	PH
1920	Borzoi	PH
2014	Chihuahua	GKS
2119	Dachshunds - pair	OM
2120	Dachshunds - pair	OM
2169	Cocker spaniel	SJ
2181	Sitting dog	PH
2270	Puppies playing	PL.H
2272	Terrier begging	CFL
2326	Bulldogs playing	KK
2373	King Charles spaniel	KK
2387	German Shepherd lying	PH
2425	Husky	KK
2506	Bulldog	
2565	Pekingese snarling	KK
2608	Dalmation puppy	KK
2621	Terrier sitting	KK
2622	Bulldog turning	KK
2627	Chuhuahua	
2667	Scottish terrier	KK
2668	Terrier head up	KK
2668a	Scottish terrier	KK
2697	Pekingese - snarling	KK
2701	Setter lying	KK
2753	West Highland terrier sitting	KK
2755	Wire haired terrier	KK
2761	Dog	KK?

2786	Terrier turning, head down	KK
2802	English bulldog sitting	KK
2803	German Shepherd	KK
2805	Spaniels - pair	KK
2806	Mastiff	KK
2830	Dog	KK
2853	Terrier standing	KK
2855	Hound scratching	
2863	English bulldog	KK
2871	Schnauzer	KK
2940	German Shepherd	KK
2941	Scottie	KK
2942	Dog	KK
2967	Wire haired terrier	PL.H
2969	Spitz	KK
2997	Peke looking up	KK
3000	Great Dane	KK
3018	Greyhound	
3020	Wire haired terrier (male)	PL.H
3062	Dog	
3063	Terrier	TM
3085	Sealyham standing	TM
3086	Sealyham squatting	TM
3087	Sealyham turning	TM
3110	Pointer	
3116	Cocker spaniel	TM
3139	Airedale terrier	TM
3140	Dachshund (sitting)	TM
3142	Spitz	TM
3161	Scottish terrier standing	TM
3162	Scottish terrier sitting	TM
3165	Wire haired terrier	TM
3169	Pug puppy	TM
3170	Wire haired terrier	TM
3235	Cairn terrier	TM
3249	Terrier	
3251	Scottie on side	TM
3252	Irish setter	TM
3261	German Shepherd	TM
3280	Bull terrier	TM
3476	Terrier with slipper	AB
3501	Dalmation	TM
3634	Boxer dog standing	HC
3635	Boxer dog lying	HC
3650	Great Dane - harlequin	HC
4593	Corgi	JG
4616	Basset hound	JG
4638	Poodle	JG
4757	Poodle	JG
4762	Chowchow	JG
4844	Scotties – black & white	
4852	Danish bird dog	JG
4917	Scottie	JG
4918	West Highland white terrier	JG
4952	Old English Sheepdog	JG
5136	Golden retriever	JG
5423	Llasa Apso	JG
20231	Westies playing	

Domesticated Animals

7a	Walking stick handle - cockerel	
130	Vase - cockerel head lid	
266	Turkey chick	AN (AP)
405	Pig	DJ
414	Pig	EJ
419	Pig lying down	EJ
432	Calf	KK
446	Cockerel & hen	CT
446	Cow	LJ
448	Calf	SJ
466	Goat	CT
471	Percheron	CJB
493	Turkey cock	
494	Turkey hen	
524	Inkstand - cockerels	CT
558	Lamb sleeping	
560	Lamb	
562	Lamb	
567	Cockerel on base	CT
580	Chicken on base	CT
600	Hen raised base	CT
605	Chicken squatting	AN (AP)
607	Donkey with baskets	TM
634	Sheep & lamb	CT
665	Goat & kid	CT
668	Chicken with frog on base	EJ
683	Pigs - pair	EJ
691	Piglets - pair	EJ
706	Calf	KK
800	Cow with calf	KK
830	Goat	KK
953	Pigs on ashtray	AN (AP)
1022	Pigs - pair	AP (AN)
1024	Hen	CT
1025	Cock	CT
1065	Turkey	CT
1072	Calf	KK
1094	Cock & hen	CT
1126	Cock head up	CT
1127	Cock head down	CT
1185	Turkey chick	IN
1195	Bull	KK
1205	Bull (head down)	LJ
1303	Cockerel	IN
1310	Cow - brown	LJ
1362	Horse	LJ
1363	Cockerel	
1399	Pig on wheatsheaf	EJ
1400	Pig	EJ
1486	Donkeys - pair	JAH
1613	Bonbon dish - pig on lid	
21516	Horse	
2309	Turkey	PL.H
2595	Cow & calf	KK
2624	Horse biting rear	KK
2686	Lamb - standing	KK
2703	Donkey	KK
2720	Lamb - sitting	KK
2735	Lamb - standing	KK
2769	Lambs - pair	KK
2993	Goat	KK
4558	Boar	HS
4559	Sow	HS
4561	Boar feeding	HS
4609	Shetland pony	JG
4611	Shetland pony sitting	JG
4653	Foal standing	JG
4678	Jersey cow standing	JG
4683	Jersey cow sitting	JG
4698	Mare & foal	JG
4726	Goat	JG
4744	Goat with kid	JG
4752	Lippizzanner	JG
4760	Kid on rock	JG
4882	Horse	JG

5690	Mare	JG
5691	Foal	JG

Fauns

0433	Faun with lizard	CT
0439	Faun with rabbit	CT
0456	Faun with squirrel	CT
0498	Faun with goat	CT
0648	Faun with bear	CT
0737	Faun on goat	CT
0752	Faun with parrot	CT
0857	Faun on tortoise & rope	CT
0858	Faun on tortoise	CT
0976	Faun backwards on bear	KK
1036	Faun with cat	KK
1061	Faun crying	KK
1119	Nymph & faun	GH
1188	Weeping faun on stand	GH
1188.1	Weeping faun	GH
1208	Faun on tree strump with rope	OM
1438	Vase - faun with kid on lid	AK
1712	Faun with snake	CT
1713	Faun with frog	CT
1736	Faun playing pipes	CT
1738	Faun on stump	TM
1804	Faun pulling bear's ear	KK
1880	Faun on tortoise	KK
1922	Faun & Squirrel clock case	CT
1929	Cherub	AM
1930	Cherub	AM
2107	Faun with owl	CT
2113	Faun with crow	CT
2146	Owl with 2 fauns	CT
2171	Faun kneeling with grapes	ST
2195	Cherub drinking	AM
2196	Cherub squatting	AM
2218	Cherub standing on a ball	AM
2228	Cherub with dolphin	AM
2230	Cherub riding a dolphin	AM
2248	Cherub drinking (no base)	AM
2249	Wood spirit	AM
2268	Cherub, toe in mouth	AM
2279	Cherub sitting (no base)	AM
2298	Faun with small girl	VW
2299	Faun with mermaid	VW
2318	Faun & bear wrestling	KK
2361	Faun with grapes	VW
2402	Faun & bear	KK
2424	Faun with parrot	KK
2496	Faun with 2 monkeys	KK
2573	2 Fauns with grapes	KK
2590	Faun with puppy	KK
2822	Faun with bear	KK
2823	Faun with goose?	KK
2852	Faun with lion cub	KK
2868	Faun with brown bear	KK
3082	Faun on tortoise	KK
3083	Faun fighting a cockerel	KK
3330	Satyr & woman	AM?
12237	Cherub with wings	AM
20230	Faun	

Figures with Animals

330	Clown & 2 dancing bears	CJB
422	'Ole' (boy with puppy)	IP
424	'Little Mother' (girl with cat)	IP
427	'Two Friends' (child with dog)	MA
440	Boy with dog	IP
443	Dairy maid	AL
465	Fish market	AL
477	Girl with puppy (kneeling)	VT
479	'Birgitte'	VT
527	Goose-girl	CT
528	Goose-girl	CT
620	Shepherd boy	CT
627	Farmer with sheep	CT
694	Girl with goats	CT
707	Children with dog	CT
772	Boy with calf	CT
779	Girl with calf	CT
782	Shepherd with dog	CT
848	Swineherd	CT
1012	Woman feeding cat	CT
1078	Gnome with cat	KK
1087	Hunter with dog	CT
1156	'Soldier & Dog'	CT
1375	Woman with collie	AL
1495	Girl with butterfly	VO
1524	Woman with lapdog	AL
1531	Girl with deer	
1762	Girl plucking a duck	CT
1849	Child sitting on cow	KK
1858	Boy with calves	CT
1875	Woman kneeling with bird	
1946	'Leda & the Swan'	
2005	Lady with bird	PH
2053	'Leda & the Swan'	HHH
2078	Man holding lamb?	CT
2111	Girl with fawn	HHH
2139	'Goose-thief'	CT
2140	Boy with terrier	CT
2188	Girl & sheep with dove on back	HHH
2189	Girl & sheep	HHH
2332	Girl holding duck	VW
2337	Mermaid riding seal with fish	KK
2347	Boy Neptune riding fish	VW
2348	Mermaid with fish	VW
2445	Boy with cockerel	VW
2537	Girl sitting with puppy	VW
3007	Boy with spaniel	TM
3686	Fisherman with fish	
4161	Maiden on seahorse	AM?
4530	'August' - boy with piglet	HHH
4631	Girl with cat	JOG
4795	Girl with butterfly	HV
5598	Girl with deer	GT
5653	Girl with rabbit	SK
5660	Boy with dog	SK
12466	'Diana'	AM
12469	Woman sitting on dog	AM
12756	Woman with piglets	AM
20244	Child with cat	
20262	Girl with cat	
20502	Man on horse	

Figures

8	Dish - woman	
19	Dish - woman lying on back	
24	Dish - merman	
30	Dish - woman	
349	Woman crying on chair	CT
369	Gnome with lamp	
370	Gnome with porridge	

400	Little girl	IP
401	Mother & child	IP
402	Reading children	IP
403	Playing children	IP
404	'Else'	IP
406	'Love refused'	IP
408	'Good morning' (girl in nightdress)	
412	'Dickie' (boy crouching)	IP
413	'Dickie's Mama'	IP
414	'Grethe' (girl on packing case)	IP
416	Woman with guitar	IP
418	'Victor' (boy on stool)	IP
421	'Only one drop' (girl with cat)	IP
426	Mason	
435	Woman sitting, thinking	CT
445	Hans Christian Andersen	HES
447	'Youthful boldness'	CW
452	Girl with milkcan	AL
453	'Headache' (white)	SL
454	'Toothache' (white)	SL
455	'Tummyache' (white)	SL
456	'Earache' (white)	SL
460	Smith	AL
466	'Spilt milk'	CW
467	'First book' (girl reading)	CW
468	'Happy trio'	MA
473	'Ida's flowers'	ES/SJ
474	Dwarf clock case	AK
478	Up to mom (girl - pick me up!)	SJ
486	Pierrot	ES/SJ
487	Harlequin	ES/SJ
488	Columbine	ES/SJ
489	Old fisherman	SJ
490	'Pardon me'	CW
491	Nurse	SJ
492	Dancing couple	CW
495	'Thirst' (thirsty man)	
508	Clown	
509	Clown	
510	Clown	
511	Clown	
525	'Tea Party'	
532	Boy with raincoat	SB
533	Girl dressed up	
544	Sisters (1 on plinth)	CT
544	Boy dressed up	
546	'The Little Gardener'	
548	Gypsy girl	
549	Witch (girl dressed up)	
561	'Mary' (spotted dress)	IP
568	Woman on a stone seat	AL
569	Women	
608	Woman	CT
620	Shepherd boy	CT
629	Little girl	CT
655	Harvest girl	CT
673	Thoughtful woman in chair	AL
685	Man with scythe	CT
744	Dish - woman	
784	Old woman with bonnet	CT
813	Man with rake	CT
815	Peasant girl with lunch	CT
822	Women	
865	Boy at lunch	CT
892	Churchgoer	CT
893	Woman with lute on pedestal	
894	Woman sitting on chair	AL
899	Milkmaid	CT

903	Girl with hay & rake	CT
905	Boy cutting stick	CT
908	Girl with sheaf	CT
922	Girl with book	CT
939	Girls with doll	CT
955	Sailor girl with book	CT
963	Sailor boy sitting	CT
990	Children sitting with doll	CT
1001	Old man, hands in pocket	CT
1010	Cross legged woman on pedestal	GH
1020	Victorian woman - curtsying	
1021	Mother holding children	BI
1042	Woman with baby?	
1043	Woman with washing	CT
1064	Old woman	
1112	'The Soldier & Witch'	CT
1114	'Princess & Swineherd'	CT
1129	'The Sandman'	CT
1132	'Wave & Rock'	TL
1145	'The Sandman'	CT
1180	'Soldier & Princess'	CT
1210	Mermaid on ice rock	CT
1212	Paperweight - mermaid in water	CT
1228	'Hans Clodhopper'	CT
1229	Girl bathing	CT
1238	'Princess & The Pea'	GGH
1244	Girl with mirror	GGH
1251	Amager girl	LB
1252	Little girl	LB
1276	'Shepherdess & Chimneysweep'	CT
1288	'Emperor's New Clothes'	CT
1300	Harvest group	CT
1307	Boy with tree	CT
1314	Girl knitting	LB
1315	Amager girl	LB
1316	Amager girls (shopping)	LB
1317	Woman knitting	LB
1319	The Gossips	CT
1323	Girl from Bornholm	LB
1324	Fanoe woman	LB
1326	Peasant couple dancing	CT
1352	Harvest group	CT
1374	Ballet dancer	LB
1382	Girl with sled	LB
1383	Victorian man	CT
1385	Victorian lady	CT
1395	Girls - pair	LB
1398	Greenland girl	LB
1404	Mother & child	CT
1413	'Nathan the Wise'	AJ
1414	Woman on plinth	
1451	'Fashionable pair'	AL
1473	Princess & Hans Clodhopper	CT
1476	Fairy Tale I	GGH
1478	King	CT
1494	Queen	CT
1517	Child sitting	ES
1518	Crawling child	ES
1521	Minister	AL
1522	Man leaning on walking stick	AL
1523	Actor	AL
1528	Woman with hoe	CT
1530	Girl in red	
1549	Woman collecting potatoes	CT
1586	Fairy Tale II	GGH
1593	Victorian couple	CT
1595	Fisherman	GT
1637	Woman standing	GT

1646	'Grief'	GGH
1648	Boy Scout at tree stump	CT
1649	Boy Scout with staff	CT
1654	Eskimo	LB
1659	Boy on rock	CT
1660	Man	CT
1663	Sultan	AL
1664	Fairy Tale III	GGH
1680	'The Proposal'	CT
1737	Children walking	CT
1739	Child, crawling	AB
1744	Boy seated eating apple	CT
1760	Woman with maid servant	GT
1761	'Flight to America'	CT
1770	Lady	CT
1783	'Hans & Trine'	CT
1785	Lady holding roses	CT
1786	Boy bathing	CT
1796	Man & woman	GGH
1818	Girl with baby	CT
1827	Woman kneeling	
1828	Boy	CT
1830	Boy with bricks	PH
1833	Boy with flowers	CT
1838	Woman kneeling	
1847	'The Nightingale'	CT
1848	Hans Christian Anderson	CT
1864	Native woman kneeling	
1866	Woman kneeling	
1871	Woman kneeling	
1878	Boy with sailing boat	PH
1879	Child sitting	CMH
1891	Girl and two soldiers	CT
1905	Old men	CT
1938	Girl with doll	AB
1969	'Lady & Beau'	CT
1982	Woman kneeling on pot base	PL.H
1983	Woman kneeling on pot lid	PL.H
1997	'Adam & Eve'	HHH
2030	Hairdresser	CT
2046	'The Kiss'	CT
2061	Girl with basket	
2071	Girl with trumpet	CT
2072	Girl with musical instrument	CT
2082	Boy with golden hair	MP
2083	Boy on a chair	MP
2085	Chinese man	GT
2086	Chinese woman	GT
2109	'The Kiss on the Hand'	GGH
2123	Woman	CT
2157	Girl with musical instrument	CT
2158	Girl with jar	CT
2162	Chinese couple	GGH
2163	'Little Matchgirl'	
2168	Man & woman on bench	CT
2211	Harlequin & Columbine	CT
2217	Woman - nude	AM
2227	Woman	PL.H
2244	Cherub	AM
2274	'Ali & Peribanu'	GGH
2303	Lamp with child & grapes	
2313	Mermaid	VW
2323	Child with grapes	VW
2342	Opium smoker (OG/BDC)	AM
2409	'The Nightingale'	GGH
2412	Mermaid sitting on rock	VW
2413	'Moon Girl'	GGH
2417	'Venus'	GGH

2423	'Susanna'	GGH
2428	Girl bathing	GGH
2444	Dancing girl	VW
2469	Card tray - woman	CT
2470	Card tray - woman	CT
2561	Girl with doll	VW
2604	Boy with pillows	HC
2824	Lady & Beau clock case	CT
2834	Greenland girl	GKS
2856	'Spring'	HHH
2857	'Summer'	HHH
2858	'Autumn'	HHH
2859	'Winter'	HHH
2970	Mother & child	AH
3009	'Rosebud'	TM
3034	Mother & child	HC
3049	'Henrik & Else'	HC
3070	Sailor boy on plinth	HC?
3171	'Knight & Maiden'	HC
3231	Dish - mermaid	HHH
3250	Boy with broom	AE
3272	Boy with sailing boat	AE
3321	Mermaid	AE
3407	Lapland boy	
3432	Dish - girl & duck	
3457	Mother with child	HC
3468	Boy with teddy bear	AB
3519	Boy with bucket & spade	AE
3539	Girl with doll standing	AB
3542	Boy with ball	AE
3556	Boy with umbrella	AB
3647	Drummer	AB
3658	Madonna (OG)	HHH
3667	Child with accordion	AB
3668	Fisherman	AL
3677	Girl with pot-cover	AB
3679	Nude female kneeling	
3689	Boy with horn	AB
4027	Girl on stone	AB
4047	Fishwife	BW
4050	Sailor with anchor	BW
4065	Woman hands on hips	BW
4066	Man standing	BW
4070	Woman with basket	BW
4071	Man with sack (white)	BW
4075	Ballet girl (OG)	HC
4082	Man with cartwheel	BW
4083	Woman with pail	BW
4087	Woman arms crossed at wrists	BW
4091	Hunter	BW
4092	Man carrying painting?	BW
4093	Woman with urn	BW
4097	Woman	BW
4100	Man with violin	BW
4102	Woman holding bowl?	BW
4109	Man	BW
4111	Blacksmith?	BW
4112	Woman with baby	BW
4113	Woman with cage	BW
4122	Old man reading	BW
4125	Man with child	BW
4126	Woman	
4131	Woman leaning on style	BW
4132	Man with saw	BW
4136	Man with wood	BW
4137	Woman with shopping	BW
4183	Woman with sickle	BW
4187	'Agnete & the Merman'	HC

4189	Old man	BW
4216	Hans Christian Andersen (OG)	HHH
4359	Woman with water jug	JH
4367	'Emperor & The Nightingale'	JH
4374	'Thumbelina'	HC
4377	Bricklayer	JH
4382	'Emperor & Nightingale'	JH
4418	Woman with eggs	JH
4424	Girl plaiting hair	JH
4431	'The Little Mermaid'	EE
4438	'Little Matchgirl'	AE
4502	Blacksmith	JMN
4503	Schoolgirl	HC
4507	Nurse	JMN
4523	'January' - girl skater	HHH
4524	'February' - boy juggler	HHH
4525	'March' - girl with posy	HHH
4526	'April' - boy with umbrella	HHH
4527	'May' - girl with flowers	HHH
4528	'June' - boy with briefcase	HHH
4529	'July' - girl bathing	HHH
4531	'September' - girl with satchel	HHH
4532	'October' - boy with fruit	HHH
4533	'November' - girl in riding habit	HHH
4534	'December' - boy with sack	HHH
4535	Carpenter	JMN
4539	Boy with gourd	JMN
4639	'Helena' - girl with mirror	HHH
4642	Ballet dancer	JOG
4645	Butcher	MB
4648	Girl dressing hair	JOG
4649	Teenagers with books	JOG
4669	Child on back	JOG
4670	Children reading	JOG
4680	Boy eating apple	JOG
4703	Nude girl turning	JOG
4704	Nude girl lying	JOG
4727	Plumber	JOG
4793	Girl sitting	HV
4794	Child in carnival dress	HV
4796	Girl with trumpet	HV
4989	Footballer	JOG
5194	Girl with pram	HV
5195	Girl with teddy	HV
5196	Boy with rocking horse	HV
5207	Girl with teddy	KJ
5245	Hans Christian Andersen	HV
5268	Ballet dancer	SK
5269	Ballet dancer	SK
5271	Ballet dancer	SK
5273	Girl with crown	SK
5284	Girl with flute	HV
5460	'See no evil'	HV
5461	'Hear no evil'	HV
5462	'Speak no evil'	HV
5599	Kneeling girl	GT
5605	'Lucy'	SK
5651	Boy on rocking horse	SK
5652	Boy with teddy	SK
5654	Girl praying	SK
5655	Girl with teddy	SK
5656	Girl with snowball	SK
5657	Footballer	SK
5658	Snowman	SK
5659	Girl on toboggan	SK
5689	'The Little Mermaid'	EE
12100	Amager man's church-going costume	CMH
12101	Amager woman's church-going costume	CMH
12102	Amager woman's market costume	CMH
12103	Amager man's market costume	CMH
12104	Amager cook's costume	CMH
12105	Amager boy's & girl's costume	CMH
12106	Amager boy's & girl's costume	CMH
12107	Amager woman's mourning costume	CMH
12110	'Asia'	
12114	'America'	
12118	'Africa'	
12127	Lady at a table	
12130	'Europe'	
12134	'Autumn'	
12136	Flute-player	
12138	Blavandshuk	CMH
12141	'Spring'	
12151	Hunter group	
12159	Mother with children	
12162	Hacdrup	CMH
12163	Hedebo	CMH
12164	Iceland	CMH
12165	Laesoe	CMH
12166	Refsnaes	CMH
12167	Woman beating baby	
12171	Skovshoved, woman	CMH
12172	Skovshoved, man & woman	CMH
12176	'Summer'	
12189	'Winter'	
12208	Man & woman	
12210	Ringe	CMH
12211	Ringkobing	CMH
12213	Roemoe	CMH
12214	The Skaw	CMH
12215	Langeland	CMH
12216	Falster	CMH
12217	Bornholm	CMH
12218	Fanoe	CMH
12219	Samsoe	CMH
12220	Als	CMH
12221	Faroe Islands woman	CMH
12222	Faroe Islands man	CMH
12223	North Slesvig	CMH
12224	Greenland woman	CMH
12225	Greenland man	CMH
12226	Denmark, Jutland, Funen, Sealand	CMH
12227	Frederiksborg	CMH
12228	Randers	CMH
12229	Lolland	CMH
12230	Horne	CMH
12231	Mors	CMH
12238	Bali dancer	AM
12242	'Girl with the Horn of Gold'	HC
12412	Amager girl	CMH
12413	Fanoe girl	CMH
12414	Amager boy	CMH
12415	Greenland girl	CMH
12416	Faroe Islands girl	CMH
12417	Slesvig girl	CMH
12418	Sealand girl	CMH
12419	Greenland boy	CMH
12420	Funen girl	CMH
12421	Jutland girl	CMH
12428	Crucifix	AM
12454	Susanna	AM
12456	'Market Girl'	AM
12458	Child arms raised ? Buddha	AM
12459	Mermaid	AM
12460	Flora	AM

12461	Huguenot girl	AM
12463	Iceland	AM
12466	"Diana"	AM
12471	Man kneeling with jackal cape	AM
12475	'Seventeen Years'	AM
12477	Cupid on scooter	AM
12480	Girl sitting	AM
12481	Dish - mermaid	AM
12485	'Europe'	AM
12486	'Asia'	AM
12487	'Africa'	AM
12488	'Australasia'	AM
12489	'America'	AM
21427	Woman in blue dress	JH

Fish

14	Lobster on ashtray	EN
14	Bonbon dish - crab lid	
282	Plaice	EN
286	Catfish open mouth	CT
288	Veil-tail (fish)	AP (AN)
329	Dish - octopus	
369	Rainbow trout	EN
371	Scorpion fish (Gurnard)	AND
372	Tench	AP (AN)
449	Trout (brown)	CT
457	Codfish	CFL
458	Cod - mouth open wide	CFL
459	Sardine	
460	Lumpsucker fish	EN
461	Carp	CT
462	Conger eel	CFL
463	Eel pout	CFL
464	Catfish	CFL
465	Common eel	CFL
480	Card tray - cod	EN
481	Card tray - cod	EN
482	Card tray - fish	EN
483	Card tray - crab	EN
484	Card tray - crayfish	EN
485	Card tray - lobster	EN
502	Salmon trout	ES
562	Bream	
618	Fish on ashtray	AK
619	Fish on ashtray	AK
621	Fish on slab	
715	Fish - pair	AAN (AP)
879	Eels - pair on ashtray	AAN (AP)
880	Frog on lily pad	
931	Fantail fish on ashtray	AAN (AP)
1023	Angel fish	AP (AN)
1138	Perch	AAN (AP)
1139	Eel on ashtray	AAN (AP)
1162	Conger eel	CFL
1182	Perch - group of 4	IN
1509	Sole	PH
1602	Trout (small)	KM
2414	Crucian carp	PL.H
2427	Pike	PL.H
2449	Bream	PL.H
2452	Bowl - fish	JAH
2465	Card tray - crab	EN
2494	Roach	PL.H
2545	Fish curled	PL.H
2553	Perch	PL.H
2674	Fish	PL.H
2675	Roach	PL.H
2676	Trout (rainbow)	PL.H
2738	Fish - pair	PL.H
2756	Grayling (fish)	PL.H
2837	Shark	PL.H
2838	Fish	PL.H
2851	Fish - pair (trout?)	PL.H
2869	Fish	PL.H
2870	Minnows	PL.H
2962	Wrasse	PL.H
3041	Minnows	
3042	Fish - pair	
3050	Flying fish	PL.H
3064	Fantail	PL.H
3084	Angel fish	PL.H
3131	Dish - crab	JOB
3164	Sunfish	PL.H
3498	Dish - lobster	JOB
5456	Leaping salmon	
12145	Sea horse	
12146	Sea horse	

Wildlife

1	Leaf dish with dragonfly	
2	Bonbon dish - snail on lid	
3	Curled snake on base	
4	Walking stick handle - mice	JAH
4	Crab	
5	Paperweight - snail	
6	Bowl hanging - snake ? handles	
6	Crab	
7	Dish - lizard	
8	Walking stick handle - mice	JAH
9	Walking stick handle - snail	
11	Bonbon dish - monkey on lid	
11	Mouse on ashtray	EN
12	Dish - snakes on lid	
12	Dish - frog	
15	Dragonfly on ashtray	
15	Frog	
16	Moth on ashtray	
16	Stag beetle	
18	Insect	
19	Snake crushing frog	EN
23	Bonbon dish - lizard on lid	
24	Dish - spider on lid	
25	Bonbon dish - lizard	
26	Dish - lizards (3)	
26	Bonbon dish - marmots ? handles	
143	Vase - snake wrapped around	
176	Vase - snake around rim	JAH
249	Rabbit (looking left)	
250	Vase - frog in relief	CT
254	Bonbon dish -grasshopper on lid	
265	Sealion	TM
267	Dragonfly	
268	Bee	
270	Moth	
272	Moth	
275	Flower holder - bat	CT
280	Card tray - insect	CT
287	Lizard on ashtray	AP (AN)
296	Bonbon dish - mouse on lid	
308	Lizard on ashtray	AP (AN)
309	Pigmy hippopotamus	PM
313	Grasshopper	AN (AP)
317	Starfish on stone	
319	Desert foxes - pair	CT

323	Jardiniere - dragonfly handles	TM
326	Vase - snakes	CT
328	Vase - butterfly wings	
343	Dish - butterfly	
344	Mouse with nut	AP (AN)
347	Paperweight - snake with frog	CT
348	Insect handles on ashtray	CT
357	Axolotl	AP (AN)
375	Rabbit	EN
377	Fruit stand - monkeys to base	
378	Rabbit scratching	EN
382	Bonbon dish - fox on lid	
382	Bonbon dish - insect? on lid	
401	Dish - snails	
415	Monkeys - pair	CT
416	Squirrels - pair	CT
417	Penguins - pair	TM
417	Penguins - triple	TM
419	Mouse white	DJ
426	Pigmy hippopotamus on rock	PM
431	Monkey holding its tail	AP (AN)
432	Monkey scratching back	AP (AN)
434	Rabbits	NN
437	Fox large barking	EN
438	Fox curled	EN
447	Elephant	TM
469	Kangaroo turning	HO
470	Stoat snarling	CFL
472	Crawling panther	CFL
479	Mice on top of sack	
487	Pen tray - bat	JAH
489	Crab	
492	Jardiniere - mouse peeping over edge	EN
501	Elephant	TM
503	Guinea-pig	JAH
504	Rabbit begging	JAH
507	Frog on stone	EN
508	Sea urchin?	
509	Curled snake	JAH
510	Mouse on sugar	EN
511	Mouse on chestnut	EN
512	Mouse on corn cob	EN
513	Mouse on fish head	EN
514	Mouse in skull	
518	Rabbits - pair	AK
521	Mice - pair	AK or AP
522	Mice - pair heads apart	AK or AP
530	Musk ox	EN
530	Lion cub	
540	Pidgeon tail down	
541	Seal on front	
542	Seal on back	
543	Seal on back	
546	Fox on hollow mound	EN
552	Tortoise	
557	Fox on small base	CT
563	Mice on ashtray	AK
573	Elephant	
575	Elephant	
576	Elephant	
598	Lemming?	TM
599	Elephant calf	TM
601	Bowl - otters	CT
604	Bonbon dish - grasshopper on lid	
615	Beaver on ashtray	TM
628	Rabbit on ashtray	TM
632	Dish - beaver?	TM
662	Panda eating	AT

663	Panda sitting	AT
664	Panda climbing	AT
665	Panda sleeping	AT
666	Panda with cubs	AT
667	Panda playing	AT
670	Bonbon dish - mouse on lid	
671	Jardiniere - dragonfly handles	AP (AN)
672	Bonbon dish - insect handles	OM
692	Monkey on ashtray	AN (AP)
695	Mice on ashtray	AN (AP)
703	Bowl - mouse on lid	
709	Seals - pairs	EN/KK?
714	Tiger	LJ
719	Otters playing	CT
721	Orangutans - pair	KK
741	Fly on rock	
746	Butterfly	
747	Grasshopper on ashtray	
756	Stag	KK
773	Polecats - pair	KK
775	Stoat with duck	KK/PM
776	Otter biting tail	KK
780	Seal pup	KK
802	Elephants - pair	KK
804	Lioness	LJ
805	Leopardess licking foot	LJ
826	Camel	KK
860	Flying insect	
878	Rabbit on ashtray	CT
881	Frog on flat base	
882	Frog on dish	
883	Frog on rock	
884	Frog on rock	
927	Fly	
928	Fly	
929	Fly	
930	Skink	AP (AN)
940	Monkeys - trio	KK
981	Squirrel on ashtray	AN (AP)
982	Squirrel with nut	AN (AP)
1019	Rabbit	CT
1034	Coati mundi	PH
1037	Bears (3) & tree stump	KK
1096	Marmot	BU
1100	Card tray - lizard	AP (AN)
1199	Monkey & baby	KK
1201	Monkeys	KK
1209	Badger	PH
1253	Bonbon dish - cats playing on lid	
1268	Lion yawning	LJ
1269	Hippos - pair	CJB
1281	Guinea-pig	PH
1286	Mole	S Spies
1327	Desert fox	CT
1329	Lynx	PH
1337	Bonbon dish - rabbit	
1338	Rabbit crouching	
1343	Leopard	LJ
1350	Leopard - crawling	CFL
1372	Elephant	AL
1373	Elephant	AL
1376	Elephant	AL
1402	Wolverine	PH
1427	Cat - wild	
1430	Fox	PH
1437	Bonbon dish - rabbit on lid	
1440	Lynx	PH
1441	Sealion	TM

1443	Musk ox	AN (AP)
1444	Monkey	NN
1455	Bonbon dish - rabbits (2) on lid	
1469	Jaguar	
1470	Bonbon dish - mouse on lid	
1475	Fox	EN
1482	Mountain lion	PH
1548	Bonbon dish - mouse on lid	
1596	Easter egg - rabbit	
1623	Male lion	JB
1691	Rabbit	PH
1771	Elephant	PH
1787	Racoons - pair	PH
1788	Vixen with cubs	PH
2036	Mouse on base	PL.H
2051	Deer on green base	HHH
2065	Tiger gnawing a bone	PH
2127	Seal scratching head	PH
2152	Baboon	PH
2166	Rabbit	PH/VW
2169	Mouse	PL.H
2175	Lion cub	PH
2180	Bison	PH
2187	Marmot on base	
2190	Inkstand - penguins	OM
2198	Squirrel	PL.H
2201	Monkeys - pair	HHH
2202	Stag jumping a mound	PH
2214	Lizards (triple) on ashtray	AN (AP)
2288	Arctic fox	PL.H
2301	Squirrel	PL.H
2319	Racoon	PL.H
2333	Otter with fish	VW
2334	Fox	VW
2336	Servil	H. Liisberg
2345	Otter with fish	KK
2365	Wolves fighting	KK
2367	Otter & duck	KK
2384	Mink	PL.H
2411	Mountain lion attacking stag	
2439	Gazelle with baby gazelle on back	KK
2443	Rabbit on haunches	
2451	Dish - frog	JAH
2460	Bonbon dish - mouse on lid	CT
2461	Bonbon dish - monkey on lid	EN
2463	Bonbon dish - lizard on lid	CT
2466	Card tray - lizard	AP (AN)
2467	Card tray - lizards	AP (AN)
2468	Card tray - lizard	AP (AN)
2477	Frog on ashtray	EN
2478	Snail on ashtray	
2480	Snail on blotter	JAH
2482	Inkstand - snake crushing frog	EN
2483	Inkstand - fly	EN
2487	Lynx	KK
2507	Chimpanzee	KK
2512	Wild cat grooming	KK
2519	Two sea-lions	GKS
2532	Dog?	KK
2539	Rabbits (3) fused	EN
2555	Panther	KK
2564	Vole	PL.H
2589	Monkey	KK
2596	Lion cub	KK
2607	Wild cat	KK
2609	Fawn	KK
2623	Squirrel	KK
2625	Weasel/ferret	KK
2636	Fawn head up	KK
2644	Dormouse	KK
2648	Fawn head down	KK
2649	Fawn asleep	KK
2650	Dish - monkey?	
2734	Lion cubs playing	KK
2741	Elephant (leg in trunk)	
2768	Fox	KK
2813	Elk	KK
2998	Elephant	KK
3005	Elephant	KK
3118	Penguins - pair	
3655	Giraffe	HC
3794	Lion Blanc de Chine	
4562	Stoat	JG
4572	Weasels - pair	JG
4643	Tiger	JG
4647	Baboon & baby	JG
4652	Guinea-pig crouching	JG
4654	Mink	JG
4659	Jaguar cub	JG
4676	Rabbit	JG
4687	Tiger & cubs	JG
4705	Rabbit	JG
4783	Puma cub	JG
5154	Kangaroo	JG
5298	Giant panda	WT
5401	Racoon	WT
5402	Koala	WT
20138	Mammoth	
20182	Hippopotamus	
20183	Fawn	
20187	Ape	
20188	Ape	
20207	Mammoth	
20217	Monkey	
20220	Elephant	KK
20223	Monkey	
20225	Elephants	
20239	Hippopotamus	
20283	Panther	
20325	Mammoth	
21400	Wild cat	
21449	Deer – pair	
20507	Stag	
22607	Fawn	
22653	Rabbit	JG
22685	Rabbit	JG
22690	Rabbit	JG
22692	Rabbit	
22693	Rabbit	
22714	Elephant	
22740	Elephant	JG
22741	Elephant	JG
22750	Badger	
22752	Fox	

Figurines

In this section the pieces are listed in numerical order The majority are underglaze decorated though some are overglaze or blanc de chine. Where possible, comprehensive information has been given (see below) but in a number of cases the reference material gives only the barest detail. The information is provided in the following order:

Piece Number – the factory numbering system has changed several times resulting in duplication. Charts of modern numbers are provided in the Appendix.

Description – a simple description of the piece. Some reference material was so indistinct that guesses have had to be made as to the subject and a ? has been inserted where appropriate. Many of the animals are difficult to identify and some of the dogs may owe more to imagination than reality.

Sculptor – in most cases the sculptor is known but in others there is some doubt and this is indicated by 2 names. Very occasionally an assumption has been made on the basis of subject and technique.

Date sculpted – this is an approximate date but not necessarily when the piece was first commercially produced.

Size – a guide only can be given. Size can vary significantly on each piece during production. Where a single size is given, this is normally the height; otherwise, height is the first figure mentioned. All sizes are in centimeters.

Comments – observations and further information.

Rating – this is very subjective, based on experience of the world market and trends in value and demand.

*	In production or Bing & Grondahl piece produced by Royal Copenhagen.
**	Piece not in production, easily obtainable.
***	Piece not in production and sometimes difficult to find.
****	Rare older pieces but with limited appeal.
*****	Rare, highly desirable subject matter.

Value – in most cases a fairly wide range has been given because the factors affecting value can make significant differences. All prices are based on the piece being perfect. In particular age, quality of decoration and availability influence prices. Sale prices at collectors fairs, auctions and on the internet have been analyzed over a long period and prices for the same piece can vary by as much as 500%. In addition some subjects for instance dogs, cats, fish and fauns appeal to a wider market not limited to Royal Copenhagen collectors. If a piece is still in production the upper figure is the 'new' cost in the UK at December 2000. Overglaze and stoneware have not been valued as the market is smaller and less reliable information is available. Suffice to say that when new overglaze was considerably more expensive and this is reflected in second hand prices. Where information is severely limited, it is impossible to give either a rating or value.

1
Leaf dish with dragonfly
pre-1910
7 x 26 cm

2
Bonbon Dish - snail on lid
pre-1910
10 cm

3
Curled snake on base
pre-1910
13 x 8 cm
*****
$300-500

4
Walking stick handle - mice
J. A. Heuch
1896
4.5 cm

4
Crab
pre-1910
8 cm
*****
$250-350

5
Paperweight - snail
pre-1910
9 x 14 cm
*****
$450-650

6
Bowl hanging - snake ? Handles
pre-1910
10 x 20 cm

6
Crab
pre-1910
3 x 5 x 17 cm
*****
$250-350

7
Walking stick handle - cockerel
pre-1910
5 x 9 cm

7
Dish - lizard
pre-1910
21 cm
*****

8
Walking stick handle - mice
J. A. Heuch
1896
5 cm

8
Dish - woman
pre-1910
11 x 20 cm
See No. 2469
****

9
Walking stick handle - snail
pre-1910
3 x 9 cm

11
Bonbon Dish - monkey on lid
pre-1910
14 cm
*****
$250-400

11
Mouse on ashtray
Erik Nielsen
pre-1910
13 cm
****
$150-200

12
Dish - snakes on lid
pre-1910
14 cm

12
Dish - frog
pre-1910
11 cm

14
Lobster on ashtray
Erik Nielsen
1895
4.5 x 16.5 cm

14
Bonbon Dish - crab lid
pre-1910
6 x 11 cm

15
Dragonfly on ashtray
1895
17 cm

15
Frog
pre-1910
8 x 16 cm
*****
$200-300

16
Moth on ashtray
1895
13 cm

16
Stag beetle
pre-1910
12 cm
*****
$250-350

18
Insect
pre-1910
16 x 20 cm

19
Dish - woman lying on back
pre-1910
10 cm

19
Snake crushing frog
Erik Nielsen
1896
7.5 x 27 x 17.5 cm
*****
$1250-1500

21
Dish - peacock
pre-1910
17 cm

23
Bonbon Dish - lizard on lid
pre-1910
11 cm

24
Dish - merman
pre-1910
15 cm

24
Dish - spider on lid
pre-1910
11 cm

25
Bonbon Dish - lizard
pre-1910
10 x 19 cm

26
Dish - lizards (3)
pre-1910
12 cm

26
Bonbon Dish - marmots ? Handles
pre-1910
10 x 19 cm

30
Dish - woman
pre-1910
12 x 19 cm

107
Sparrow
7 cm
In production 1991
*
$45-75

130
Vase - cockerel head lid
pre-1910
20 cm

143
Vase - snake wrapped around
pre-1910
25 cm

176
Vase - snake around rim
J. A. Heuch
1898
14 cm

232
Bear on side
5 cm
In production 2000
*
$50-75

233
Bear sitting arm up
9 cm
In production 2000
*
$50-70

234
Bear on back
6 cm
In production 2000
*
$50-70

235
Bear upright
7 cm
In production 2000
*
$50-70

236
Vase - peacock heads at waist
pre-1910
29 cm

237
Bear standing
18 cm
In production 2000
*
$120-180

238
Bear sitting
13 cm
In production 2000
*
$120-180

249
Rabbit (looking left)
7 x 7 cm
In production 1994
**
$75-105

250
Vase - frog in relief
Chr. Thomsen
1899
23.5 x 2.7 x 6.5 cm

254
Bonbon Dish -grasshopper on lid
pre-1910
13 cm h

259
Pointer puppy
Erik Nielsen
1900
20 cm
In production 2000
*
$120-270

260
Pointer puppies - pair
Erik Nielsen
1900
15 cm
In production 1988
**
$90-200

263
Icelandic Falcon
Chr. Thomsen
1900
29 cm
In production 2000
*
$350-900

265
Sealion
Th. Madsen
1900
29 cm
In production 1981
**
$400-500

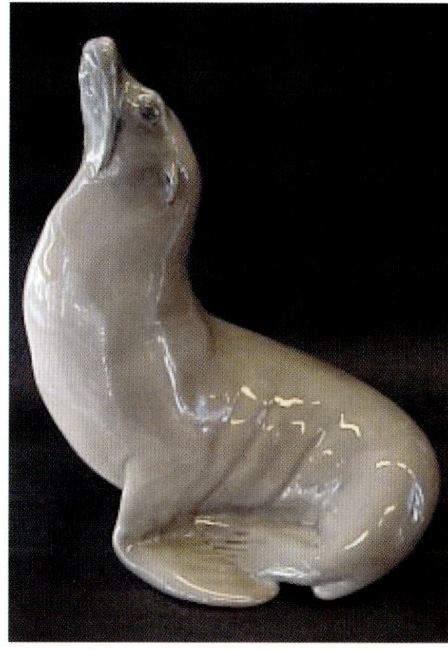

266
Turkey chick
A. Nielsen (AP)
1900
4.5 x 9 cm
In production 1981
**
$50-80

267
Dragonfly
pre-1910
7 x 11 cm
*****
$150-250

268
Bee
pre-1910
3.5 x 7 cm
*****
$100-200

270
Moth
pre-1910
2.5 x 4 cm
*****
$100-200

272
Moth
pre-1910
4.5 x 8.5 cm
*****
$150-250

273
Barn owl
Chr. Thomsen
1900
22 cm
In production 1981
***
$300-450

274
Flower holder - barn owls
Chr. Thomsen or Arnold Krog
1900
20 x 23 cm
*****

275
Flower holder - bat
Chr. Thomsen
1900
17 x 20 cm
*****
$450-600

280
Card tray - insect
Chr. Thomsen
1901
5.3 x 24.3 x 22.7 cm

282
Plaice
Erik Nielsen
1901
18 cm
*****
$400-550

283
Owls - pair
Arnold Krog
1901
33.5 x 20 cm
In production 1981
****
$500-750

284
Cat curled
Erik Nielsen
1901
8 x 21 cm
Also in tabby
*****
$400-550

286
Catfish open mouth
Chr. Thomsen
1901
16 cm
****
$400-600

287
Lizard on ashtray
A. Pedersen (AN)
1901
13 cm

288
Veil-tail (Fish)
A. Pedersen (AN)
1901
17 cm
*****
$400-550

296
Bonbon Dish - mouse on lid
pre-1910
10 cm

301
Cat Sitting (white)
Allan Therkelsen
1993
15 cm
In production 1997
*
$90-130

301
Cat sitting (tabby)
Allan Therkelsen
1993
13 x 15 cm
In production 2000
*
$165-240

302
Kitten lying (tabby)
Allan Therkelsen
1993
7.5 x 7.5 cm
In production 2000
*
$95-130

302
Kitten lying (white)
Allan Therkelsen
1993
8 cm
In production 1997
*
$90-130

303
Kittens lying (white)
Allan Therkelsen
1993
5 cm
In production 1997
*
$90-130

303
Kittens lying (tabby)
Allan Therkelsen
1993
10.8 x 5.4 cm
In production 2000
*
$90-130

304
Kittens (3) lying (white)
Allan Therkelsen
1993
5 cm
In production 1997
*
$90-140

304
Kittens (3) lying (tabby)
Allan Therkelsen
1993
5 cm
In production 2000
*
$90-140

305
Kitten standing (white)
Allan Therkelsen
1993
10 cm
In production 1997
*
$90-130

305
Kitten standing (tabby)
Allan Therkelsen
1993
10 cm
In production 2000
*
$90-130

306
Cat sneaking (white)
Allan Therkelsen
1993
4 cm
In production 1997
*
$95-130

306
Cat sneaking (tabby)
Allan Therkelsen
1993
4 cm
In production 2000
*
$95-130

306
Vase - bird handles
pre-1910
12 x 17 cm

307
Cat
Erik Nielsen
1901
19 cm
***
$350-500

308
Lizard on ashtray
A. Pedersen (AN)
1901
13 cm

309
Pigmy Hippopotamus
Marie Prinzessin
1901
18 x 34 cm
*****
$750-1000

313
Grasshopper
A. Nielsen (AP)
pre-1910
5 x 7 cm
*****
$250-400

317
Starfish on stone
pre-1910
10 cm

318
Labrador puppy 'Bob'
Chr. Thomsen
1901
14 x 23 cm
****
$350-500

319
Desert Foxes - pair
Chr. Thomsen
1901
11 x 18 cm
***
$300-400

320
Polar bear walking
Carl J. Bonnesen
1900
9 x 18 cm
In production 2000
*
$50-110

321
Polar bear feeding
Carl J. Bonnesen
1900
9 x 14 cm
In production 2000
*
$50-110

322
Cat lying - white
Erik Nielsen
1901
13 x 26 cm
See #332
*****
$450-600

323
Jardiniere - dragonfly handles
Th. Madsen
1901
12 x 31 x 14 cm

324
Cat seated
pre-1910
11 cm
*****
$300-500

326
Vase - snakes
Chr. Thomsen
1901
14 x 16 cm

327
Bonbon Dish - Cat lid
1901
14 x 18 cm

328
Vase - butterfly wings
pre-1910
10 cm

329
Dish - octopus
pre-1910
6 x 17 cm

330
Clown & 2 Dancing Bears
Carl J. Bonnesen
1901
30 x 25 cm
*****
$1500-2000

332
Cat lying
Erik Nielsen
1901
13 x 26 cm
See #322
*****
$450-600

340
Cat
Erik Nielsen
1901
19 cm
In production 2000
*
$175-260

343
Dish - butterfly
pre-1910
13 cm

344
Mouse with nut
A. Pedersen (AN)
1901
5 cm
***
$100-200

345
Bear - sitting
Hermissen?
1901
14 cm
****
$250-350

347
Paperweight - snake with frog
Chr. Thomsen
1901
11 cm
*****
$450-600

348
Insect handles on ashtray
Chr. Thomsen
1901
16 cm

349
Woman crying on chair
Chr. Thomsen
1901
17 x 21 cm
*****
$400-550

351
Bear chewing toe
Erik Nielsen
1901
16 cm
****
$250-400

357
Axolotl
A. Pedersen (AN)
1901
3 x 25 cm
*****
$800-1200

358
Card tray -ducklings
Chr. Thomsen
1901
10 x 28 cm
****
$275-375

359
Swan male
Allan Therkelsen
1995
14 cm
In production 2000
*
$115-160

360
Swan with cygnets
Allan Therkelsen
1995
14 cm
In production 2000
*
$100-200

361
Cygnet stretching
Allan Therkelsen
1995
8 cm
In production 2000
*
$65-85

362
Cygnet
Allan Therkelsen
1995
7 cm
In production 2000
*
$65-85

363
Cygnets
Allan Therkelsen
1995
10 cm
In production 2000
*
$75-105

364
Cygnet with raised wing
Allan Therkelsen
1995
8 cm
In production 2000
*
$75-105

365
Crow
Chr. Thomsen
1901
16 x 35 cm
In production 1981
***
$350-500

366
Bear cubs playing
Erik Nielsen
1901
22 cm
****
$350-500

367
Barn Owl - small
Th. Madsen
1902
9 cm
*****
$200-400

368
Bonbon Dish - pigeon on lid
pre-1910
27 x 15 cm

369
Rainbow Trout
Erik Nielsen
1902
23 cm
***
$200-300

369
Gnome with lamp
1997
7 x 10 cm
**
$100-150

370
Gnome with porridge
1997
7 x 10 cm
**
$100-150

370
Seagull wings spread
Kjaer
1902
25 x 32 x 38 cm
*****
$450-600

371
Scorpion Fish (Gurnard)
Andresen
1902
9 x 20 cm
****
$350-500

372
Tench
A. Pedersen (AN)
1902
7 x 17 cm
****
$150-250

373
Card tray - finches
Th. Madsen
1902
15 x 20.7 x 18 cm
****
$400-500

375
Rabbit
Erik Nielsen
1902
9 x 19 cm
***
$200-300

376
Bird with long tail on ashtray
Th. Madsen
1901
15 cm

377
Fruit stand - monkeys to base
pre-1910
31 x 29 cm

378
Rabbit Scratching
Erik Nielsen
1902
9 cm
***
$250-350

382
Bonbon Dish - fox on lid
pre-1929
15 cm w

382
Bonbon Dish - insect? on lid
pre-1910
12 cm

388
Cat Crawling
C. F. Liisberg
1896
12 cm
*****
$600-750

400
Little girl
Ingeborg Plockross
11 cm
B&G piece in production in 2000
*
$80-170

401
Dish - snails
pre-1910
7 cm

401
Mother & child
Ingeborg Plockross
28 cm
B&G piece in production 1994
*
$150-250

402
Lovebirds
Th. Madsen
1902
14 cm
In production 2000
*
$75-205

402
Reading children
Ingeborg Plockross
1900
10 cm
B&G piece in production in 2000
*
$85-240

403
Playing children
Ingeborg Plockross
1900
12 cm
B&G piece in production in 2000
*
$100-240

404
'Else'
Ingeborg Plockross
17 cm
B&G piece Blue or white dress
*
$100-150

405
Pig
Dahl Jensen
12 cm
B&G piece in production in 1991
*
$40-100

406
'Love refused'
Ingeborg Plockross
1900
17 cm
B&G piece in production in 2000
*
$120-350

407
Kingfisher
Dahl Jensen
11 cm
B&G piece in production in 2000
*
$75-150

408
'Good morning' (Girl in nightdress)
Michaela Ahlmann
20 cm
B&G piece in production in 2000
*
$50-150

409
Polar bear sitting
Dahl Jensen
19 cm
B&G piece in production in 2000
*
$90-175

410
Titmouse - 'Optimist'
Dahl Jensen
1904
13 cm
B&G piece in production in 2000
*
$45-100

411
Titmouse - 'Pessimist'
Dahl Jensen
1904
13 cm
B&G piece in production in 2000
*
$40-100

411
Fantail Pigeon
A. Pedersen (AN)
1902
21 x 19 cm
*****
$350-500

412
Drake & duck
C. F. Liisberg
1902
19 cm
In production 1981
****
$450-650

412
'Dickie' (boy crouching)
Ingeborg Plockross
12 cm
B&G piece in production in 2000
*
$60-215

413
'Dickie's Mama'
Ingeborg Plockross
22 cm
B&G piece in production in 2000
*
$215-605

414
Pig
Erik Nielsen
1902
16 cm
In production 1988
***
$300-400

414
'Grethe' (girl on packing case)
Ingeborg Plockross
17 cm
B&G piece in production in 2000
*
$155-235

415
Monkeys - pair
Chr. Thomsen
1902
13 cm
***
$200-350

415
'Protection' - 3 birds
Dahl Jensen
18 cm
B&G piece in production in 2000
*
$130-270

416
Squirrels - pair
Chr. Thomsen
1902
19 cm
In production 1981
****
$400-550

416
Woman with guitar
Ingeborg Plockross
24 cm
B&G piece in production 1994
*
$220-350

417
Polar bear sniffing
Niels Nielsen
19 cm
B&G piece in production in 2000
*
$60-115

417
Penguin
Th. Madsen
1902
24 cm
In production 1981
***
$200-300

417a
Penguins - pair
Th. Madsen
1902
24 x 16 cm
****
$250-350

417b
Penguins - triple
Th. Madsen
1902
24 x 24 cm
****
$300-400

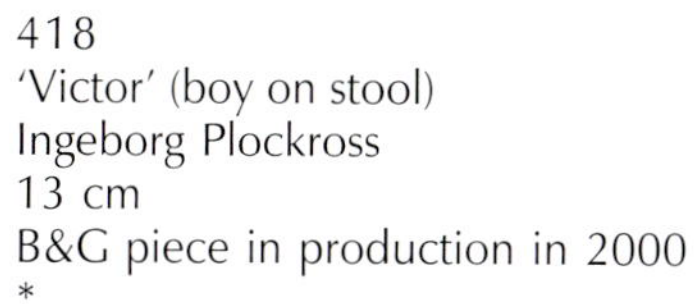

418
'Victor' (boy on stool)
Ingeborg Plockross
13 cm
B&G piece in production in 2000
*
$80-215

419
Pig lying down
Erik Nielsen
1902
34 cm
*****
$400-600

419
Mouse white
Dahl Jensen
5 cm
B&G piece in production 1997
*
$20-55

420
Black Grouse
Dahl Jensen
41 cm
B&G piece in production 1994
*
$450-600

421
'Only one drop' (girl with cat)
Ingeborg Plockross
15 cm
B&G piece in production in 2000
*
$150-380

422
Cat
Erik Nielsen
1902
8 x 13 cm
In production 2000
*
$75-125

422
'Ole' (boy with puppy)
Ingeborg Plockross
1911
17 cm
B&G piece in production in 2000
*
$80-255

422
Cat - Tabby
Erik Nielsen
1902
8 cm
In production 2000
*
$90-130

423
Cuckoo
Dahl Jensen
24 cm
B&G piece in production 1994
*
$100-150

424
'Little Mother' (girl with cat)
Ingeborg Plockross
17 cm
B&G piece in production in 2000
*
$75-215

425
Polar bear walking
Niels Nielsen
30 cm
B&G piece in production in 2000
*
$70-270

426
Pigmy Hippopotamus on rock
Marie Prinzessin
1902
17 x 43 cm
Prone to damage on back legs
*****
$850-1100

426
Mason
29 cm
B&G piece in production 1994
*
$250-350

427
Walking stick handle - duck
pre-1910
5 x 7 cm

427
'Two friends' (child with dog)
Michaela Ahlmann
12 cm
B&G piece in production in 2000
*
$125-300

428
Walking stick handle - gull
pre-1910
6 x 9 cm

428
Gull with fish
Dahl Jensen
14 cm
B&G piece in production in 2000
*
$65-85

429
Blackheaded gull
Chr. Thomsen
1902
11 x 24 cm
***
$200-300

429
Gull crying
Dahl Jensen
9 cm
B&G piece in production in 2000
*
$25-65

430
Gull
Dahl Jensen
9 cm
B&G piece in production 1997
*
$75-100

431
Monkey holding its tail
A. Pedersen (AN)
1902
15 cm
****
$250-400

431
Penguin
Sveistrup Madsen
8 cm
B&G piece in production in 2000
*
$50-95

432
Monkey scratching back
A. Pedersen (AN)
1902
15 cm
****
$250-400

432
Calf
Knud Kyhn
18 cm
B&G piece in production in 2000
*
$110-360

433
Faun with lizard
Chr. Thomsen
1903
21 cm
In production 1981
***
$250-350

433
Polar bear (large)
Knud Kyhn
34 cm
B&G piece in production in 2000
*
$300-820

434
Rabbits
Niels Nielsen
6 cm
B&G piece in production in 1991
*
$50-75

435
Woman sitting, thinking
Chr. Thomsen
1903
23 cm
*****
$350-500

435
Cat sitting
Ingeborg Plockross
12 cm
B&G piece in production in 2000
*
$65-120

436
Kingfisher
Niels Nielsen
1916
11 cm
B&G piece in production in 2000
*
$70-165

437
Goose (small)
Niels Nielsen
9 cm
B&G piece in production in 2000
*
$30-75

437
Fox large barking
Erik Nielsen
1903
27 cm
In production 1981
**
$250-400

438
Fox curled
Erik Nielsen
1902
9 x 17 cm
In production 1981
****
$300-400

438
Bullfinch
Niels Nielsen
12 cm
B&G piece in production in 1997
*
$45-100

439
Faun with rabbit
Chr. Thomsen
1903
14 cm
In production 1963
***
$350-450

439
St. Bernard
Niels Nielsen
1918
12 cm
B&G piece in production in 2000
*
$50-115

440
Boy with dog
Ingeborg Plockross
13 cm
B&G piece in production in 2000
*
$100-150

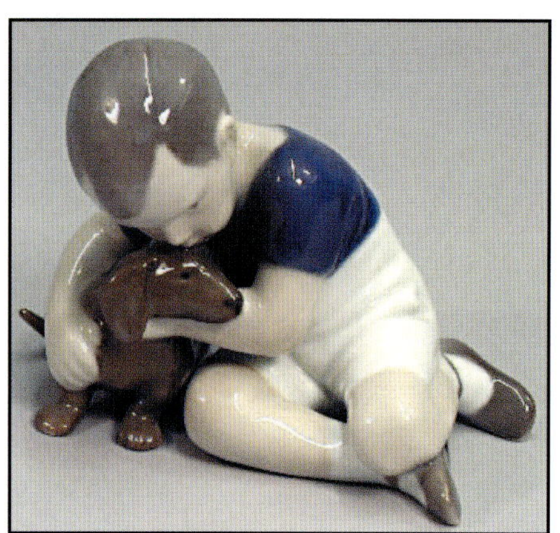

441
Gerfalcon
Knud Moller
36 cm
B&G piece in production 1994
*
$2000-3000

442
Pekingese
Erik Nielsen
1903
15 x 53 cm
*****
$750-1000

442
Polar bear
Niels Nielsen
43 cm
B&G piece in production in 2000
*
$2000-4250

443
Dairy maid
Axel Locher
19 cm
B&G piece in production in 1997
*
$350-450

444
Pointer
Lauritz Jensen
1925
16 cm
B&G piece in production in 2000
*
$125-200

445
Pekingese puppy
Erik Nielsen
1903
13 cm
****
$300-400

445
Hans Christian Andersen
Henning Seidelin
1925
23 cm
B&G piece in production in 2000
*
$225-1000

446
Cockerel & hen
Chr. Thomsen
1903
25 cm
*****
$350-500

446
Cow
Lauritz Jensen
25 cm
B&G piece in production in 1991
*
$200-275

447
Elephant
Th. Madsen
1903
30 x 42 cm
*****
$800-1500

447
'Youthful boldness'
Claire Weiss
1932
20 cm
B&G piece in production in 2000
*
$85-410

448
Pekingese puppy
Erik Nielsen
1903
13 cm
****
$300-400

448
Calf
Svend Jespersen
8 cm
B&G piece in production 1994
*
$25-75

449
Trout (brown)
Svend Jespersen
15 cm
B&G piece in production in 2000
*
$60-105

450
Owl & mice on base
Chr. Thomsen
1903
11 x 11 cm
*****
$450-600

450
Cocker Spaniel
Svend Jespersen
1932
11 cm
B&G piece in production in 2000
*
$40-105

451
Sealyham
Lauritz Jensen
6 cm
B&G piece in production in 2000
*
$50-70

452
Girl with milkcan
Axel Locher
21 cm
B&G piece in production 1994
*
$225-350

453
Pointer puppies playing
Erik Nielsen
pre-1910
9 cm
In production 2000
*
$90-135

453
'Headache' (white)
Svend Lindhardt
11.5 cm
B&G piece in production in 1991
*
$20-60

454
'Toothache' (white)
Svend Lindhardt
11.5 cm
B&G piece in production in 1991
*
$20-60

455
'Tummyache' (white)
Svend Lindhardt
11.5 cm
B&G piece in production in 1991
*
$20-60

456
'Earache' (white)
Svend Lindhardt
11.5 cm
B&G piece in production in 1991
*
$20-60

456
Faun with squirrel
Chr. Thomsen
1903
23 cm
In production 1981
***
$250-350

457
Codfish
C. F. Liisberg
1888
25 cm
****
$350-500

457
Budgerigar - blue
Svend Jespersen
15 cm
B&G piece in production in 2000
*
$60-150

458
Cod - mouth open wide
C. F. Liisberg
1888
25 cm
****
$375-500

458
Polar bear sitting
Svend Jespersen
11 cm
B&G piece in production in 2000
*
$65-80

459
Sardine
pre-1910
16 cm
****
$200-300

459
Polar bear
Svend Jespersen
12 cm
B&G piece in production in 2000
*
$40-80

460
Lumpsucker fish
Erik Nielsen
1890
8.5 x 29 cm
****
$500-750

460
Blacksmith
Axel Locher
29 cm
B&G piece in production 1994
*
$255-325

461
Carp
Chr. Thomsen
1899
9 x 19 cm
****
$250-400

462
Conger Eel
C. F. Liisberg
1889
10 cm
*****
$250-350

463
Eel Pout
C. F. Liisberg
1889
19 cm
*****
$275-375

464
Catfish
C. F. Liisberg
1889
18 cm
****
$300-450

465
Common eel
C. F. Liisberg
1888
11 cm
*****
$250-350

465
Fish market
Axel Locher
20 cm
B&G piece in production in 2000
*
$400-1200

466
Goat
Chr. Thomsen
1900
15 x 27 cm
In production 1963
***
$300-400

466
'Spilt milk'
Claire Weiss
1938
18 cm
B&G piece in production in 2000
*
$80-285

467
Snowy Owl
J. A. Heuch
1895
22 x 17.8 cm
****
$400-550

467
'First book' (girl reading)
Claire Weiss
11 cm
B&G piece in production in 2000
*
$95-220

468
Guillemot
Chr. Thomsen
1899
27 cm
***
$350-450

468
'Happy trio'
Michaela Ahlmann
20 cm
B&G piece in production in 2000
*
$265-915

469
Kangaroo turning
Howitz
1885
18 x 24 cm
*****
$300-450

470
Stoat snarling
C. F. Liisberg
1897
13 x 25 cm
****
$450-650

471
Percheron
Carl J. Bonnesen
1895
29 x 35 cm
In production 1981
****
$650-950

472
Crawling panther
C. F. Liisberg
1898
10.5 x 47 cm
Also in white & brown
****
$800-1000

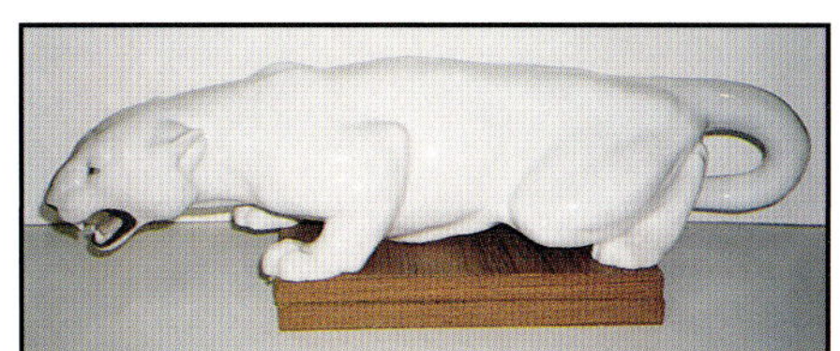

473
Cat crawling
C. F. Liisberg
1896
12 x 46 cm
In production 2000
*
$400-600

473
'Ida's flowers'
Else Sandholt/Svend Jespersen
15 cm
B&G piece in production in 2000
*
$85-255

474
Dwarf clock case
Arnold Krog
1899
17 cm h
*****
$800-1000

474
Robin
Svend Jespersen
10 cm
B&G piece in production in 2000
*
$25-85

477
Girl with puppy (kneeling)
Vita Thymann
13 cm
B&G piece in production in 2000
*
$50-220

478
Up to mom (girl - pick me up!)
Svend Jespersen
11 cm
B&G piece in production in 2000
*
$70-210

479
Mice on top of sack
pre-1910
12 cm
*****
$350-450

479
'Birgitte'
Vita Thymann
13 cm
B&G piece
*
$100-150

480
Card tray - cod
Erik Nielsen
1890
27 cm
****
$350-450

481
Card tray - cod
Erik Nielsen
1890
27 cm

481
Titmouse
10 cm
B&G piece in production in 2000
*
$50-75

482
Card tray - fish
Erik Nielsen
1896
26 cm w

482
Titmouse
7 cm
B&G piece in production in 2000
*
$50-75

483
Card tray - crab
Erik Nielsen
1896
29 cm w

483
Titmouse
7 cm
B&G piece in production in 2000
*
$50-75

484
Card tray - crayfish
Erik Nielsen
1896
26 cm w

484
Titmouse
6 cm
B&G piece in production in 2000
*
$50-75

485
Card tray - lobster
Erik Nielsen
1896
5 x 28 x 26 cm
In production 1981

485
Titmouse
6 cm
B&G piece in production in 2000
*
$50-75

486
Pierrot
Else Sandholt/Svend Jespersen
23 cm
B&G piece in production in 1991
*
$100-200

487
Pen tray - bat
J. A. Heuch
1895
22 cm h
*****
$500-750

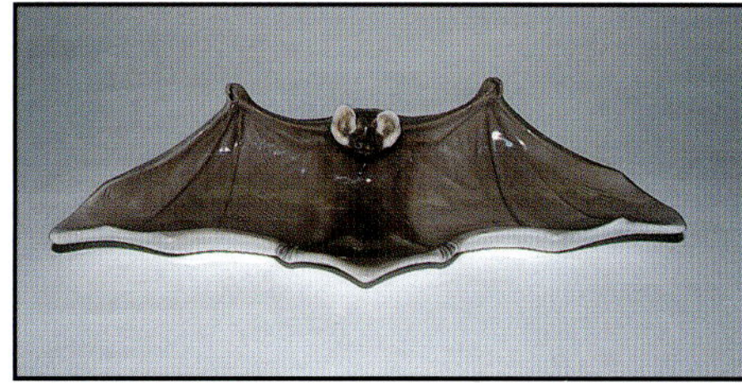

487
Harlequin
Else Sandholt/Svend Jespersen
28 cm
B&G piece in production in 1991
*
$150-250

488
Columbine
Else Sandholt/Svend Jespersen
25 cm
B&G piece in production in 1991
*
$150-250

489
Crab
pre-1910
10 x 16 cm
*****
$400-600

489
Old fisherman
Svend Jespersen
22 cm
B&G piece in production 1994
*
$200-350

490
'Pardon me'
Claire Weiss
1932
20 cm
B&G piece in production in 2000
*
$100-400

491
Nurse
Svend Jespersen
23 cm
B&G piece
*
$150-200

492
Jardiniere - mouse peeping over edge
Erik Nielsen
1894
12 x 20 cm

492
Dancing couple
Claire Weiss
1932
20 cm
B&G piece in production in 2000
*
$150-410

493
Turkey Cock
B&G piece
*

494
Turkey Hen
B&G piece
*

495
'Thirst' (thirsty man)
21 cm
B&G piece in production 1994
*

498
Faun with goat
Chr. Thomsen
1906
13 cm
In production 1981
***
$400-550

499
Cat white
11 cm
B&G piece in production in 2000
*
$50-85

500
Cat grey
11 cm
B&G piece in production in 2000
*
$50-100

501
Elephant
Th. Madsen
1903
18 x 20 cm
****
$225-400

502
Polar bear
C. F. Liisberg
1894
31.8 x 14.5 x 8.5 cm
In production 2000
*
$200-350

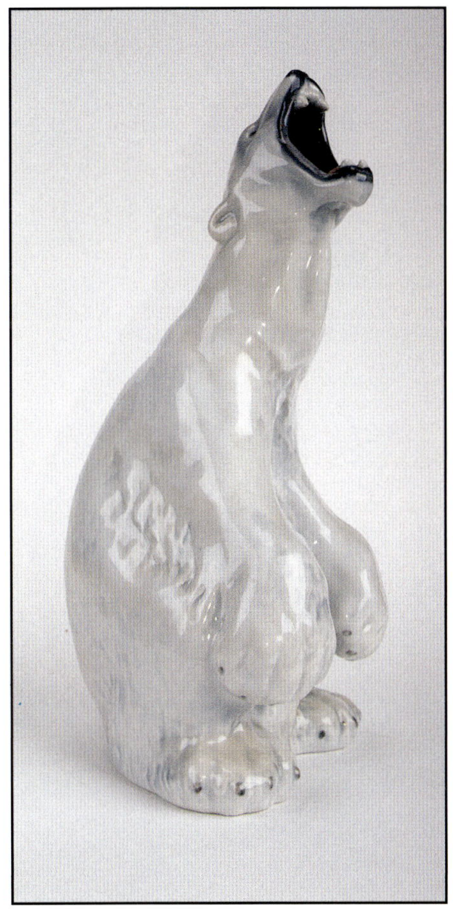

502
Salmon trout
Else Sandholt
1964
22 cm
B&G piece in production in 2000
*
$150-200

503
Guinea-pig
J. A. Heuch
1895
8 x 13 cm
*****
$350-450

503
Blue Ara
Armand Petersen
1977
42 cm
B&G piece in production in 2000
*
$500-1500

504
Rabbit begging
J. A. Heuch
1895
18 cm
****
$250-350

504
Kitten lying
8 cm
B&G piece in production in 2000
*
$60-105

505
Duck
Arnold Krog
1895
9 x 20 cm
****
$250-400

505
Kitten sitting
12 cm
B&G piece in production in 2000
*
$75-105

506
Kitten standing
13 cm
B&G piece in production in 2000
*
$80-115

507
Frog on stone
Erik Nielsen
1891
4 cm
In production 2000
*
$30-60

507
Kitten tail up
14 cm
B&G piece in production in 2000
*
$80-115

508
Sea Urchin?
pre-1910
4 x 6.5 cm

508
Clown
22 cm
B&G piece
*
$25-75

509
Curled snake
J. A. Heuch
pre-1910
6 x 7 cm
*****
$250-400

509
Clown
23 cm
B&G piece
*
$25-75

510
Mouse on sugar
Erik Nielsen
1890
4.5 cm
In production 2000
*
$30-85

510
Clown
24 cm
B&G piece
*
$25-75

511
Mouse on chestnut
Erik Nielsen
1890
7 cm
In production 2000
*
$40-85

511
Clown
25 cm
B&G piece
*
$25-75

512
Mouse on corn cob
Erik Nielsen
1890
5.5 x 14 cm
In production 1981
**
$60-95

513
Mouse on fish head
Erik Nielsen
1890
4.5 x 8 cm
*****
$250-400

514
Mouse in skull
pre-1910
6 x 12 cm
*****
$400-600

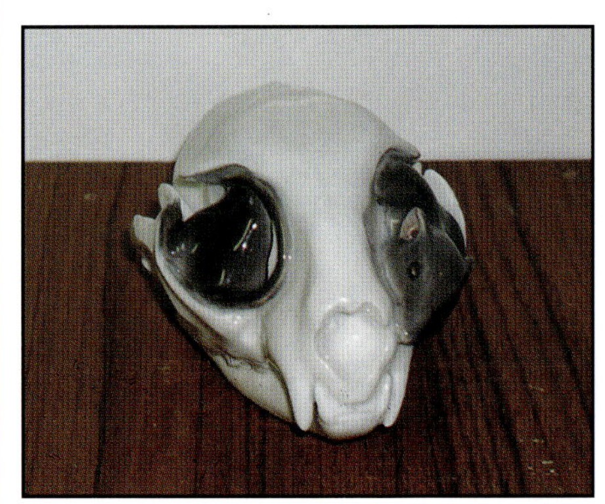

514
Kitten lying
8 cm
B&G piece in production in 2000
*
$90-130

515
Duck
Erik Nielsen
1898
5 x 12 cm
****
$100-150

515
Kitten sitting
12 cm
B&G piece in production in 2000
*
$90-130

516
Ducklings
Erik Nielsen
1897
4.5 x 9 cm
In production 1997
**
$50-100

516
Kitten standing
13 cm
B&G piece in production in 2000
*
$90-130

517
Duckling
Erik Nielsen
1898
5 x 7 cm
****
$175-225

517
Kitten tail up
14 cm
B&G piece in production in 2000
*
$90-130

518
Rabbits - pair
Arnold Krog
1895
5 x 10 cm
In production 2000
*
$40-100

521
Mice - pair
Arnold Krog or A. Pedersen
1903
4.5 x 8 cm
In production 1981
***
$150-250

522
Mice - pair heads apart
Arnold Krog or A. Pedersen
1903
10 cm
*****
$200-300

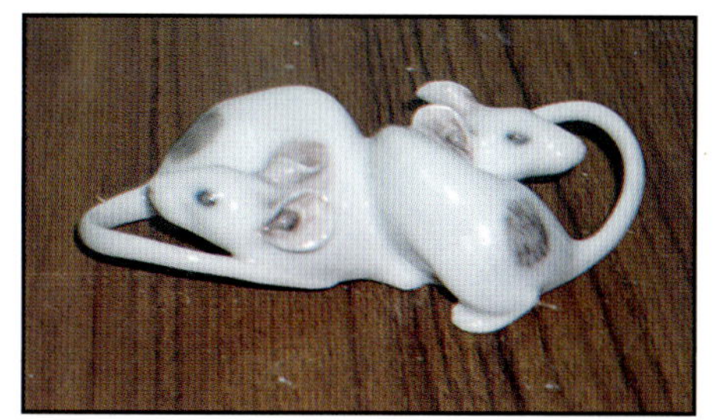

524
Inkstand - cockerels
Chr. Thomsen
1903
11 x 23 cm
*****
$1000-1300

525
'Tea Party'
26 cm
B&G piece
*

527
Goose-girl
Chr. Thomsen
1903
24 cm
Also in overglaze. Underglaze still in production
*
$150-525

527
Cat
5 cm
B&G piece in production in 1997
*

528
Goose-girl
Chr. Thomsen
1903
19 cm
Also in overglaze. Underglaze still in production
*
$75-350

530
Musk Ox
Erik Nielsen
1903
18 x 29 cm
*****
$750-1000

530
Lion Cub
B&G piece
*

532
Heron
Th. Madsen
1903
27 x 12 cm
In production 2000
*
$500-725

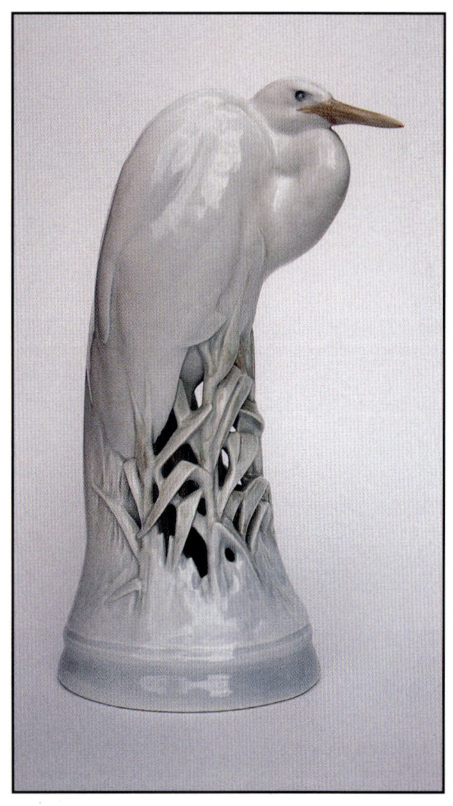

532
Boy with raincoat
Soren Brunoe
1985
18 cm
B&G piece in production in 2000
*
$100-215

533
Girl dressed up
20 cm
B&G piece in production in 1991
*

535
Polar bear cub standing
Merete Agergaard
1985
16 cm
B&G piece in production in 2000
*
$75-120

536
Polar bear cub feet up
Merete Agergaard
1985
13 cm
B&G piece in production in 2000
*
$80-120

537
Polar bear cub on back
Merete Agergaard
1985
15 cm
B&G piece in production in 2000
*
$80-120

538
Polar bear cub on back
Merete Agergaard
1985
16 cm
B&G piece in production in 2000
*
$80-120

539
Pidgeon tail up
14 cm
B&G piece in production in 1997
*

540
Pidgeon tail down
6 cm
B&G piece in production 1994
*

541
Seal on front
15 cm
B&G piece in production 1994
*
$30-75

542
Seal on back
15 cm
B&G piece in production in 1991
*
$30-75

543
Seal on back
14 cm
B&G piece in production in 1991
*
$30-75

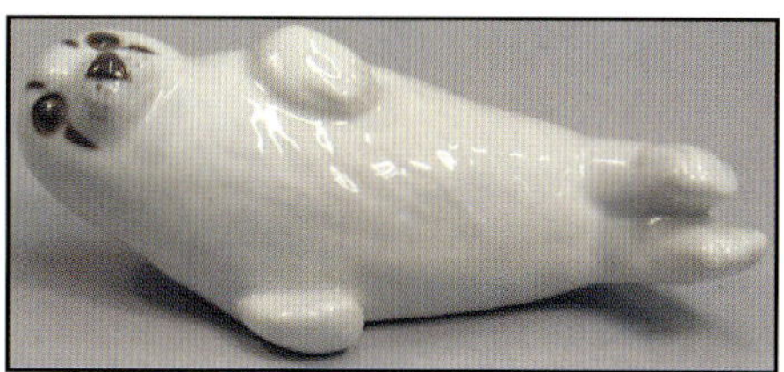

544
Sisters (1 on plinth)
Chr. Thomsen
1904
26 x 11 cm
****
$450-550

544
Boy dressed up
20 cm
B&G piece in production in 1991
*
$100-150

546
Fox on hollow mound
Erik Nielsen
1904
16 x 10 cm
*****
$350-500

546
'The Little Gardener'
B&G piece in production in 1991
*

547
Cats playing
Erik Nielsen
1904
8 x 8 cm
*****
$300-400

547
Spaniel white
5 cm
B&G piece
*
$50-75

548
Gypsy girl
18 cm
B&G piece in production in 1991
*
$100-150

549
Witch (girl dressed up)
20 cm
B&G piece in production in 1991
*
$100-150

552
Tortoise
pre-1910
6 x 16 cm
*****
$350-500

557
Fox on small base
Chr. Thomsen
pre-1910
5 x 7 cm
****
$250-400

558
Lamb sleeping
B&G piece in production in 1991
*

560
Lamb
B&G piece in production in 1991
*

561
'Mary' (spotted dress)
Ingeborg Plockross
1900
19 cm
B&G piece in production in 200(lso with blue dress
*
$95-210

562
Bream
pre-1910
10 x 18 cm
*****
$250-350

562
Lamb
B&G piece in production in 1991
*

563
Mice on ashtray
Arnold Krog
pre-1910
12 x 7 cm
*****
$300-400

564
Beagle standing
10 cm
B&G piece in production in 2000
*
$150-240

565
Beagle lying
9 cm
B&G piece in production in 2000
*
$200-240

566
Cockerel on clock case
Chr. Thomsen
1904
21 x 10 cm
*****
$800-1000

567
Cockerel on base
Chr. Thomsen
1904
21 x 8 cm
****
$300-400

568
Woman on a stone seat
Axel Locher
pre-1910
26 cm
*****
$500-600

569
Women
pre-1910
28 cm
*****
$600-750

573
Elephant
B&G piece
*

575
Elephant
B&G piece
*
$75-125

576
Elephant
B&G piece
*

580
Chicken on base
Chr. Thomsen
pre-1910
16 x 8 cm
*****
$250-350

598
Lemming?
Th. Madsen
1904
6 x 8 cm
*****
$250-350

599
Elephant calf
Th. Madsen
1904
17 x 17 cm
****
$100-175

600
Hen with chicks raised base
Chr. Thomsen
1904
15 x 8 cm
*****
$300-400

601
Bowl - otters
Chr. Thomsen
1904
11 x 18 cm
*****

604
Bonbon Dish - grasshopper on lid
pre-1910
10 x 14 cm

605
Chicken squatting
A. Nielsen (AP)
1904
5 x 8 cm
In production 1981
**
$50-80

606
Swan
Th. Madsen
1904
9 x 23 cm
****
$250-400s

607
Donkey with baskets
Th. Madsen
1904
13 x 17 cm
****
$650-800

608
Woman
Chr. Thomsen
1904
19 x 10 cm
*****
$300-450

609
Geese
Ingeborg Nielsen
1904
14 x 19 cm
In production 1988
***
$150-250

610
Owl & 3 mice on ashtray
Chr. Thomsen
1904
14 x 13 cm
*****
$450-600

615
Beaver on ashtray
Th. Madsen
1904
9 x 13 cm
*****
$250-350

618
Fish on ashtray
Arnold Krog
1905
15 cm

619
Fish on ashtray
Arnold Krog
1905
15

620
Shepherd boy
Chr. Thomsen
1904
22 x 8 cm
Also in overglaze.
**
$100-200

621
Fish on slab
pre-1910
9 x 27 cm
*****
$400-500

627
Farmer with sheep
Chr. Thomsen
1905
19 x 11 cm
Also in overglaze.
***
$225-375

628
Rabbit on ashtray
Th. Madsen
1905
7 x 13 cm
*****
$250-350

629
Little girl
Chr. Thomsen
1905
26 x 11 cm
*****
$300-400

632
Dish - beaver?
Th. Madsen
pre-1910
7 x 11 cm

634
Sheep & Lamb
Chr. Thomsen
1905
12 x 15 cm
*****
$500-600

635
Common gull
Chr. Thomsen
1905
10 x 28 cm
***
$200-300

648
Faun with bear
Chr. Thomsen
1905
16 cm
In production 1981
***
$250-500

649
Parrots on branches
Th. Madsen
1905
19 cm
In production 1981
**
$200-300

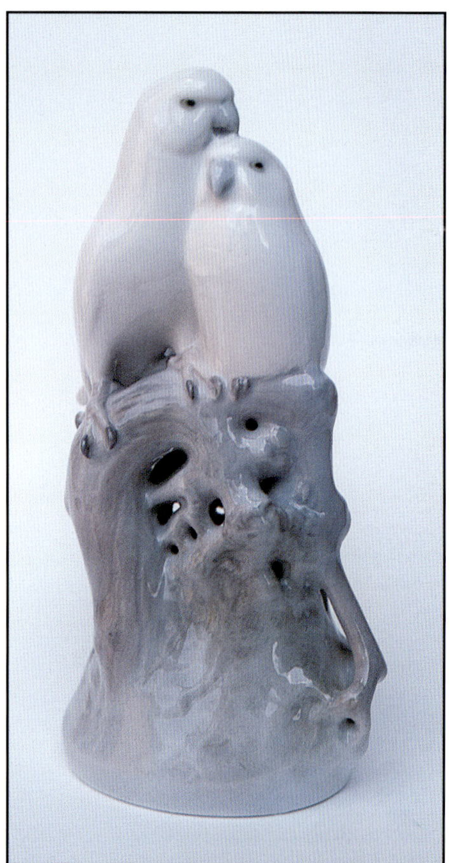

652
Bonbon Dish - eagle spread wings
pre-1910
18 cm

655
Harvest girl
Chr. Thomsen
1905
19 cm
***
$150-250

662
Panda eating
Allan Therkelsen
1994
18 cm
In production 2000
*
$110-230

663
Panda sitting
Allan Therkelsen
1994
9 cm
In production 2000
*
$70-105

664
Panda climbing
Allan Therkelsen
1994
13 cm
In production 2000
*
$100-170

665
Goat & kid
Chr. Thomsen
1905
11 x 16 cm
*****
$500-600

665
Panda sleeping
Allan Therkelsen
1994
12 cm
In production 2000
*
$60-90

666
Panda with cubs
Allan Therkelsen
1994
13 cm
In production 2000
*
$100-260

667
Cat yawning
Erik Nielsen
1905
17 cm
Also in white
*****
$350-500

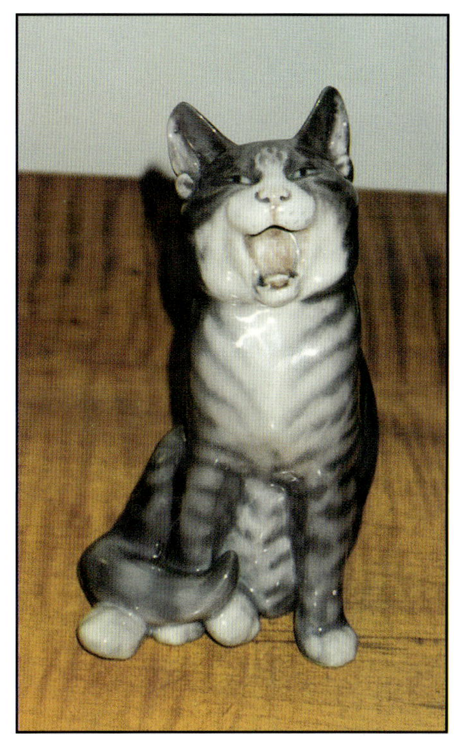

667
Panda playing
Allan Therkelsen
1994
9 cm
In production 2000
*
$150-190

668
Chicken with frog on base
Erik Nielsen
1905
22 cm
*****
$500-650

670
Bonbon Dish - mouse on lid
pre-1910
9 cm

671
Jardiniere - dragonfly handles
A. Pedersen (AN)
1905
5 x 16 cm

672
Bonbon Dish -insect handles
Olaf Mathiesen
1905
7.5 x 16 x 10 cm

673
Thoughtful woman in chair
Axel Locher
1905
21 x 24 cm
*****
$350-500

674
Jardiniere - swallows
A. Pedersen (AN)
1905
12 x 30.5 x 16 cm

683
Pigs - pair
Erik Nielsen
1906
6 x 12 cm
In production 1981
***
$125-175

685
Man with scythe
Chr. Thomsen
1905
25 cm
In production 1981
***
$150-250

691
Piglets - pair
Erik Nielsen
1905
5 x 10 cm
***
$125-175

692
Monkey on ashtray
A. Nielsen (AP)
1905
8 cm h
*****
200-300

693
Dog looking in basket
Erik Nielsen
1905
11 cm h

694
Girl with goats
Chr. Thomsen
1905
24 x 19 cm
Also in overglaze & Blanc de Chine.
*
$350-780

695
Mice on ashtray
A. Nielsen (AP)
1905
6 x 12 cm

703
Bowl - mouse on lid
pre-1910
22 x 20 cm

704
Dog chewing bone
Chr. Thomsen
1905
9 x 23 cm
****
$400-550

706
Calf
Knud Kyhn
1905
6 x 15 cm
**
$150-200

707
Children with dog
Chr. Thomsen
1905
15 cm
In production 2000
*
$200-460

709
Seals - pairs
Erik Nielsen/KK?
1906
10 x 27 cm
*****
$300-450

714
Tiger
Lauritz Jensen
1906
14 x 31 cm
In production 1981
**
$350-550

715
Fish - pair
A. Nielsen (AP)
pre-1910
5 x 15 cm

719
Otters playing
Chr. Thomsen
1906
10 x 21 cm
*****
$400-600

721
Orangutans - pair
Knud Kyhn
1906
10 x 14 cm
*****
$450-600

727
Cat playing
A. Nielsen (AP)
1906
6 x 10 cm
In production 2000
*
$75-140

729
Polar bear cub
Knud Kyhn
1904
6 x 11 cm
In production 2000
*
$50-130

737
Faun on goat
Chr. Thomsen
1906
20 x 22 cm
In production 1981
***
$400-650

741
Fly on rock
pre-1910
8 x 13 cm
*****
$250-350

744
Dish - woman
pre-1910
8 x 16 cm

746
Butterfly
pre-1910
5 x 2.5 cm
*****
$150-250

747
Grasshopper on ashtray
pre-1929

750
Hound puppies
Erik Nielsen
1906
23 x 26 cm
*****
$600-800

751
Peacock on globe base
Arnold Krog
pre-1910
57 x 34 cm

752
Faun with parrot
Chr. Thomsen
1906
19 x 13 cm
In production 1981
***
$300-500

753
Terrier sitting
Lauritz Jensen
1906
23 x 18 cm
*****
$300-450

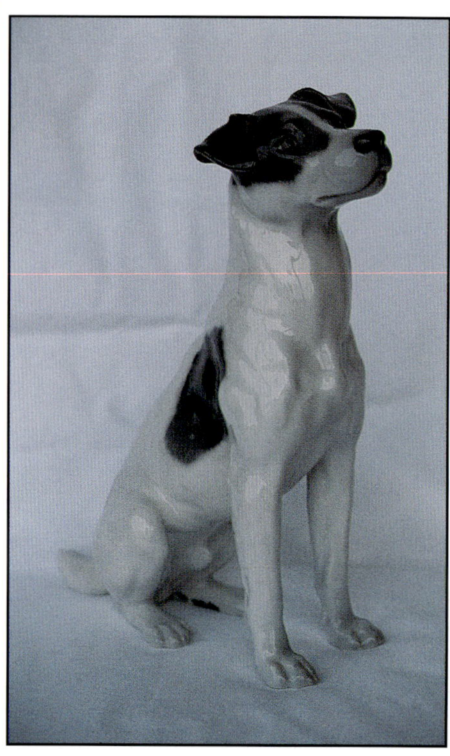

755
Swan
Erik Nielsen
1906
10 x 17 cm
In production 1988
**
$60-125

756
Stag
Knud Kyhn
1906
14 x 16 cm
In production 1988
**
$100-150

757
Bear lying
Knud Kyhn
1906
9 x 27 cm
*****
$450-650

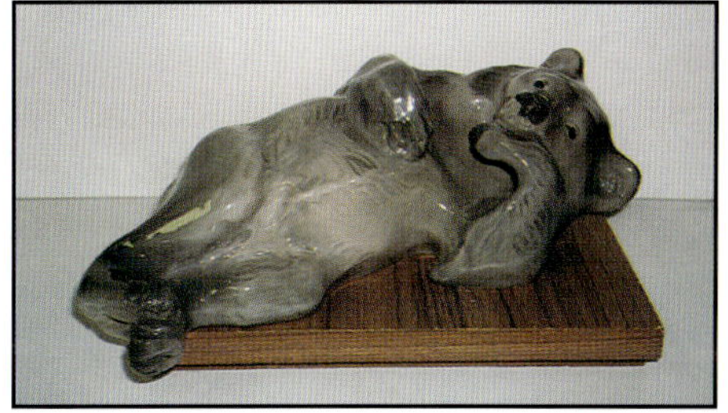

758
Cat looking up for food
Knud Kyhn
1906
13 x 12 cm
****
$350-500

772
Boy with calf
Chr. Thomsen
1906
17 x 16 cm
Also in overglaze. Underglaze still in production
*
$200-550

773
Polecats - pair
Knud Kyhn
1906
6 x 19 cm
*****
$350-500

774
Cat - white grooming
Knud Kyhn
1906
16 x 24 cm
*****
$500-750

775
Stoat with duck
Knud Kyhn/Pr. Marie
1906
6 x 16 cm
*****
$275-400

776
Otters biting tail
Knud Kyhn
1906
7 x 19 cm
*****
$350-550

778
English bulldog sitting
Knud Kyhn
1906
18 x 33 cm
****
$450-600

779
Girl with calf
Chr. Thomsen
1906
16 x 17 cm
Also in overglaze. Underglaze still in production
*
$200-550

780
Seal pup
Knud Kyhn
1900
7 x 20 cm
****
$300-400

781
Dachshund asleep
Knud Kyhn
1906
8 x 20 cm
****
$200-350

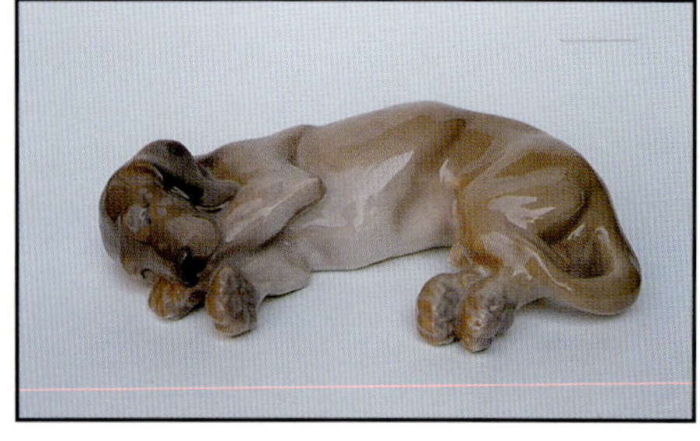

782
Shepherd with dog
Chr. Thomsen
1906
19 cm
In production 1981
***
$150-250

784
Old woman with bonnet
Chr. Thomsen
1906
20 cm
*****
$400-600

800
Cow with calf
Knud Kyhn
1907
12 x 27 cm
In production 1981
**
$300-450

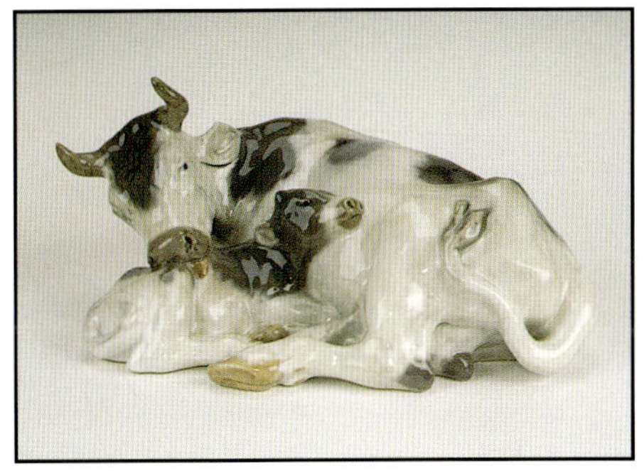

801
English Bulldog
Knud Kyhn
1907
23 x 38 cm
*****
$1250-1750

802
Elephants - pair
Knud Kyhn
1907
20 x 26 cm
*****
$800-1100

804
Lioness
Lauritz Jensen
1907
16 x 31 cm
In production 1988
***
$300-450

805
Leopardess licking foot
Lauritz Jensen
1907
17 x 17 cm
****
$350-450

812
Ducks - trio
pre-1910
5.5 x 13 cm
*****
$400-500

813
Man with rake
Chr. Thomsen
1907
25 cm
****
$300-400

815
Peasant girl with lunch
Chr. Thomsen
1907
22 cm
In production 1981
***
$200-300

822
Women
pre-1910
26 cm
*****
$600-750

824
Bears standing
Erik Nielsen
1907
13 x 8 cm
*****
$350-550

825
Polar bear looking up
Knud Kyhn
1907
29 x 23 cm
***
$250-400

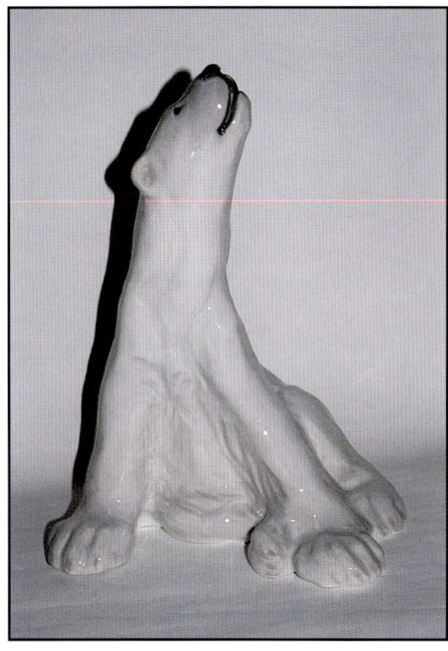

826
Camel
Knud Kyhn
1907
19 x 30 cm
*****
$450-600

827
Tern squatting
Chr. Thomsen
1907
11 x 26 cm
In production 2000
*
$175-225

829
Duck
Knud Kyhn
1907
11 x 20 cm
****
$250-400

830
Goat
Knud Kyhn
1907
14 x 21 cm
***
$300-450

832
Cat lying with ball of wool
Christian Thomsen
pre-1910
9 x 21 cm
*****
$450-600

834
Owls - pair
Th. Madsen
1907
9 x 7 cm
In production 2000
*
$50-165

848
Swineherd
Chr. Thomsen
1907
20 x 19 cm
In production 1981
****
$400-600

850
Dachshund
Erik Nielsen
1907
22 x 30 cm
****
$650-850

856
Dachshund
Lauritz Jensen
1907
19 x 30 cm
In production 2000
*
$275-425

857
Faun on tortoise & rope
Chr. Thomsen
1905
10 x 9 cm
*****
$450-550

858
Faun on tortoise
Chr. Thomsen
1907
10 x 9 cm
In production 1981
***
$150-225

860
Flying Insect
pre-1910
6 x 5 cm
*****
$200-300

862
Pheasants
A. Nielsen (AP)
1907
14 x 17 cm
In production 1981
***
$250-400

865
Boy at lunch
Chr. Thomsen
1907
11 x 20 cm
Also in overglaze.
***
$150-250

866
Blue Parrot on column
Chr. Thomsen
1907
29 cm
****
$900-1200

878
Rabbit on ashtray
Chr. Thomsen
pre-1910
10 x 14 cm

879
Eels - pair on ashtray
A. Nielsen (AP)
1908
3 x 13 cm

880
Frog on lily pad
pre-1910
5 x 10 cm
*****
$200-300

881
Frog on flat base
pre-1910
4.5 x 13 cm
*****
$200-300

882
Frog on dish
pre-1910
5 x 11 cm
*****
$200-300

883
Frog on rock
pre-1910
7 x 10 cm
*****
$200-300

884
Frog on rock
pre-1910
6 x 9 cm
*****
$200-300

892
Churchgoer
Chr. Thomsen
1908
21 x 11 cm
In production 1963
***
$250-450

893
Woman with lute on pedestal
pre-1910
39 x 15 cm
*****
$600-800

894
Woman sitting on chair
Axel Locher
1908
21 x 16 cm
*****
$350-450

899
Milkmaid
Chr. Thomsen
1905
29 x 15 cm
In production 1981
***
$250-350

903
Girl with hay & rake
Chr. Thomsen
1905
21 x 12 cm
****
$250-350

905
Boy cutting stick
Chr. Thomsen
1908
19 x 9 cm
Also in overglaze. Underglaze still in production.
*
$100-350

908
Girl with sheaf
Chr. Thomsen
1908
19 x 9 cm
Also in overglaze.
***
$150-250

922
Girl with book
Chr. Thomsen
1905
17 cm
In production 1981
***
$125-225

927
Fly
pre-1910
5 cm
*****
$150-250

928
Fly
pre-1910
4 cm
*****
$150-250

929
Fly
pre-1910
5 cm
*****
$150-250

930
Skink
A. Pedersen (AN)
1905
7 cm
*****
$150-250

931
Fantail fish on ashtray
A. Nielsen (AP)
pre-1910
5 x 12 cm
In production 1981
***
$75-125

939
Girls with doll
Chr. Thomsen
1905
16 x 9 cm
In production 1981
***
$150-250

940
Monkeys - trio
Knud Kyhn
1908
16 x 28 cm
*****
$600-850

953
Pigs on ashtray
A. Nielsen (AP)
1908
6 x 11 cm

955
Sailor girl with book
Chr. Thomsen
1905
17 x 8 cm
*****
$150-300

956
French Bulldog
Knud Kyhn
1908
17 x 15 cm
***
$300-450

957
French Bulldogs - fused
Knud Kyhn
1908
15 x 21 cm
*****
$750-1000

963
Sailor boy sitting
Chr. Thomsen
1905
11 x 9 cm
*****
$150-300

975
Cat playing with ball of wool
Chr. Thomsen
1908
9 x 21 cm
*****
$450-600

976
Faun backwards on bear
Knud Kyhn
1908
19 x 17 cm
***
$175-300

977
Spitz/Husky
A. Pedersen (AN)
1908
18 x 16 cm
****
$400-500

981
Squirrel on ashtray
A. Nielsen (AP)
1908
8 x 13 cm
***
$100-150

982
Squirrel with nut
A. Nielsen (AP)
1908
7 x 6 cm
In production 1988
**
$25-70

990
Children sitting with doll
Chr. Thomsen
1908
11 x 12 cm
*****
$150-300

1001
Old man, hands in pocket
Chr. Thomsen
pre-1910
16 x 8 cm
****
$150-250

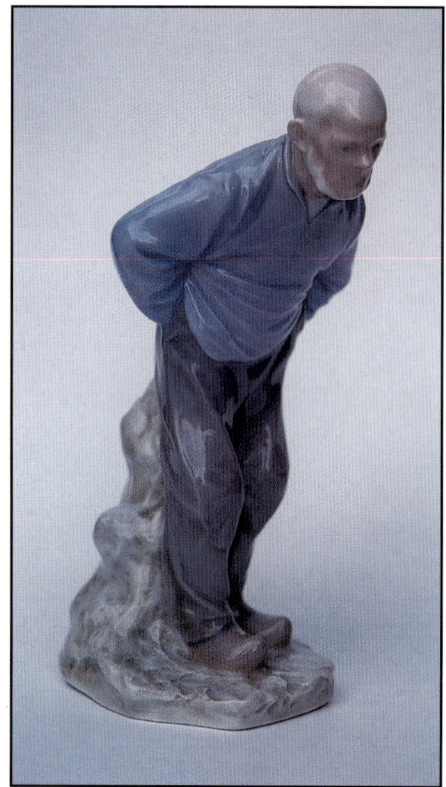

1008
Pigeon
Anna Trap
1907
14 x 15 cm
***
$200-350

1010
Cross legged woman on pedestal
Gerhard Henning
1908
31 cm
Overglaze

1012
Woman feeding cat
Chr. Thomsen
1909
14 x 13 cm
*****
$350-500

1019
Rabbit
Chr. Thomsen
1909
9 x 6 cm
In production 2000
*
$50-100

1020
Victorian woman - curtsying
pre-1910
20 x 11 cm
*****
$450-550

1021
Mother holding children
Bisson
1895
15 x 7 cm
*****
$350-500

1022
Pigs - pair
A. Pedersen (AN)
1909
5 x 9 cm
***
$125-175

1023
Angel Fish
A. Pedersen (AN)
1909
4 x 9 cm
****
$150-250

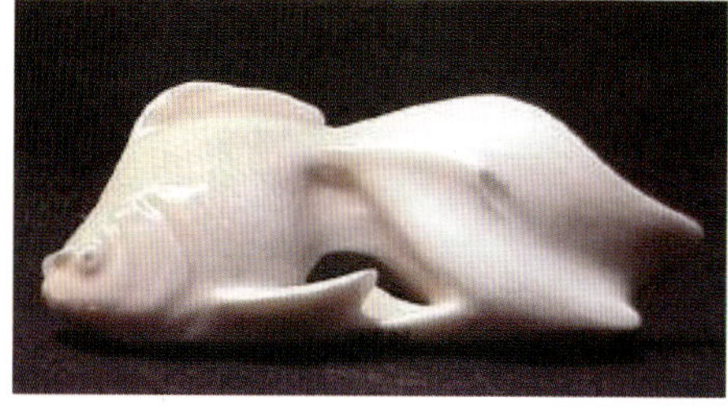

1024
Hen
Chr. Thomsen
1909
14 x 12 cm
In production 1988
**
$90-150

1025
Cock
Chr. Thomsen
1909
18 x 14 cm
In production 1988
**
$90-160

1034
Coati Mundi
Peter Herold
1909
7 x 11 cm
*****
$150-250

1036
Faun with cat
Knud Kyhn
1909
13 x 17 cm
****
$400-600

1037
Tree Stump & 3 Bears
Knud Kyhn
1909
22 x 19 cm
****
$1000-1500

1040
Finch
A. Nielsen (AP)
1909
5 x 6 cm
In production 2000
*
$50-65

1041
Finch preening
A. Nielsen (AP)
1909
4 x 6 cm
In production 1988
**
$50-75

1042
Woman with baby?
pre-1910
*****

1043
Woman with washing
Chr. Thomsen
1909
19 x 10 cm
****
$400-500

1044
Ptarmigan
Anna Trap
1909
10 x 16 cm
****
$250-400

1045
Finch group
A. Nielsen (AP)
1909
5 x 10 cm
In production 1988
**
$75-125

1061
Faun crying
Knud Kyhn
1909
11 x 9 cm
***
$300-400

1064
Old woman
pre-1910
11 x 13 cm
*****
$250-350

1065
Turkey
Chr. Thomsen
1909
18 x 17 cm
*****
$400-600

1071
Eider Duck
Anna Trap
1909
12 x 18 cm
****
$250-400

1072
Calf
Knud Kyhn
1909
10 x 17 cm
In production 2000
*
$100-265

1078
Gnome with cat
Knud Kyhn
1909
10 x 12 cm
*****
$500-750

1081
Sparrow tail up
A. Nielsen (AP)
1909
8 cm
In production 1997
**
$50-75

1086
Guinea-fowl
Peter Herold
1909
15 x 12 cm
In production 1981
**
$100-150

1087
Hunter with dog
Chr. Thomsen
1909
20 x 10 cm
In production 2000
*
$300-1200

1088
Goose
Ingeborg Nielsen
1909
11 x 12 cm
In production 1981
***
$150-225

1094
Cock & hen
Chr. Thomsen
1903
21 x 18 cm
In production 1981
***
$350-500

1096
Marmot
Brussemins?
1909
20 x 11 cm
*****
$375-550

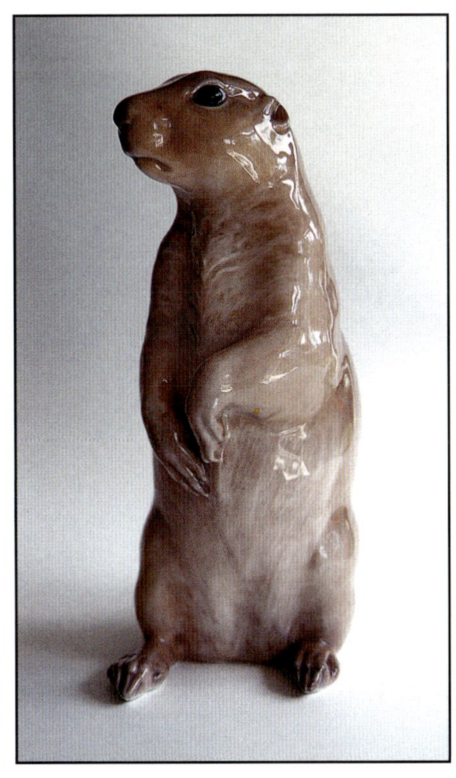

1100
Card tray - lizard
A. Pedersen (AN)
1909
21 cm

1101
Owl on ball
pre-1910
28 x 20 cm
*****
$800-1000

1103
Magpie
A. Pedersen (AN)
1909
23 x 22 cm
****
$450-600

1107
Polar Bears cubs playing
Knud Kyhn
1907
14 cm
In production 2000
*
$75-200

1108
Polar bear & seal
Knud Kyhn
1909
23 cm
In production 2000
*
$750-1500

1112
'The Soldier & Witch'
Chr. Thomsen
1909
32 x 11 cm
Also in overglaze.
****
$450-550

1114
'Princess & Swineherd'
Chr. Thomsen
1909
28 x 11 cm
Also in overglaze.
***
$400-500

1119
Nymph & Faun
Gerhard Henning
1909
27 cm
Overglaze

1124
Bear
Knud Kyhn
pre-1910
6 x 8 cm
In production 1988
**
$60-90

1126
Cock head up
Chr. Thomsen
pre-1910
11 x 8 cm
In production 1991
**
$60-150

1127
Cock head down
Chr. Thomsen
pre-1910
10 x 12 cm
In production 1988
**
$50-160

1129
'The Sandman'
Chr. Thomsen
pre-1910
18 x 7 cm
Also in overglaze.
**
$75-200

1132
'Wave & Rock'
Theodor Lundberg
1895
46 cm
In production 2000
*
$850-3350

1137
Polar bear standing
Knud Kyhn
pre-1910
17 cm
In production 2000
*
$150-280

1138
Perch
A. Nielsen (AP)
pre-1910
7 x 15 cm
In production 1981
***
$150-225

1139
Eel on ashtray
A. Nielsen (AP)
pre-1910
11 cm
****
$150-200

1145
'The Sandman'
Chr. Thomsen
pre-1910
16 x 8 cm
Also in overglaze.
**
$100-200

1156
'Soldier & Dog'
Chr. Thomsen
pre-1910
31 x 9 cm
Also in overglaze.
****
$400-500

1157
Barn owls - trio
Olaf Mathiesen
pre-1910
9 x 7 cm
*****
$300-500

1162
Conger Eel
C. F. Liisberg
1888

1180
'Soldier & Princess'
Chr. Thomsen
pre-1910
28 x 14 cm
Also in overglaze.
***
$450-550

1182
Perch - group of 4
Ingeborg Nielsen
pre-1910
15 x 7 cm
*****
$450-600

1185
Turkey chick
Ingeborg Nielsen
pre-1910
11 x 8 cm
**
$50-100

1188
Weeping Faun on Stand
Gerhard Henning
1910
16 cm
Overglaze

1188.1
Weeping Faun
Gerhard Henning
pre-1910
16 cm
Overglaze

1189
Finches - pair
Peter Herold
pre-1910
6 cm
In production 2000
*
$65-145

1190
Penguins - pair
Anna Trap
1911
10 cm
In production 2000
*
$70-135

1192
Duck
Olaf Mathiesen
pre-1910
10 cm
In production 2000
*
$50-140

1195
Bull
Knud Kyhn
pre-1910
22 cm
In production 1981
***
$700-950

1199
Monkey & baby
Knud Kyhn
pre-1910
30 x 19 cm
Baby is dark blue.
*****
$1000-1500

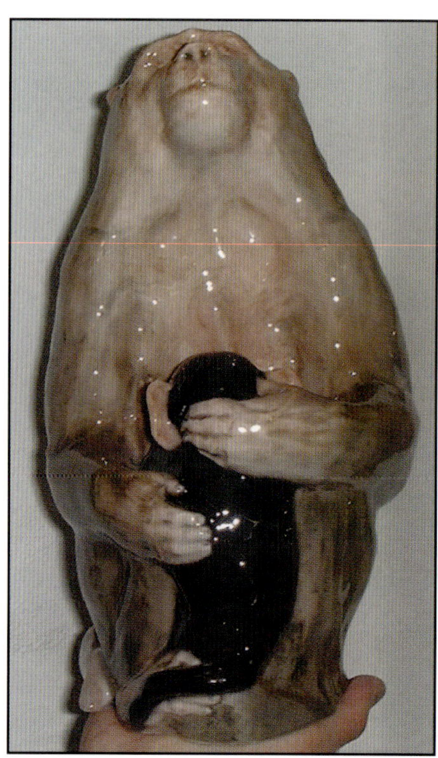

1201
Monkeys
Knud Kyhn
pre-1910
29 x 24 cm
*****
$1000-1500

1204
Bassett puppy
Peter Herold
pre-1910
7 x 18 cm
****
$250-350

1205
Bull (head down)
Lauritz Jensen
pre-1910
22 x 37 cm
****
$500-750

1208
Faun on tree strump with rope
Olaf Mathiesen
pre-1929
9 cm
*****
$300-500

1209
Badger
Peter Herold
pre-1910
8 x 20 cm
*****
$300-450

1210
Mermaid on ice rock
Chr. Thomsen
pre-1910
26 x 10 cm
****
$400-500

1212
Mermaid in water - paperweight
Chr. Thomsen
pre-1910
8 x 20 cm
***
$250-350

1228
'Hans Clodhopper'
Chr. Thomsen
pre-1910
18 x 14 cm
Also in overglaze.
***
$250-400

1229
Girl bathing
Chr. Thomsen
pre-1910
14 x 9 cm
****
$200-300

1232
Marabou Storks
Martha Hasted
1911
11 x 13 cm
*****
$500-700

1235
Redwing
Ingeborg Nielsen
1911
15 x 13 cm
In production 1988
**
$200-300

1238
'Princess & The Pea'
Gerhard Henning
1911
43 cm
Overglaze-most expensive single piece ever made

1244
Girl with mirror
Gerhard Henning
1911
18 cm
Overglaze

1251
Amager girl
Lotte Benter
1911
20 cm
In production 1988
**
$150-250

1252
Little girl
Lotte Benter
1911
21 x 11 cm
*****
$300-450

1253
Bonbon Dish - cats playing on lid
pre-1929
11 x 16 cm

1254
Bonbon Dish - finches (3) on lid
1911
11 x 16 cm

1268
Lion yawning
Lauritz Jensen
1911
16 x 36 cm
****
$500-650

1269
Hippos - pair
Carl J. Bonnesen
1911
13 x 33 cm
*****
$850-1100

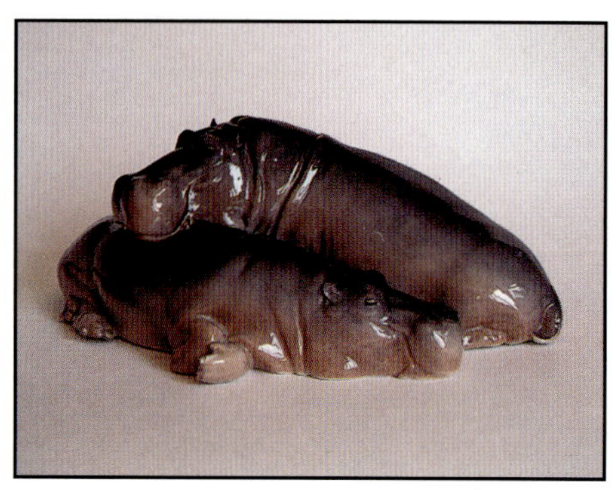

1276
'Shepherdess & Chimneysweep'
Chr. Thomsen
1911
24 x 12 cm
Also in overglaze.
*****
$600-700

1281
Guinea-pig
Peter Herold
1911
10 x 21 cm
*****
$300-450

1283
Penguin
Anna Trap
1911
10 x 7 cm
In production 1988
**
$40-135

1190, 1283, and 1284 form as set.

1284
Penguins - trio
Anna Trap
1911
10 x 9 cm
In production 1981
**
$75-140

1286
Mole
Sophie Spies
1911
5 x 14 cm
*****
$250-400

1288
'Emperor's New Clothes'
Chr. Thomsen
1911
20 x 15 cm
Also in overglaze.
***
$300-450

1289
Night Heron
Martha Hasted
1911
12 x 7 cm
*****
$200-300

1300
Harvest group
Chr. Thomsen
1905
20 x 11 cm
In production 1988
***
$350-550

1303
Cockerel
Ingeborg Nielsen
1911
37 x 30 cm
*****
$600-800

1304
Tawny Owl
A. Pedersen (AN)
1911
21 x 20 cm
****
$350-650

1307
Boy with tree
Chr. Thomsen
1911
18 cm
****
$350-500

1309
Sparrows - pair
A. Nielsen (AP)
1911
6 cm
In production 2000
*
$75-185

1310
Cow - brown
Lauritz Jensen
1911
15 x 28 cm
***
$250-400

1311
Pointer puppy
Erik Nielsen
1911
6 cm
In production 2000
*
$40-100

1314
Girl knitting
Lotte Benter
1911
15 cm
Also in overglaze. Still in production.
*
$100-350

1315
Amager girl
Lotte Benter
1911
16 cm
In production 2000
*
$130-400

1316
Amager girls (shopping)
Lotte Benter
1911
17 cm
In production 2000
*
$140-530

1317
Woman knitting
Lotte Benter
1911
18 cm
In production 1994
***
$150-325

1319
The Gossips
Chr. Thomsen
1911
30 x 22 cm
In production 1981
***
$400-550

1322
Bloodhound - female
Lauritz Jensen
1911
23 x 19 cm
In production 1981
****
$400-500

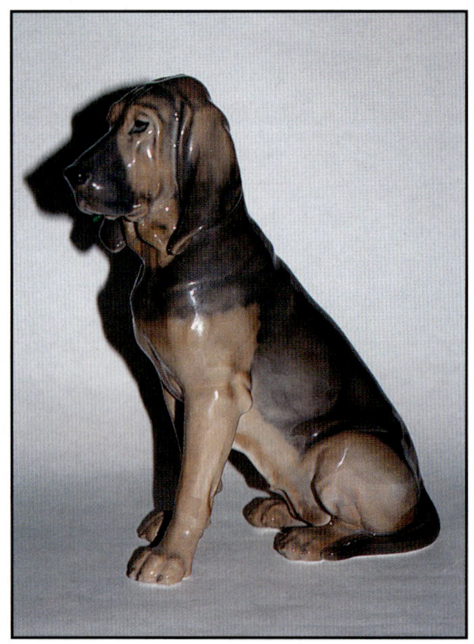

1323
Girl from Bornholm
Lotte Benter
1911
22 cm
In production 1988
***
$150-300

1324
Fanoe Woman
Lotte Benter
1911
21 x 16 cm
****
$300-400

1326
Peasant couple dancing
Chr. Thomsen
1920
24 x 18 cm
****
$500-650

1327
Desert Fox
Chr. Thomsen
1911
24 x 17 cm
****
$600-750

1329
Lynx
Peter Herold
1911
12 x 17 cm
In production 1963
****
$225-350

1331
Owl long eared
Peter Herold
1912
36 x 18 cm
In production 1981
****
$700-950

1337
Bonbon Dish - rabbit
pre-1929
7 x 11 cm

1338
Rabbit crouching
1911/12
6 cm
**
$100-150

1341
Bloodhound Sniffing - male
Lauritz Jensen
1912
25 x 32 cm
Tail often damaged
*****
$500-650

1343
Leopard
Lauritz Jensen
1912
14 x 25 cm
****
$700-900

1350
Leopard - crawling
C. F. Liisberg
1901
11 x 18 cm
****
$800-1000

1352
Harvest group
Chr. Thomsen
1912
43 cm
In production 1981
***
$600-1000

1362
Horse
Lauritz Jensen
1912
19 cm
In production 1963
***
$450-700

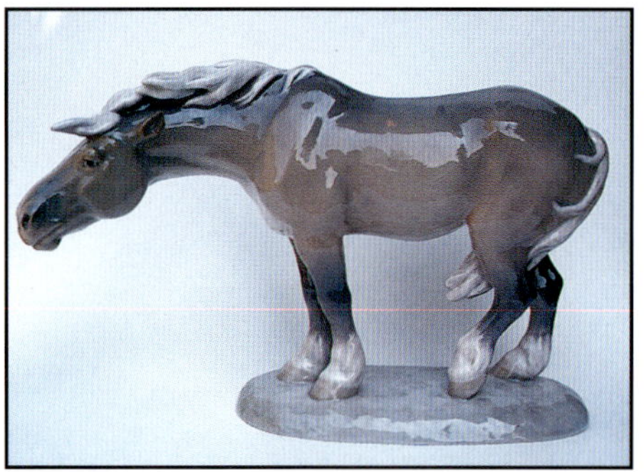

1363
Cockerel
1912
*****

1372
Elephant
Axel Locher
1912
9 x 12 cm
****
$80-175

1373
Elephant
Axel Locher
1912
24 x 32 cm
****
$300-500

1374
Ballet dancer
Lotte Benter
1912
30 x 19 cm
****
$600-700

1375
Woman with collie
Axel Locher
1912
26 cm
*****
$700-800

1376
Elephant
Axel Locher
1912
11 x 21 cm
***
$200-300

1382
Girl with sled
Lotte Benter
1912
24 cm
****
$300-450

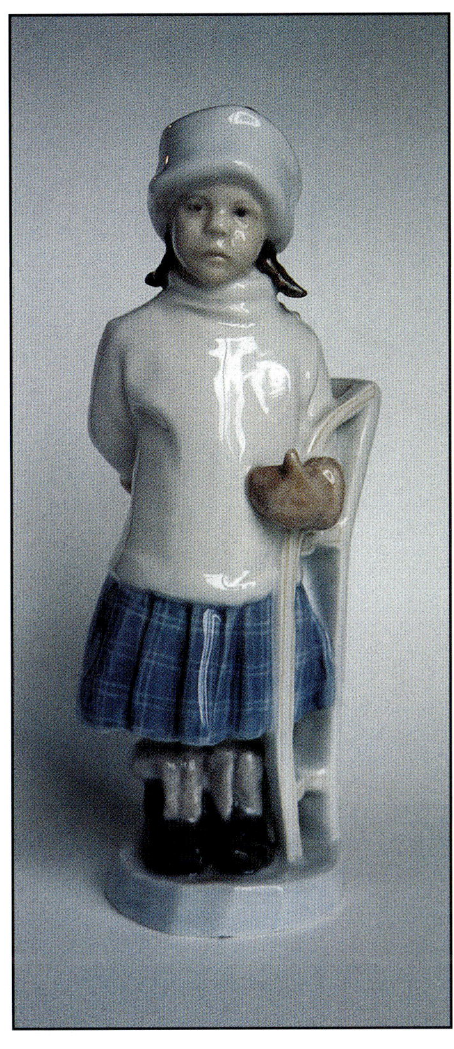

1383
Victorian man
Chr. Thomsen
1912
29 cm
****
$300-450

1385
Victorian lady
Chr. Thomsen
1912
34 cm
****
$600-800

1395
Girls - pair
Lotte Benter
1912
18 cm
In production 2000
*
$170-630

1398
Greenland girl
Lotte Benter
1912
15 x 14 cm
****
$300-400

1399
Pig on wheatsheaf
Erik Nielsen
1912
15 cm
*****
$300-450

1400
Pig
Erik Nielsen
1912
7 cm
In production 2000
*
$60-145

1402
Wolverine
Peter Herold
1912
20 x 22 cm
*****
$750-950

1404
Mother & child
Chr. Thomsen
1912
28 cm
*****
$500-600

1407
Dachshund
Olaf Mathiesen
1912
11 cm
In production 2000
*
$60-150

1408
Dachshund
Olaf Mathiesen
1912
11 cm
In production 2000
*
$60-160

1413
'Nathan the Wise'
Adolf Jahn
1913
35 cm
In production 1981
****
$500-600

1414
Woman on plinth
22 x 9 cm
*****
$400-600

1427
Cat - wild

1430
Fox
Peter Herold
1913
7 x 12 cm
*****
$250-400

1437
Bonbon Dish - rabbit on lid
1913
19 x 13 cm

1438
Vase - faun with kid on lid
Arnold Krog
1897
29.5 x 19 cm
Lid 498 Chr. Thomsen

1440
Lynx
Peter Herold
1913
12 x 21 cm
*****
$325-500

1441
Sealion
Th. Madsen
1913
12 x 10 cm
In production 1981
**
$40-100

1443
Musk Ox
A. Nielsen (AP)
1913
9 x 20 cm
*****
$500-750

1444
Monkey
Niels Nielsen
1913
13 x 8 cm
In production 1981
**
$150-250

1448
Bonbon Dish - cockerel on lid
1913
16 x 16 cm

1450
Dachshund
Knud Moller
1913
11 x 19 cm
*****
$300-450

1451
'Fashionable pair'
Axel Locher
Overglaze

1455
Bonbon Dish - rabbits (2) on lid
1913
12 x 16 cm

1457
Boston Terrier
Knud Moller
1913
11 x 13 cm
In production 1981
****
$200-300

1463
Bonbon Dish - bird on lid
pre-1929

1464
Bonbon Dish - sparrow on lid
pre-1929

1465
French bulldog standing
Lauritz Jensen
1913
17 x 20 cm
***
$350-500

1466
French bulldog sitting
Lauritz Jensen
1913
20 x 18 cm
***
$350-500

1468
Seagull
Peter Herold
1913
6 cm
In production 1997
***
$60-90

1469
Jaguar
10 x 20 cm
*****
$400-600

1470
Bonbon Dish - mouse on lid
1913
15 x 10 cm

1473
Princess & Hans Clodhopper
Chr. Thomsen
1913
24 x 24 cm
Also in overglaze
*****
$800-1000

1475
Fox
Erik Nielsen
1913
15 x 8 cm
In production 1988
**
$125-200

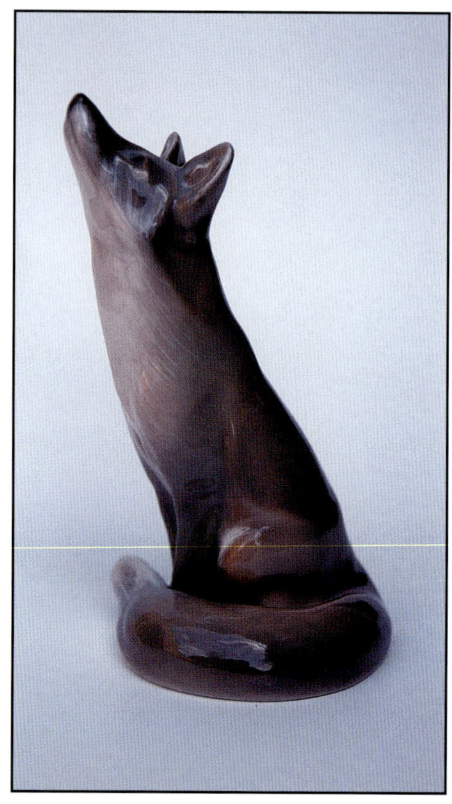

1476
Fairy Tale I
Gerhard Henning
1913
22 cm
Overglaze

1478
King
Chr. Thomsen
1913
25 cm
Also in overglaze
*****
$900-1200

1479
Cockatoo
Edinger Jensen
1915
20 x 11 cm
*****
$250-350

1482
Mountain Lion
Peter Herold
1913
11 x 19 cm
****
$350-500

1486
Donkeys - pair
J. A. Heuch
1913
18 x 21 cm
*****
$900-1200

1493
Lark
Peter Herold
1913
11 x 13 cm
****
$125-225

1494
Queen
Chr. Thomsen
1913
25 cm
Also in overglaze
*****
$900-1200

1495
Girl with butterfly
V Oppenheim
1913
11 x 11 cm
****
$150-300

1504
Wren
Peter Herold
1913
4 x 8 cm
In production 1988
***
$75-125

1505
Bluetit
Peter Herold
1913
4 x 10 cm
In production 1988
***
$50-100

1506
Crested tit
Peter Herold
1913
6 x 8 cm
In production 1988
***
$75-125

1507
Wagtails - pair
Peter Herold
1913
6 x 16 cm
****
$200-300

1509
Sole
Peter Herold
1913
8 x 17 cm
*****
$450-600

1516
Robin
Peter Herold
1913
8 x 7 cm
In production 1988
***
$125-225

1517
Child sitting
Else Sandholt
1913
9 x 11 cm
**
$100-200

1518
Crawling child
Else Sandholt
1913
7 cm
In production 2000
*
$100-175

1519
Sparrow
A. Nielsen (AP)
1913
6 cm
In production 2000
*
$40-105

1521
Minister
Axel Locher
Overglaze

1522
Man leaning on walking stick
Axel Locher
Overglaze

1523
Actor
Axel Locher
Overglaze

1524
Woman with lapdog
Axel Locher
Overglaze

1528
Woman with hoe
Chr. Thomsen
1913
27 cm
****
$300-400

1530
Girl in red
1913
30 cm
*****
$600-800

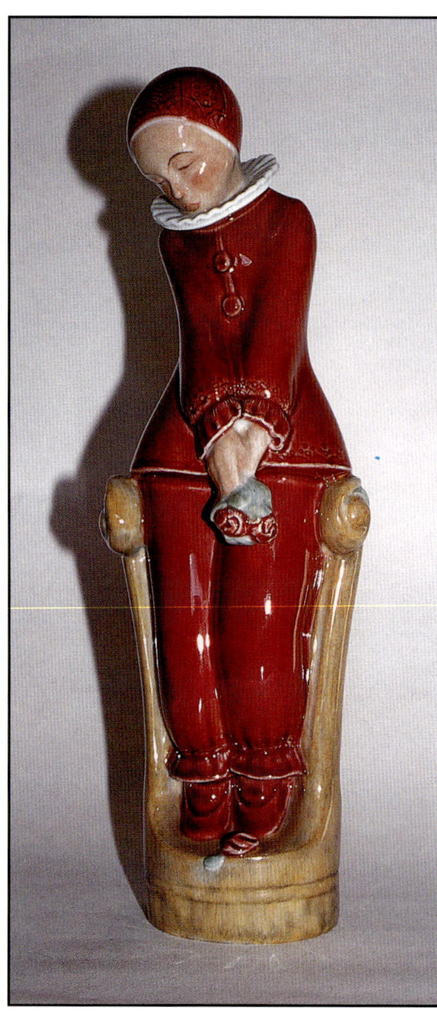

1531
Girl with deer

1533
Setter with pheasant
Knud Moller
1913
8 cm
In production 1981
**
$150-300

1548
Bonbon Dish - mouse on lid
1913
14 x 13 cm

1549
Woman collecting potatoes
Chr. Thomsen
1913
27 x 20 cm
In production 1988
***
$400-500

1558
Terrier sitting
Knud Moller
1913
12 x 11 cm
****
$250-350

1586
Fairy Tale II
Gerhard Henning
1913
23 cm
Overglaze

1593
Victorian Couple
Chr. Thomsen
1914
29 cm
In production 1981
***
$550-650

1595
Fisherman
Georg Thylstrup
17 cm
****
$250-350

1596
Easter egg - rabbit
pre-1929
15 x 15 cm

1600
Partridge - pair
Peter Herold
1914
9 x 22 cm
***
$250-350

1602
Trout (small)
Knud Moller
1914
12 cm
In production 1988
**
$50-75

1613
Bonbon Dish - pig on lid
pre-1929
12 x 16 cm

1622
Collie dog lying
Jessie Borlwiych
1914
15 x 47 cm
*****
$750-1000

1623
Male Lion
Jessie Borlwiych
1914

1634
Pointer (head down)
Lauritz Jensen
1914
6 x 20 cm
In production 1981
***
$300-400

1635
Pointer (head up)
Lauritz Jensen
1914
13 x 24 cm
In production 1988
***
$250-350

1637
Woman standing
Georg Thylstrup
1914
22.5 cm
****
$300-450

1646
'Grief'
Gerhard Henning
1914
25 cm
Overglaze

1648
Boy Scout at tree stump
Chr. Thomsen
1914
25 cm
*****
$300-450

1649
Boy Scout with staff
Chr. Thomsen
1914
25 cm
*****
$300-450

1652
Hound standing
Peter Herold ? L. Jensen
1914
14 cm
****
$250-350

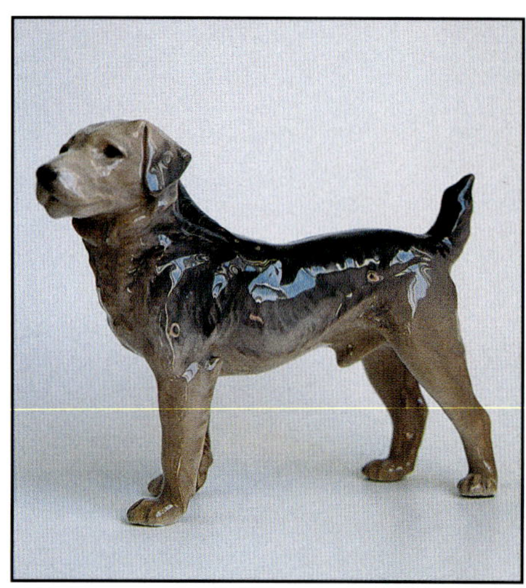

1653
Peahen
Knud Moller
1914
12 cm
*****
$250-350

1654
Eskimo
Lotte Benter
1914
26 x 10 cm
*****
$400-550

1659
Boy on rock
Chr. Thomsen
1914
30 cm
In production 1988
***
$300-400

1660
Man
Chr. Thomsen
1914
28 cm
*****
$300-450

1661
Falcon
Peter Herold
1914
41 cm
In production 2000
*
$850-2000

1662
Pekingese reclining
Erik Nielsen
1914
27 x 11 cm
****
$300-400

1663
Sultan
Axel Locher
Overglaze

1664
Fairy Tale III
Gerhard Henning
1914
20 cm
Overglaze

1670
Birds - triple

1678
Bird - pair
Knud Moller
1914
9 cm
****
$200-300

1679
Great Dane
Peter Herold
1914
11 cm
In production 1981
****
$175-300

1680
'The Proposal'
Chr. Thomsen
1914
26 cm
In production 1981
***
$350-500

1684
Poodle Dog Sitting
Peter Herold
1914
15 cm
*****
$250-400

1688
German Shepherd dog sitting
Peter Herold
1914
19 cm
***
$250-350

1690
Jay
Knud Moller
1914
19 cm
*****
$400-550

1691
Rabbit
Peter Herold
1915
7 cm
In production 2000
*
$50-65

1701
Collie
Peter Herold
1915
13 cm
In production 1981
***
$250-400

1712
Faun with snake
Chr. Thomsen
1915
12 cm
In production 1963
***
$250-500

1713
Faun with frog
Chr. Thomsen
1915
12 cm
In production 1981
***
$200-300

1719
Poodle
Peter Herold
1915
17 x 25 cm
*****
$400-500

1736
Faun playing pipes
Chr. Thomsen
1915
14 cm
In production 1981
***
$200-350

1737
Children walking
Chr. Thomsen
1915
20 x 16 cm
***
$300-400

1738
Faun on stump
Th. Madsen
1915
9 cm
In production 1981
***
$150-225

1739
Child, crawling
Ada Bonfils
1915
6 cm
In production 2000
*
$70-125

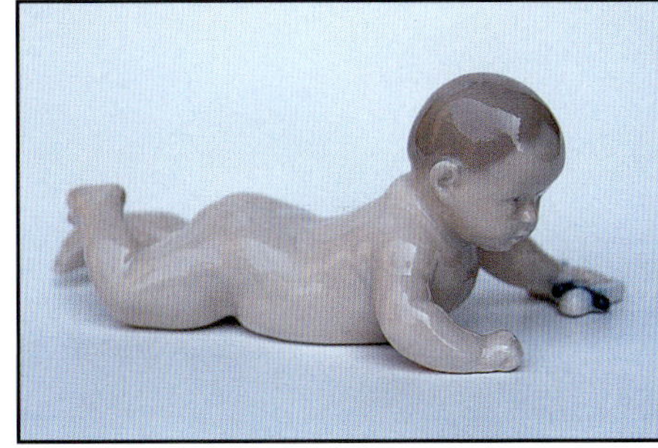

1741
Owl
Th. Madsen
1915
9 cm
In production 2000
*
$40-80

1742
Owl asleep
Th. Madsen
12 x 7 cm
**
$75-150

1744
Boy seated eating apple
Chr. Thomsen
1915
20 x 9 cm
*****
$300-450

1752
Cats playing
Erik Nielsen
1915
12 x 10 cm
*****
$300-400

1760
Woman with maid servant
Georg Thylstrup
1915
19 cm
****
$300-450

1761
'Flight to America'
Chr. Thomsen
1915
21 x 11 cm
Also in overglaze.
***
$200-450

1762
Girl plucking a duck
Chr. Thomsen
1915
22 x 12 cm
*****
$250-400

1769
Kingfishers
Peter Herold
1915
11 cm
In production 2000
*
$110-230

1770
Lady
Chr. Thomsen
1915
23 x 10 cm
*****
$300-400

1771
Elephant
Peter Herold
1915
15 x 22 cm
In production 1981
***
$140-220

1772
Pekingese sitting
Peter Herold
1915
12 x 12 cm
In production 1981
***
$200-300

1776
Pekingese
Peter Herold
1916
12 x 6 cm
In production 1981
**
$80-150

1778
Bonbon Dish - turkey chick
A. Nielsen (AP)
1916
7 x 8 cm

1783
'Hans & Trine'
Chr. Thomsen
1916
22 x 14 cm
Also in overglaze.
***
$250-500

1785
Lady holding roses
Chr. Thomsen
1916
23 cm
*****
$350-500

1786
Boy bathing
Chr. Thomsen
1916
16 cm
****
$150-300

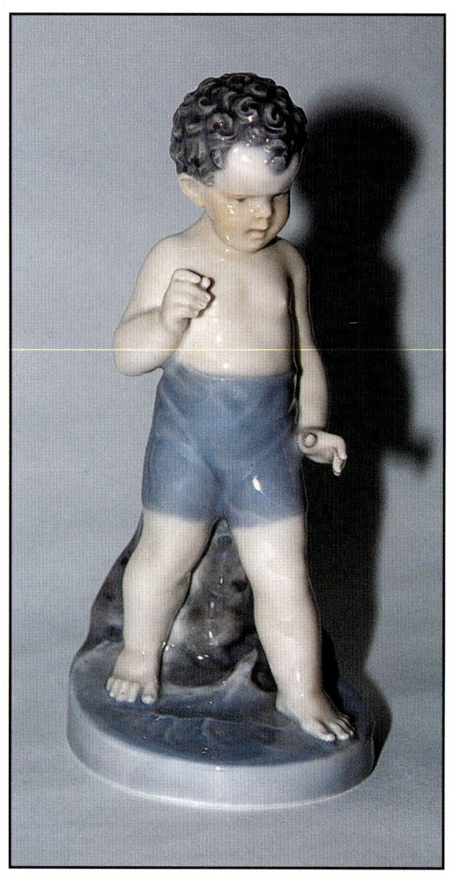

1787
Racoons - pair
Peter Herold
1916
7 x 11 cm
*****
$450-600

1788
Vixen with cubs
Peter Herold
1916
13 x 13 cm
In production 1988
***
$450-550

1796
Man & woman
Gerhard Henning
1916
23 cm
Overglaze

1798
Belgian Shepherd Dog reclining
Peter Herold
1916
11 x 24 cm
***
$250-350

1803
Cat, plain grey
A. Nielsen (AP)
1916
13 cm
In production 2000
*
$50-125

1804
Faun pulling bear's ear
Knud Kyhn
1916
19 cm
****
$400-600

1818
Girl with baby
Chr. Thomsen
1916
17 cm
*****
$250-400

1827
Woman kneeling
Overglaze

1828
Boy
Chr. Thomsen
1916
17 cm
*****
$150-300

1829
Snowy Owl
Peter Herold
1917
40 cm
In production 2000
*
$650-1700

1830
Boy with bricks
Peter Herold
1917
14 cm
*****
$250-400

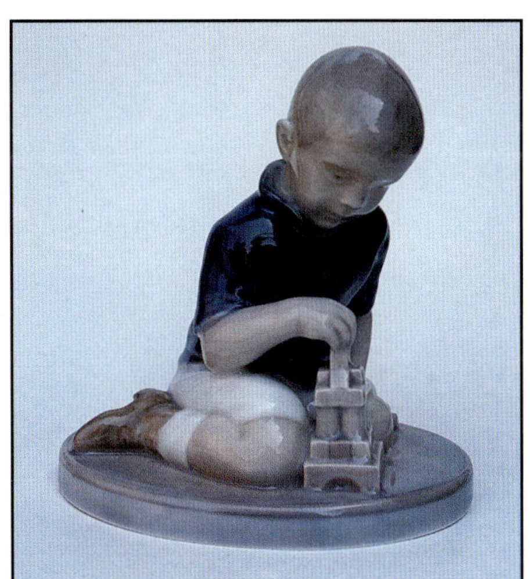

1833
Boy with flowers
Chr. Thomsen
1917
17 cm
*****
$150-300

1838
Woman kneeling
Overglaze

1846
Basket - herons
Peter Herold
1917
42 cm w
*****
$1000-1500

1847
'The Nightingale'
Chr. Thomsen
1917
22 cm
Also in overglaze & partial overglaze.
****
$500-650C

1848
Hans Christian Anderson
Chr. Thomsen
1917
18 x 18 cm
****
$400-500

1849
Child sitting on cow
Knud Kyhn
1917
17 x 30 cm
*****
$950-1350

1858
Boy with calves
Chr. Thomsen
1917
23 x 18 cm
In production 1994
**
$200-350

1859
Dog
Peter Herold
1917
11 x 20 cm
*****
$450-600

1860
Pekingese puppy
Peter Herold
1917
13 cm
*****
$300-450

1863
Mandarin ducks
Peter Herold
1917
19 x 20 cm
In production 1963
****
$450-650

1864
Native woman kneeling
16 cm
Overglaze & grey glaze

1866
Woman kneeling
Overglaze

1871
Woman kneeling
Overglaze

1875
Woman kneeling with bird
Overglaze

1878
Boy with sailing boat
Peter Herold
1917
14 x 11 cm
****
$250-400

1879
Girl with teddy
Carl Martin-Hansen
1917
13 x 15 cm
Only known underglaze by CMH
*****
$300-450

1880
Faun on tortoise
Knud Kyhn
1917
13 x 13 cm
****
$400-500

1881
Pheasant
A. Nielsen (AP)
1917
19 x 30 cm
In production 1981
****
$300-400

1882
Huskies - pair
Peter Herold
1917
17 x 21 cm
*****
$450-600

1891
Girl and two soldiers
Chr. Thomsen
1917
20 x 15 cm
*****
$500-750

1905
Old men
Chr. Thomsen
1918
21 x 14 cm
*****
$350-550

1920
Borzoi
Peter Herold
1918
13 x 21 cm
*****
$500-750

1922
Faun & Squirrel clock case
Chr. Thomsen
1918
25 x 11 cm
*****
$800-1000

1924
Duck - tufted
Peter Herold
1918
6 cm
In production 2000
*
$70-150

1925
Duck
Peter Herold
1918
6 x 15 cm
****
$200-350

1926
Eider Duck
Peter Herold
1918
9 x 15 cm
****
$200-350

1928
Robin

1929
Cherub
Arno Malinowski

1930
Cherub
Arno Malinowski
12 cm

1933
Duck - drake
Peter Herold
1918
8 cm
In production 2000
*
$110-160

1934
Mallard
Peter Herold
1918
10 cm
In production 2000
*
$90-210

1938
Girl with doll
Ada Bonfils
1918
13 cm
In production 2000
*
$125-350

1941
Duck tufted
Peter Herold
1918
12 cm
In production 2000
*
$50-200

1946
'Leda & the Swan'
18 cm
Overglaze

1951
Pheasants on base
Peter Herold
1918
22 x 21 cm
***
$300-450

1969
Lady & Beau
Chr. Thomsen
1918
25 x 20 cm
****
$650-750

1982
Woman kneeling on pot base
Platen Hallermundt
1918
25 cm
*****
$350-500

1983
Woman kneeling on pot lid
Platen Hallermundt
1918
16 cm
*****
$350-500

1997
'Adam & Eve'
Hans H. Hansen
1919
14 cm
Overglaze

2005
Lady with bird
Peter Herold

2014
Chihuahua
G. K. Strand
1919
21 x 7 cm
*****
$800-1200

2030
Hairdresser
Chr. Thomsen
20 cm
*****
$500-650

2033
Golden eagle (Blue)
Vilhelm Thdr Fischer
50 cm
In production 2000
*
$7000-8900

2036
Mouse on base
Platen Hallermundt
1919
7 cm
*****
$150-250

2039
Cat grooming
G. K. Strand
1919
9 x 11 cm
*****
$300-450

2046
'The Kiss'
Chr. Thomsen
1919
22 x 17 cm
In production 1963
***
$500-600

2051
Deer on green base
Hans H. Hansen
1919
13 x 17 cm
In production 1963
****
$200-300

2053
'Leda & the Swan'
Hans H. Hansen
1919
28 x 33 cm
*****
$900-1200

2061
Girl with basket
17 cm
*****
$300-450

2064
Dove
Hans H. Hansen
1919
13 x 16 cm
*****
$300-400

2065
Tiger gnawing a bone
Peter Herold
1919
36 cm
****
$500-750

2068
Geese
Peter Herold
1919
19 x 21 cm
In production 1981
***
$250-400

2071
Girl with trumpet
Chr. Thomsen
1920
26 cm
****
$250-350

2072
Girl with musical instrument
Chr. Thomsen
1920
26 cm
****
$250-350

2078
Man holding lamb?
Chr. Thomsen
1920
21 cm
*****
$350-500

2082
Boy with golden hair
Michael Pedersen
***
$200-250

2083
Boy on a chair
Michael Pedersen
***
$200-250

2084
Finch
Peter Herold?

2085
Chinese man
Georg Thylstrup
1920
19 x 10 cm
****
$200-300

2086
Chinese woman
Georg Thylstrup
1920
18 x 9 cm
****
$200-300

2107
Faun with owl
Chr. Thomsen
1920
16 x 11 cm
In production 1981
***
$300-500

2108
Parrot
Martha Hasted
1920
9 x 11 cm
*****
$300-450

2109
'The Kiss on the Hand'
Gerhard Henning
1920
38 cm
Overglaze

2111
Girl with fawn
Hans H. Hansen
1920
20 x 22 cm
*****
$350-450

2113
Faun with crow
Chr. Thomsen
1920
17 x 13 cm
In production 1963
***
$250-400

2119
Dachshunds - pair
Olaf Mathiesen
1920
11 x 16 cm
*****
$350-500

2120
Dachshunds - pair
Olaf Mathiesen
1920
11 x 15 cm
*****
$350-500

2122
Drake
Olaf Mathiesen
1920
15 x 9 cm
***
$150-225

2123
Woman
Chr. Thomsen
1920
21 x 13 cm
*****
$300-500

2125
Guinea Fowl
Peter Herold
1920
17 x 12 cm
****
$250-400

2126
Cat looking back
Peter Herold
1920
11 cm
*****
$300-450

2127
Seal scratching head
Peter Herold
1920
13 x 10 cm
****
$250-350

2128
Drake & duck
Olaf Mathiesen
1920
11 x 12 cm
In production 1988
****
$200-250

2133
Pied Flycatcher
Platen Hallermundt
1920
11 x 8 cm
****
$150-250

2138
Wagtail
Platen Hallermundt
1920
12 x 13 cm
****
$150-250

2139
'Goose-thief'
Chr. Thomsen
1920
18 x 12 cm
Also in overglaze.
***
$150-300

2140
Boy with terrier
Chr. Thomsen
1920
17 x 10 cm
****
$300-400

2144
Flycatcher
Platen Hallermundt
1920
9 x 12 cm
In production 1981
**
$125-225

2146
Owl with 2 fauns
Chr. Thomsen
1920
20 x 11 cm
*****
$900-1200

2152
Baboon
Peter Herold
1920
17 cm
*****
$300-500

2157
Girl with musical instrument
Chr. Thomsen
1921
26 cm
****
$250-350

2158
Girl with jar
Chr. Thomsen
1921
26 cm
****
$250-350

2162
Chinese couple
Gerhard Henning
1921
33 cm
Overglaze

2163
'Little Matchgirl'
1921
14 x 9 cm
*****
$150-300

02/525

2165
Duck
Platen Hallermundt
1921
4.5 cm
****
$100-200

2166
Rabbit
Peter Herold/Vwaldorff
1921
4 x 4 cm
2 color versions
****
$75-150

2167
Seagull
Georg K. Strand
1921
4 x 4 cm
****
$75-150

2168
Man & woman on bench
Chr. Thomsen
1921
24 cm
*****
$500-800

2169
Cocker spaniel
Svend Jespersen

2169
Mouse
Platen Hallermundt
1919
5 cm
*****
$100-200

2171
Faun kneeling with grapes
Storch
1921
16 x 11 cm
*****
$450-650

2175
Lion cub
Peter Herold
1920
16 x 13 cm
***
$250-350

2177
Inkstand - barn owls
Olaf Mathiesen
1921
30 cm

2178
Falcon on rock
Platen Hallermundt
1921
31 cm
*****
$750-1000

2180
Bison
Peter Herold
1920
17 x 32 cm
*****
$600-1000

2181
Sitting dog
Peter Herold
1920
20 x 12 cm
****
$400-600

2187
Marmot on base
15 cm
*****
$300-400

2188
Girl & sheep with dove on back
Hans H. Hansen
1921
21 x 10 cm
*****
$350-450

2189
Girl & sheep
Hans H. Hansen
1921
15 x 14 cm
*****
$350-450

2190
Inkstand - penguins
Olaf Mathiesen
1921
32 cm
*****
$1100-1300

2195
Cherub drinking
Arno Malinowski
1921
7 cm
*****
$250-350

2196
Cherub squatting
Arno Malinowski
pre-1929
9 cm
*****
$250-350

2198
Squirrel
Platen Hallermundt
1921
18 x 11 cm
*****
$400-600

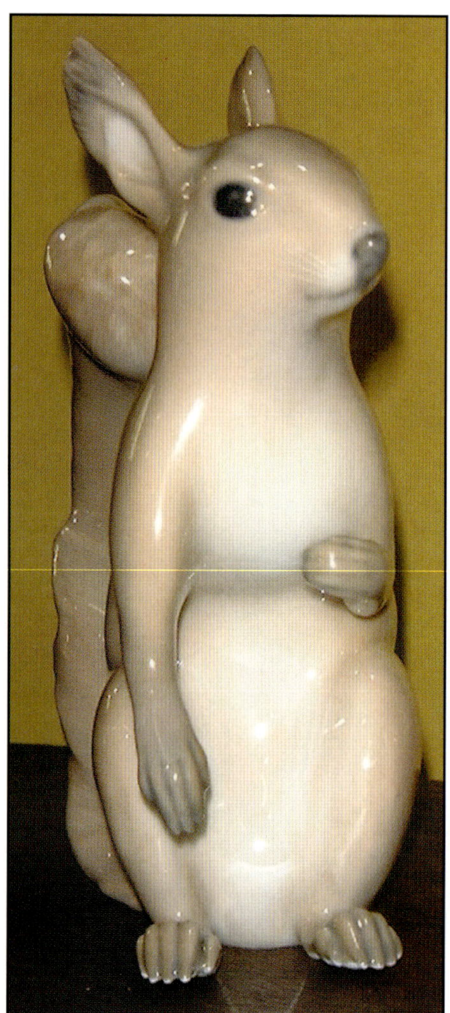

2201
Monkeys - pair
Hans H. Hansen
1920
11 cm
*****
$300-450

2202
Stag jumping a mound
Peter Herold
1920
20 x 11 cm
****
$250-400

2208
Sparrow on base
O. Jensen
1921
4 cm
****
$75-150

2211
Harlequin & Columbine
Chr. Thomsen
1922
17 x 11 cm
*****
$350-450

2214
Lizards (triple) on ashtray
A. Nielsen (AP)
1922
12 cm

2215
Duck - flying
Platen Hallermundt
3 cm
In production 1997
***
$50-150

2216
Woodpecker
Platen Hallermundt
1923
5 x 5.5 cm
****
$100-200

2217
Woman - nude
Arno Malinowski
Overglaze

2218
Cherub standing on a ball
Arno Malinowski
1922
10 cm
*****
$250-350

2220
Cat
Platen Hallermundt
1922
5 cm
****
$100-200

2224
Cat playing with ball
Platen Hallermundt
1922
7 cm
2 color versions
*****
$100-200

2227
Woman
Platen Hallermundt
1921
28 cm
*****
$350-500

2228
Cherub with dolphin
Arno Malinowski
1922
11 x 9 cm
*****
$300-400

2230
Cherub riding a dolphin
Arno Malinowski
1922
6 x 14 cm
*****
$300-400

2232
Jay on perch
Peter Herold
1920
16 x 8 cm
****
$250-350

2238
Robin
Platen Hallermundt
1922
4 cm
In production 2000
*
$25-75

2239
Woodpecker on ashtray
pre-1929

2240
Sparrow on ashtray
pre-1929

2242
Duck - flying on ashtray
Platen Hallermundt
pre-1929
4 cm
In production 1981
**

2244
Cherub
Arno Malinowski
6 cm
*****
$250-350

2248
Cherub drinking (no base)
Arno Malinowski
5 cm
*****
$250-350

2249
Wood spirit
Arno Malinowski
1922
6 cm
*****
$250-350

2250
Robin on ashtray
pre-1929

2251
Cat on ashtray
pre-1929

2257
Kingfisher holding fish
Peter Herold
1915
18 cm
In production 2000
*
$75-140

2258
Nuthatch?
Platen Hallermundt
1922
10 x 9 cm
****
$125-225

2259
Tit
Platen Hallermundt
1922
9 x 11 cm
****
$150-250

2260
Warbler?
Platen Hallermundt
1922
10 x 12 cm
****
$150-250

2261
Partridge
Peter Herold
1914
9 x 18 cm
In production 1981
***
$200-300

2262
Robin squatting
Platen Hallermundt
1922
5 x 8 cm
***
$50-100

2264
Thrush on base
Platen Hallermundt
1922
11 x 11 cm
****
$150-250

2265
Bunting on base
Platen Hallermundt
1922
10 x 11 cm
****
$150-250

2266
Robin
Platen Hallermundt
1922
8 cm
In production 2000
*
$30-105

2268
Cherub, toe in mouth
Arno Malinowski
1922
11 cm
*****
$250-350

2270
Puppies playing
Platen Hallermundt
1922
8 x 6 cm
*****
$250-350

2272
Terrier begging
C. F. Liisberg
1922
12 x 5 cm
*****
$250-350

2274
'Ali & Peribanu'
Gerhard Henning
1922
23 cm
Overglaze

2279
Cherub sitting (no base)
Arno Malinowski
6 cm
*****
$250-350

2284
Cat on back
C. F. Liisberg
1922
13 x 18 cm
*****
$450-650

2285
Bear squatting
V. Waldorff
1922
10 x 9 cm
***
$125-200

2286
Sparrow
Platen Hallermundt
1922
7 x 9 cm
****
$50-100

2288
Arctic Fox
Platen Hallermundt
1923
5.5 cm
***
$50-150

2298
Faun with small girl
V. Waldorff
1923
8 x 6 cm
*****
$500-800

2299
Faun with mermaid
V. Waldorff
1923
11 x 9 cm
****
$500-800

2301
Squirrel
Platen Hallermundt
1923
3 x 5.5 cm
****
$100-200

2303
Lamp with Child & grapes
pre-1929
19 cm

2309
Turkey
Platen Hallermundt
1923
5.5 cm
***
$75-150

2310
Cockerels fighting?
Platen Hallermundt
1923
6 x 7 cm
*****
$100-200

2313
Mermaid
V. Waldorff
1923
5 cm
In production 2000
*
$35-90

2317
Polar bears
Knud Kyhn
1923
16 x 14 cm
In production 1988
***
$150-250

2318
Faun & bear wrestling
Knud Kyhn
1923
18 x 14 cm
****
$400-600

2319
Racoon
Platen Hallermundt
1923
4 cm
****
$100-200

2322
Cat? licking
C. F. Liisberg
1923
10 x 9 cm
*****
$250-400

2323
Child with grapes
V. Waldorff
1923
5 cm
****
$150-250

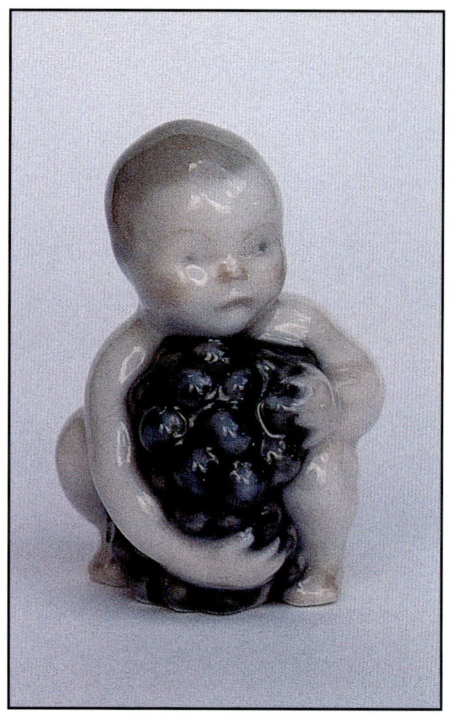

2326
Bulldogs playing
Knud Kyhn
1923
19 x 22 cm
*****
$600-900

2330
Cuckoo being fed
Knud Kyhn
1923
17 cm
*****
$500-700

2332
Girl holding duck
V. Waldorff
1923
6.5 cm
****
$100-200

2333
Otter with fish
V. Waldorff
1923
5.5 cm
In production 1988
**
$50-75

2334
Fox
V. Waldorff
1923
2.5 x 4 cm
*****
$100-200

2335
Duck
Platen Hallermundt
1922
4 x 4 cm
****
$75-150

2336
Servil
H. Liisberg
1923
24 x 11 cm
*****
$1000-1250

2337
Mermaid riding seal with fish
Knud Kyhn
1923
24 x 18 cm
*****
$600-900

2342
Opium smoker
Arno Malinowski
14 cm
Overglaze/Blanc de Chine

2345
Otter with Fish
Knud Kyhn
16 x 16 cm
*****
$800-1000

2347
Boy Neptune riding fish
V. Waldorff
1923
13 x 13 cm
****
$400-500

2348
Mermaid with fish
V. Waldorff
1923
7 cm
In production 1981
***
$75-125

2360
Bear
Knud Kyhn
1923
17 x 17 cm
*****
$275-400

2361
Faun with grapes
V. Waldorff
1923
14 x 13 cm
In production 1981
***
$200-350

2365
Wolves fighting
Knud Kyhn
1923
20 x 23 cm
*****
$450-650

2366
Warbler?
Platen Hallermundt
1923
4 x 9 cm
****
$100-200

2367
Otter & Duck
Knud Kyhn
1923
20 x 21 cm
*****
$400-500

2373
King Charles Spaniel
Knud Kyhn
1923
18 x 17 cm
*****
$350-500

2374
Swallow
Platen Hallermundt
1923
4 cm
In production 2000
*
$30-95

2384
Mink
Platen Hallermundt
1923
4 x 7 cm
****
$100-200

2387
German Shepherd lying
Peter Herold
1917
11 x 17 cm
*****
$400-550

2394
Pheasant
Peter Herold
1918
19 x 20 cm
***
$200-300

2402
Faun & bear
Knud Kyhn
1924
15 x 14 cm
*****
$550-750

2409
'The Nightingale'
Gerhard Henning
1924
30 cm
Overglaze

2411
Mountain Lion attacking Stag
20 cm
*****
$600-800

2412
Mermaid sitting on rock
V. Waldorff
1924
27 x 13 cm
*****
$300-450

2413
'Moon Girl'
Gerhard Henning
1924
30 cm
Overglaze

2414
Crucian Carp
Platen Hallermundt
1924
6 x 10 cm
In production 1981
***
$75-125

2417
'Venus'
Gerhard Henning
1924
21 cm
Overglaze

2423
'Susanna'
Gerhard Henning
1924
19 cm
Overglaze

2424
Faun with parrot
Knud Kyhn
1924
16 x 16 cm
*****
$500-750

2425
Husky
Knud Kyhn
1925
14 x 19 cm
*****
$500-600

2427
Pike
Platen Hallermundt
1924
3 x 13 cm
In production 1981
**
$50-100

2428
Girl bathing
Gerhard Henning
1924
33 cm
Overglaze

2439
Gazelle with baby gazelle on back
Knud Kyhn
20 cm
*****
$750-900

2443
Rabbit on haunches
12.5 cm
**
$30-65

2444
Dancing girl
V. Waldorff
1924
21 cm
In production 2000
*
$110-340

2445
Boy with cockerel
V. Waldorff
1925
6 cm
****
$100-200

2449
Bream
Platen Hallermundt
1924
7 x 15 cm
****
$200-300

2451
Dish - frog
J. A. Heuch
1895
6 x 18 cm

2452
Bowl - fish
J. A. Heuch
1895
8 x 27 cm

2460
Bonbon Dish - mouse on lid
Chr. Thomsen
1898
11 cm w

2461
Bonbon Dish - monkey on lid
Erik Nielsen
1896
14 cm w

2462
Dish - swan?
Chr. Thomsen
1902
12 cm w

2463
Bonbon Dish - lizard on lid
Chr. Thomsen
1898
11 cm h

2465
Card tray - Crab
Erik Nielsen
1894
6.5 x 24 x 20 cm
In production 1981
***
$100-195

2466
Card tray - lizard
A. Pedersen (AN)
1899
10 x 19 cm

2467
Card tray - lizards
A. Pedersen (AN)
1899
10 x 19 cm

2468
Card tray - lizard
A. Pedersen (AN)
1898
21 cm w

2469
Card tray - Woman
Chr. Thomsen
1899
11 x 20 cm
See No. 8
*****
$300-450

2470
Card tray - woman
Chr. Thomsen
1899
12 x 19 cm

2477
Frog on ashtray
Erik Nielsen
pre-1929
3 x 10 cm
In production 1981
**
$25-120

2478
Snail on ashtray
pre-1929
3 x 10 cm
*****
$75-150

2480
Snail on blotter
J. A. Heuch
1896
14 cm

2482
Inkstand - snake crushing frog
Erik Nielsen
1896
16 x 27 cm

2483
Inkstand - fly
Erik Nielsen
1896
16 x 20 cm

2487
Lynx
Knud Kyhn
1924
29 x 31 cm
*****
$750-1000

2494
Roach
Platen Hallermundt
1924
7 x 17 cm
***
$200-300

2496
Faun with 2 monkeys
Knud Kyhn
1924
18 x 21 cm
*****
$750-1000

2506
Bulldog
20 cm
*****
$500-650

2507
Chimpanzee
Knud Kyhn
1924
18 x 14 cm
*****
$300-400

2512
Wild Cat grooming
Knud Kyhn
1924
11 x 18 cm
*****
$300-400

2519
Sea-lions
Georg K. Strand
1918
11 x 11 cm
In production 1981
**
$75-125

2524
Bird - long tailed
Platen Hallermundt
1924
6 x 16 cm
****
$100-200

2532
Wild Dog?
Knud Kyhn
1924
20 x 19 cm
*****
$500-750

2537
Girl sitting with puppy
V. Waldorff
1924
15 x 12 cm
****
$250-350

2539
Rabbits (3) fused
Erik Nielsen
1925
10 x 11 cm
*****
$200-300

2545
Fish curled
Platen Hallermundt
1924
6 x 10 cm
***
$75-125

2549
Snowy Owl
Knud Kyhn
1925
51 cm
*****
$750-1000

2553
Perch
Platen Hallermundt
1925
6 x 8 cm
In production 1988
***
$50-100

2555
Panther
Knud Kyhn
1925
21 x 23 cm
In production 1963
****
$750-1000

2561
Girl with doll
V. Waldorff
1925
15 x 12 cm
*****
$200-300

2562
Gull?
Platen Hallermundt
1925
8 x 13 cm
****
$150-200

s2564
Vole
Platen Hallermundt
1925
4 x 7 cm
In production 1981
***
$100-150

2565
Pekingese snarling
Knud Kyhn
18 x 23 cm
See #2697
*****
$450-600

2573
2 Fauns with grapes
Knud Kyhn
1925
14 x 11 cm
*****
$750-1000

2574
Toucan
Georg K. Strand
1925
10 x 11 cm
In production 1963
****
$100-200

2589
Monkey
Knud Kyhn
1925
14 cm
*****
$200-300

2590
Faun with puppy
Knud Kyhn
*****

2595
Cow & calf
Knud Kyhn
1925
22 x 35 cm
*****
$500-700

2596
Lion cub
Knud Kyhn
1925
10 x 15 cm
****
$200-300

2604
Boy with pillows
Holger Christensen
17 x 9 cm
****
$150-200

2607
Wild Cat
Knud Kyhn
1925
11 x 18 cm
*****
$300-400

2608
Dalmation Puppy
Knud Kyhn
15 cm
*****
$650-800

2609
Fawn
Knud Kyhn
1925
13 cm
In production 1988
**
$75-125

2621
Terrier sitting
Knud Kyhn
8 cm
****
$150-250

2622
Bulldog Turning
Knud Kyhn
1925
11 x 10 cm
*****
$250-350

2623
Squirrel
Knud Kyhn
1925
15 x 10 cm
*****
$300-400

2624
Horse biting rear
Knud Kyhn
1925
12 x 19 cm
*****
$300-400

2625
Weasel/Ferret
Knud Kyhn
1925
16 cm
*****
$200-300

2627
Chuhuahua
1925
6 x 18 cm
*****
$300-400

2636
Fawn head up
Knud Kyhn
1925
9 x 11 cm
**
$100-150

2638
Cat turning
Knud Kyhn
1925
11 x 17 cm
*****
$300-400

2644
Dormouse
Knud Kyhn
1925
7 x 6 cm
****
$125-200

2648
Fawn head down
Knud Kyhn
1925
9 cm
In production 1981
**
$75-125

2649
Fawn asleep
Knud Kyhn
1925
11 x 15 cm
**
$125-175

2650
Dish - monkey?
pre-1929
9 x 19 cm

2667
Scottish Terrier
Knud Kyhn
1926
16 x 15 cm
****
$250-350

2668
Terrier head up
Knud Kyhn
1926
13 x 13 cm
****
$200-300

2668
Scottish Terrier
Knud Kyhn
1926
16. x 15 cm
****
$200-300

2674
Fish
Platen Hallermundt
1926
6.5 x 11 cm
*****
$200-300

2675
Roach
Platen Hallermundt
1926
7 x 15 cm
In production 1981
***
$80-150

2676
Trout (rainbow)
Platen Hallermundt
1926
20 cm
In production 1997
**
$50-125

2686
Lamb - standing
Knud Kyhn
1926
11 x 11 cm
*****
$250-350

2697
Pekingese - snarling
Knud Kyhn
1926
12 x 15 cm
See #2565
*****
$300-500

2701
Setter lying
Knud Kyhn
1926
11 x 20 cm
*****
$350-500

2703
Donkey
Knud Kyhn
1926
12 x 15 cm
*****
$200-300

2720
Lamb - sitting
Knud Kyhn
1926
8 x 13 cm
*****
$200-300

2734
Lion cubs playing
Knud Kyhn
1926
14 x 14 cm
*****
$250-350

2735
Lamb - standing
Knud Kyhn
1926
9 x 16 cm
*****
$200-300

2738
Fish - pair
Platen Hallermundt
1926
10 x 13 cm
*****
$250-350

2741
Elephant (leg in trunk)
6 x 9 cm
In production 1994
**
$100-150

2741
Cat
Knud Kyhn
1926
14 x 14 cm
*****
$250-350

2742
Cat
pre-1929
13 x 15 cm
*****
$250-350

2743
Peewit
Knud Kyhn
17 x 19 cm
****
$200-300

2751
Seagull
Knud Kyhn
1926
14 x 13 cm
*****
$100-200

2753
West Highland Terrier sitting
Knud Kyhn
1926
10 x 12 cm
*****
$200-300

2755
Wire Haired Terrier
Knud Kyhn
1926
13 x 9 cm
*****
$200-300

2756
Fish Grayling
Platen Hallermundt
1926
7 x 19 cm
*****
$200-300

2761
Dog
Knud Kyhn?
192?

2768
Fox
Knud Kyhn
10 x 15 cm
*****
$250-350

2769
Lambs - pair
Knud Kyhn
1926
5.5 x 10 cm
In production 2000
*
$95-165

2786
Terrier turning, head down
Knud Kyhn
1927
11 x 17 cm
*****
$250-350

2802
English Bulldog sitting
Knud Kyhn
1927
11 x 12 cm
****
$200-300

2803
German Shepherd Dog
Knud Kyhn
1927
19 x 23 cm
*****
$500-600

2805
Spaniels - pair
Knud Kyhn
1927
12 x 10 cm
*****
$300-400

2806
Mastiff
Knud Kyhn
1928
12 x 22 cm
*****
$450-600

2811
Owl
Knud Kyhn
1927
39 x 19 cm
*****
$500-700

2813
Elk
Knud Kyhn
1928
21 x 24 cm
In production 1981
***
$300-400

2822
Faun with bear
Knud Kyhn
1927
12 x 10 cm
*****
$500-800

2823
Faun with goose?
Knud Kyhn
1927
15 x 10 cm
*****
$450-700

2824
Lady & Beau clock case
Chr. Thomsen
30 x 20 cm

2830
Dog
Knud Kyhn
1928
11 x 11 cm
*****
$300-400

2834
Greenland girl
Georg K. Strand
1927
10 x 7.5 cm
****
$150-250

2837
Shark
Platen Hallermundt
1927
4 x 12 cm
*****
$150-250

2838
Fish
Platen Hallermundt
1927
5 cm
*****
$150-250

2841
Bear walking
Knud Kyhn
1927
10 x 15 cm
In production 1981
**
$75-150

2842
Bear with paw raised
Knud Kyhn
1928
9 x 9 cm
***
$150-250

2851
Fish - pair (Trout?)
Platen Hallermundt
1928
5 x 17 cm
*****
$150-250

2852
Faun with lion cub
Knud Kyhn
1927
14 x 18 cm
*****
$500-800

2853
Terrier standing
Knud Kyhn
1927
14 x 21 cm
****
$200-275

2855
Hound scratching
7 x 12 cm
****
$200-300

2856
'Spring'
Hans H. Hansen
1927
6.5 x 3 cm
****
$150-250

2857
'Summer'
Hans H. Hansen
1927
9 x 7 cm
****
$150-250

2858
'Autumn'
Hans H. Hansen
1927
8 x 5 cm
****
$150-250

2859
'Winter'
Hans H. Hansen
1927
6.5 x 3.5 cm
****
$150-250

2862
Siamese cat
Th. Madsen
1928
11 cm
In production 1988
***
$75-150

2863
English Bulldog
Knud Kyhn
1927
12 x 15 cm
****
$200-300

2868
Faun with brown bear
Knud Kyhn
1927
9 x 11 cm
****
$450-600

2869
Fish
Platen Hallermundt
1927
3.5 x 7 cm
*****
$150-200

2870
Minnows
Platen Hallermundt
1927
4.5 x 9 cm
In production 1988
**
$50-100

2871
Schnauzer
Knud Kyhn
1927
15 x 10 cm
****
$200-275

2872
Siamese cat playing
Th. Madsen
1928
12 x 21 cm
***
$200-300

2911
Cat

2918
Penguins
Th. Madsen
1927
18 x 14 cm
In production 1981
***
$150-250

2940
German Shepherd
Knud Kyhn
1928
12 x 18 cm
*****
$350-450

2941
Scottie
Knud Kyhn
1928
12 x 15 cm
****
$200-300

2942
Dog
Knud Kyhn
1928
11 x 12 cm
*****
$300-400

2952
Dove - faience
10 cm

2962
Wrasse
Platen Hallermundt
1928
11 x 10 cm
*****
$200-300

2965
Cat creeping
Th. Madsen
1928
10 x 24 cm
*****
$250-350

2967
Wirehaired Terrier
Platen Hallermundt
1928
17 cm
In production 1963
***
$200-300

2969
Spitz
Knud Kyhn
1928
17 x 16 cm
*****
$350-500

2970
Mother & child
A. Hofmann
1928
14 x 16 cm
*****
$300-400

2975
Penguin
Th. Madsen
20 x 12 cm
***
$250-350

2989
Snowy Owl
Knud Kyhn
1928
30 x 30 cm
*****
$550-750

2991
Bears - pair
Knud Kyhn
1928
12 x 14 cm
*****
$250-350

2993
Goat
Knud Kyhn
1928
15 x 24 cm
*****
$600-800

2997
Peke looking up
Knud Kyhn
1928
10 x 11 cm
*****
$250-350

2998
Elephant
Knud Kyhn
1928
11 cm
In production 1988
**
$45-75

2999
Owl
Th. Madsen
14 cm
White version still in production
*
$50-115

3000
Great Dane?
Knud Kyhn
1928
11 x 23 cm
*****
$500-600

3002
Heron
Th. Madsen
1928
29 cm
In production 2000
*
$250-725

3003
Penguin
Th. Madsen
1928
7 cm
In production 2000
*
$25-55

3005
Elephant
Knud Kyhn
1928
8 x 10 cm
***
$75-125

3007
Boy with spaniel
Th. Madsen
1928
12 x 13 cm
*****
$300-400

3009
'Rosebud'
Th. Madsen
1928
14 cm
In production 1981
****
$200-300

3014
Bear cub eating
Knud Kyhn
1928
9 cm
In production 1988
**
$40-70

3015
Bear squatting
Knud Kyhn
1928
9 x 8.5 cm
**
$100-175

3018
Greyhound
10 cm
*****
$650-800

3020
Wirehaired Terrier (m)
Platen Hallermundt
1928
13 cm
In production 1963
***
$200-300

3034
Mother & child
Holger Christensen
1929
21 x 12 cm
*****
$350-450

3041
Minnows
3 x 7 cm
***
$100-150

3042
Fish - pair
5 cm
***
$150-250

3049
'Henrik & Else'
Holger Christensen
42 cm
In production 1981
***
$750-1200

3050
Flying Fish
Platen Hallermundt
3 x 15 cm
In production 1963
****
$100-150

3062
Dog
10.5 cm
*****
$250-350

3063
Terrier
Th. Madsen
10 cm
****
$150-250

3064
Fantail
Platen Hallermundt
5 cm
In production 1981
***
$40-70

3070
Sailor boy on plinth
Holger Christensen?

3082
Faun on tortoise
Knud Kyhn
1929
46.5 x 32 cm
*****
$3500-4500

3083
Faun fighting a cockerel
Knud Kyhn
30 x 32 cm
Also Blanc de Chine
*****
$3000-4000

3084
Angel Fish
Platen Hallermundt
10 x 12 cm
*****
$250-300

3085
Sealyham standing
Th. Madsen
5 cm
***
$100-150

3086
Sealyham squatting
Th. Madsen
5 cm
***
$100-150

3087
Sealyham turning
Th. Madsen
5 cm
***
$100-175

3110
Pointer
18 cm
*****
$300-400

3116
Cocker Spaniel
Th. Madsen
12 x 13 cm
In production 1963
***
$150-200

3118
Penguins - pair

3128
French Bulldog
11 cm
****

3131
Dish - Crab
Jorgen Balslov
16 cm
In production 1981
**
$100-150

3139
Airedale Terrier
Th. Madsen
15 cm
In production 1981
***
$150-200

3140
Dachshund (sitting)
Th. Madsen
10 cm
In production 2000
*
$55-135

3142
Spitz
Th. Madsen
12 x 12 cm
***
$200-300

3161
Scottish Terrier standing
Th. Madsen
10 cm
In production 1981
***
$100-150

3162
Scottish Terrier sitting
Th. Madsen
8 cm
In production 1981
***
$100-150

3164
Sunfish
Platen Hallermundt
11 cm
****
$250-350

3165
Wirehaired Terrier
Th. Madsen
12 cm
In production 1981
***
$65-100

3169
Pug puppy
Th. Madsen
8 cm
In production 1988
***
$85-160

3170
Wirehaired Terrier
Th. Madsen
8 cm
In production 1981
***
$50-105

3171
Knight & Maiden
Holger Christensen
45 cm
In production 1981
***
$800-1000

3194
Grebe with young
Platen Hallermundt
****
$400-550

3231
Dish - mermaid
Hans H. Hansen
6 x 15 cm
***
$100-150

3234
Kingfisher
Platen Hallermundt
10 cm
In production 1981
**
$60-115

3235
Cairn Terrier
Th. Madsen
9 x 10 cm
***
$100-200

3249
Terrier
****
$200-300

3250
Boy with broom
Aage Erhardt
11 cm
In production 2000
*
$35-150

3251
Scottie on side
Th. Madsen
4 cm
*****
$150-200

3252
Irish Setter
Th. Madsen
13 cm
In production 1981
***
$150-200

3261
German Shepherd
Th. Madsen
16 cm
In production 1981
***
$150-250

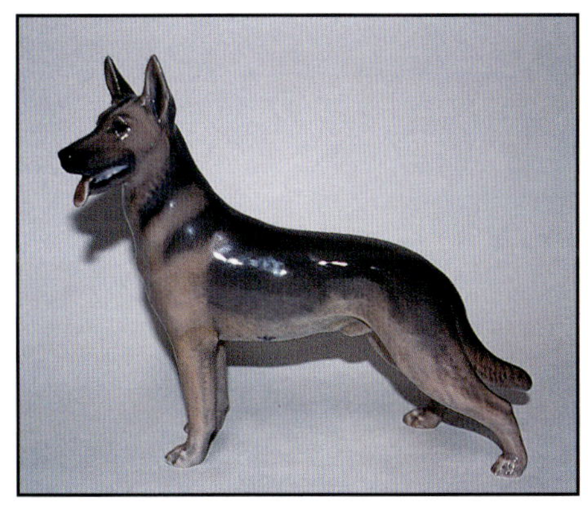

3263
Grebe
Platen Hallermundt
10 x 17 cm
In production 1981
***
$85-175

3270
Starling fledgling
Platen Hallermundt
8 x 14 cm
In production 1981
***
$100-150

3272
Boy with sailing boat
Aage Erhardt
10 cm
**
$50-85

3280
Bull Terrier
Th. Madsen
13 cm
In production 1981
***
$100-150

3281
Siamese Cat
Th. Madsen
19 cm
In production 2000
*
$50-165

3321
Mermaid
Aage Erhardt
11 cm
In production 1981
***
$150-200

3330
Satyr & woman
Arno Malinowski?
Blanc de Chine

3407
Lapland Boy
22 cm
*****
$300-400

3432
Dish - girl & duck
6 x 15 cm
****
$150-200

3457
Mother with child
Holger Christensen
21 cm
In production 1963
***
$200-300

3468
Boy with teddy bear
Ada Bonfils
18 cm
In production 2000
*
$120-375

3476
Terrier with slipper
Ada Bonfils
10 cm
In production 2000
*
$80-130

3498
Dish - lobster
Jorgen Balslov
19 cm
In production 1963
**
$150-200

3501
Dalmation
Th. Madsen
12 cm
In production 1981
**
$100-200

3510
Pigeon
Th. Madsen
15 cm
In production 1963. Color variations.
**
$150-200

3519
Boy with bucket & spade
Aage Erhardt
9 cm
****
$200-300

3539
Girl with doll standing
Ada Bonfils
15 cm
In production 2000
*
$50-210

3542
Boy with ball
Aage Erhardt
16 cm
In production 1981
**
$85-105

3556
Boy with umbrella
Ada Bonfils
18 cm
In production 2000
*
$100-350

3634
Boxer Dog standing
Holger Christensen
14 cm
In production 1981
***
$150-250

3635
Boxer Dog lying
Holger Christensen
9 cm
In production 1981
***
$160-205

3647
Drummer
Ada Bonfils
9 cm
In production 2000
*
$60-155

3650
Great Dane - harlequin
Holger Christensen
20 x 23 cm
***
$250-350

3654
Cat - faience
12 cm

3655
Giraffe
Holger Christensen
22 cm
In production 1963
****
$350-500

3658
Madonna (OG)
Hans H. Hansen
1939
23 cm
Overglaze & Blanc de Chine

3667
Child with accordion
Ada Bonfils
11 cm
In production 1988
***
$60-155

3668
Fisherman
Axel Locher
26 cm
In production 1981
**
$140-185

3677
Girl with pot-cover
Ada Bonfils
9 cm
In production 1988
***
$60-155

3679
Nude female kneeling
Blanc de Chine

02/716

3686
Fisherman with fish
16 cm
****
$400-550

3689
Boy with horn
Ada Bonfils
11 cm
In production 1988
***
$60-155

3794
Lion B de Chine
10 x 20 cm
***
$125-175

4027
Girl on stone
Ada Bonfils
15 cm
In production 1981
***
$100-150

4047
Fishwife
Bode Willumsen
1941
20 cm
Blanc de Chine
***
$250-350

4050
Sailor with anchor
Bode Willumsen
18 cm
Blanc de Chine
$250-350

4065
Woman hands on hips
Bode Willumsen
15 cm
Blanc de Chine
***
$250-350

4066
Man standing
Bode Willumsen
15 cm
Blanc de Chine
***
$250-350

4070
Woman with basket
Bode Willumsen
16 cm
Blanc de Chine
***
$250-350

4071
Man with sack (white)
Bode Willumsen
16 cm
Blanc de Chine
***
$250-350

4075
Ballet girl
Holger Christensen
1942
21.5 cm
Overglaze & Blance de Chine only

4082
Man with cartwheel
Bode Willumsen
15 cm
Overglaze/Blanc de Chine
****
$250-350

4083
Woman with pail
Bode Willumsen
15 cm
Overglaze/Blanc de Chine
***
$250-350

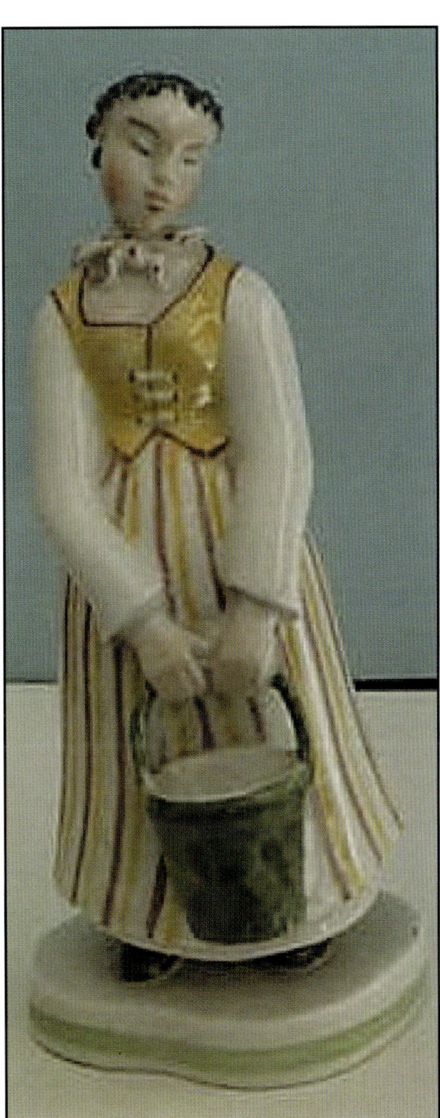

4087
Woman arms crossed at wrists
Bode Willumsen
16 cm
Overglaze/Blanc de Chine
****
$250-350

4091
Hunter
Bode Willumsen
16 cm
Overglaze/Blanc de Chine
****
$250-350

4092
Man carrying painting?
Bode Willumsen
15 cm
Blanc de Chine
***
$250-350

4093
Woman with urn
Bode Willumsen
15 cm
Blanc de Chine
****
$250-350

4097
Woman
Bode Willumsen
15 cm
Blanc de Chine
***
$250-350

4100
Man with violin
Bode Willumsen
15 cm
Blanc de Chine
***
$250-350

4102
Woman holding bowl?
Bode Willumsen
18 cm
Blanc de Chine
***
$250-350

4109
Man
Bode Willumsen
18 cm
Blanc de Chine
***
$250-350

4111
Blacksmith?
Bode Willumsen
18 cm
Blanc de Chine
***
$250-350

4112
Woman with baby
Bode Willumsen
18 cm
Blanc de Chine
***
$250-350

4113
Woman with cage
Bode Willumsen
17 cm
Blanc de Chine
***
$250-350

4122
Old man reading
Bode Willumsen
17 cm
Blanc de Chine
***
$250-350

4125
Man with child
Bode Willumsen
18 cm
Blanc de Chine
***
$250-350

4126
Woman
19 cm
Blanc de Chine

4131
Woman leaning on style
Bode Willumsen
17 cm
Blanc de Chine
***
$250-350

4132
Man with saw
Bode Willumsen
17 cm
Blanc de Chine
***
$250-350

4136
Man with wood
Bode Willumsen
18 cm
Blanc de Chine
***
$250-350

4137
Woman with shopping
Bode Willumsen
18 cm
Blanc de Chine
***
$250-350

4161
Maiden on seahorse
Arno Malinowski?
Blanc de Chine

4183
Woman with sickle
Bode Willumsen
20 cm
Blanc de Chine
***
$250-350

4187
'Agnete & the Merman'
Holger Christensen
55 cm
In production 1981
***
$750-1200

4189
Old man
Bode Willumsen
15 cm
Blanc de Chine
***
$250-350

4216
Hans Christian Andersen (OG)
Hans H. Hansen
1948
26 cm
Overglaze & Blance de Chine only
**
$200-300

4359
Woman with water jug
Johannes Hedegaard
31 cm
In production 1963
***
$250-300

4367
'Emperor & The Nightingale'
Johannes Hedegaard
1953
31 cm
Overglaze. See #4382.
****
$450-550

4374
'Thumbelina'
Holger Christensen
9 cm
In production 1988
***
$65-100

4377
Bricklayer
Johannes Hedegaard
25 cm
In production 1981
***
$150-200

4382
'Emperor & Nightingale'
Johannes Hedegaard
1953
31 cm
Underglaze. See #4367.
****
$500-800

4418
Woman with eggs
Johannes Hedegaard
31 cm
In production 1963
***
$250-350

4424
Girl plaiting hair
Johannes Hedegaard
32 cm
In production 1963
***
$275-375

4431
'The Little Mermaid'
Edvard Eriksen
22 cm
In production 2000
*
$200-1200

4438
'Little Matchgirl'
Aage Erhardt
11 x 5 cm
***
$150-200

02/739

4502
Blacksmith
J. M. Nissen
22 cm
In production 2000
*
$140-260

4503
Schoolgirl
Holger Christensen
19 cm
In production 1963
**
$165-225

4507
Nurse
J. M. Nissen
21 cm
In production 1994
***
$150-200

4523
'January' - girl skater
Hans H. Hansen
16 cm
In production 1981
***
$140-200

4524
'February' - boy juggler
Hans H. Hansen
16 cm
In production 1981
***
$140-200

4525
'March' - girl with posy
Hans H. Hansen
17 cm
In production 1981
***
$140-200

4526
'April' - boy with umbrella
Hans H. Hansen
16 cm
In production 1981
***
$140-200

4527
'May' - girl with flowers
Hans H. Hansen
16 cm
In production 1981
***
$140-200

4528
'June' - boy with briefcase
Hans H. Hansen
17 cm
In production 1981
***
$140-200

4529
'July' - girl bathing
Hans H. Hansen
16 cm
In production 1981
***
$140-200

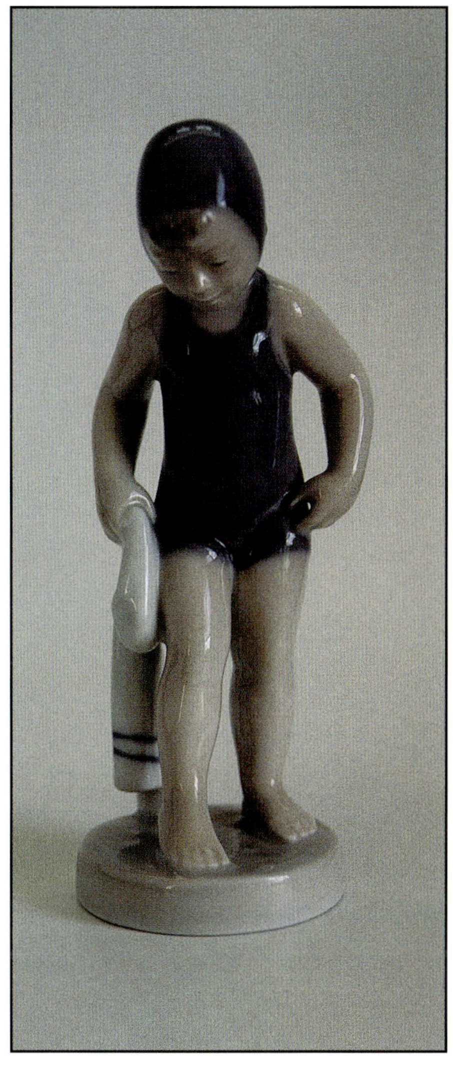

4530
'August' - boy with piglet
Hans H. Hansen
17 cm
In production 1981
***
$140-200

4531
'September' - girl with satchel
Hans H. Hansen
18 cm
In production 1981
***
$140-200

4532
'October' - boy with fruit
Hans H. Hansen
16 cm
In production 1981
***
$140-200

4533
'November' - girl in riding habet
Hans H. Hansen
17 cm
In production 1981
***
$140-200

4534
'December' - boy with sack
Hans H. Hansen
17 cm
In production 1981
***
$140-200

4535
Carpenter
J. M. Nissen
23 cm
In production 1994
***
$150-200

4539
Boy with gourd
J. M. Nissen
12 cm
In production 2000
*
$140-245

4558
Boar
Helen Schou
15 cm
In production 1963
****
$400-500

4559
Sow
Helen Schou
15 cm
In production 1963
****
$400-500

4561
Boar feeding
Helen Schou
18 cm
In production 1963
****
$400-500

4562
Stoat
Jeanne Grut
post 1950
10 cm
In production 1963
****
$150-175

4572
Weasels - pair
Jeanne Grut
post 1950
11 x 17 cm
***
$300-400

4593
Corgi
Jeanne Grut
post 1950
13 cm
In production 1981
***
$125-225

4609
Shetland Pony
Jeanne Grut
post 1950
15 cm
In production 1981
***
$300-400

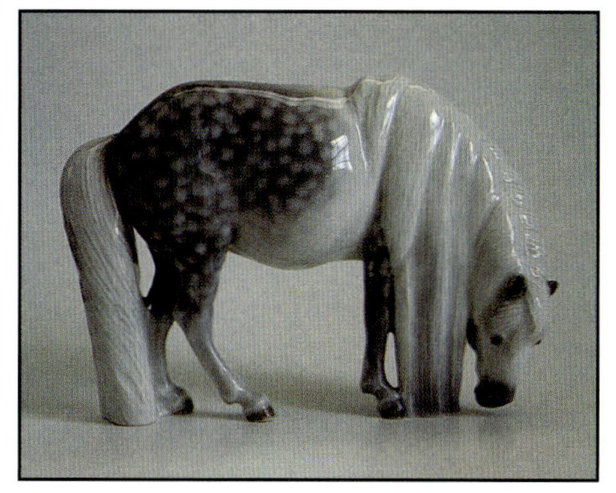

4611
Shetland Pony sitting
Jeanne Grut
post 1950
6 cm
In production 1981
***
$250-350

4616
Basset Hound
Jeanne Grut
post 1950
12 cm
In production 1981
***
$200-300

4631
Girl with cat
John Galster
15 cm
In production 1988
***
$200-250

4638
Poodle
Jeanne Grut
post 1950
18 cm
In production 1963
***
$200-300

4639
'Helena' - girl with mirror
Hans H. Hansen
29 cm
In production 1963
***
$250-350

4642
Ballet dancer
John Galster
17 cm
In production 1981
***
$275-375

4643
Tiger
Jeanne Grut
post 1950
***
$150-250

4645
Butcher
M. Bovenschulte
20 cm
**
$150-200

4647
Baboon & baby
Jeanne Grut
post 1950
8 cm
****
$300-450

4648
Girl dressing hair
John Galster
12 cm
In production 1981
***
$135-180

4649
Teenagers with books
John Galster
11 cm
In production 1981
***
$160-290

4652
Guinea-pig crouching
Jeanne Grut
post 1950
9 x 13 cm
In production 1981
***
$200-300

4653
Foal standing
Jeanne Grut
post 1950
12 cm
In production 1981
***
$190-400

4654
Mink
Jeanne Grut
1959
10 x 17 cm
In production 1981
***
$175-250

4659
Jaguar cub
Jeanne Grut
7 x 21 cm
In production 1981
***
$225-325

4669
Child on back
John Galster
8 x 14 cm
***
$100-200

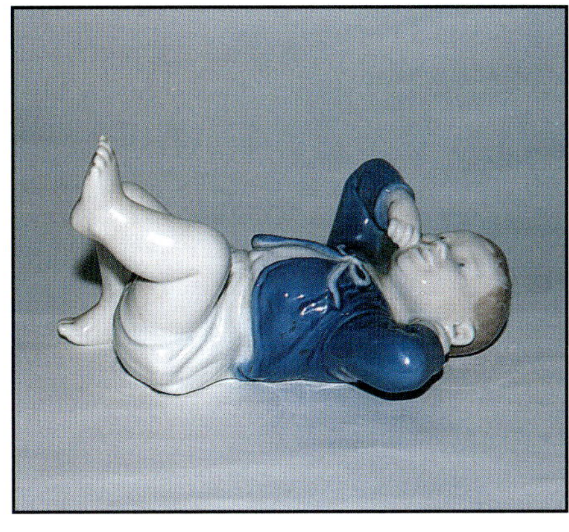

4670
Children reading
John Galster
15 cm
In production 1988
***
$275-375

4676
Rabbit
Jeanne Grut
post 1950
15 cm
In production 1988
***
$150-250

4678
Jersey Cow standing
Jeanne Grut
post 1950
16 cm
***
$250-350

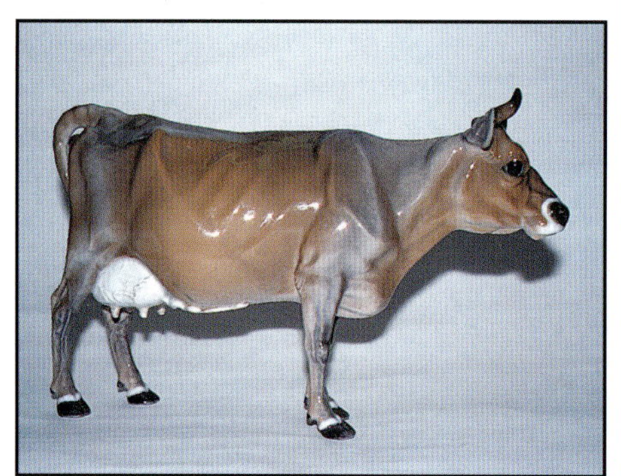

4680
Boy eating apple
John Galster
12.5 cm
****
$150-200

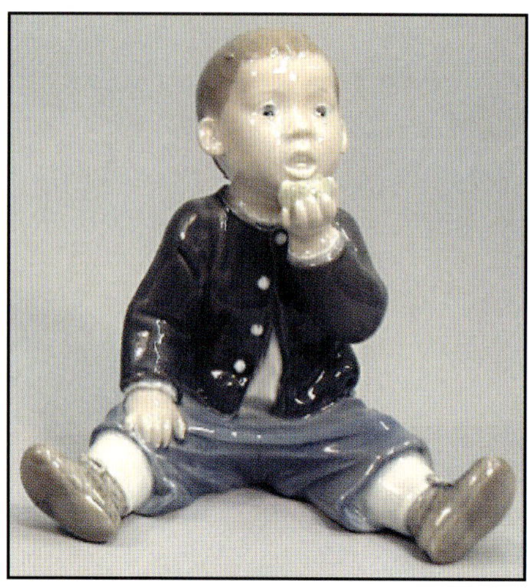

4682
Budgie on gourd
Jeanne Grut
post 1950
14 x 10 cm
In production 1981
***
$150-300

4683
Jersey cow sitting
Jeanne Grut
post 1950
9 x 23 cm
In production 1981
***
$250-350

4687
Tiger & cubs
Jeanne Grut
post 1950
28 x 18 cm
In production 1981
****
$1000-1500

4698
Mare & foal
Jeanne Grut
post 1950
10 x 18 cm
In production 1981
***
$300-450

4703
Nude girl turning
John Galster
9 x 22 cm
***
$240-345

4704
Nude girl lying
John Galster
9 x 18 cm
***
$200-300

4705
Rabbit
Jeanne Grut
post 1950
7 cm
In production 2000
*
$40-70

4726
Goat
Jeanne Grut
post 1950
16 x 19 cm
***
$250-350

4727
Plumber
John Galster
25 cm
In production 1981
**
$200-250

4744
Goat with kid
Jeanne Grut
post 1950
11 x 15 cm
In production 1981
***
$300-400

4746
Hoopoe
Jeanne Grut
post 1950
12 x 17 cm
In production 1981
***
$200-250

4752
Lippizzanner
Jeanne Grut
post 1950
19 cm
In production 1981
***
$250-350

4753
Polar bear
Jeanne Grut
post 1950
20 x 30 cm
In production 1981
***
$300-400

4757
Poodle
Jeanne Grut
post 1950
12 cm
In production 1981
***
$125-170

4760
Kid on rock
Jeanne Grut
post 1950
11 x 8 cm
In production 1981
***
$100-175

4762
Chowchow
Jeanne Grut
post 1950
15 cm
***
$450-550

4780
Polar Bear & Cubs
Jeanne Grut
post 1950
5 x 6 cm
In production 1988
***
$75-125

4783
Puma cub
Jeanne Grut
post 1950
7 cm
***
$125-225

4784
Turkey
Jeanne Grut
post 1950
7 cm
In production 1981
***
$75-125

4787
Pigeon
Jeanne Grut
post 1950
4 cm
In production 1981
***
$40-75

4793
Girl sitting
Hanne Varming
9 cm
In production 1981
***
$100-150

4794
Child in carnival dress
Hanne Varming
15 cm
In production 1981
***
$100-150

4795
Girl with butterfly
Hanne Varming
15 cm
In production 1981
***
$100-150

4796
Girl with trumpet
Hanne Varming
10 cm
In production 1981
***
$100-150

4844
Scotties - black & white
12 cm
*****
$350-450

4852
Danish bird dog
Jeanne Grut
post 1950
15 cm
In production 1981
***
$250-350

4882
Horse
Jeanne Grut
post 1950
In production 1981
***
$75-125

4917
Scottie
Jeanne Grut
post 1950
11 cm
***
$150-200

4918
West Highland White Terrier
Jeanne Grut
post 1950
11 cm
In production 1981
***
$100-150

4952
Old English Sheepdog
Jeanne Grut
post 1950
20 cm
In production 1981
***
$300-400

4989
Footballer
John Galster
18 cm
In production 1981
***
$300-450

5136
Golden Retriever
Jeanne Grut
post 1950
In production 1981
***
$400-550

5154
Kangaroo
Jeanne Grut
post 1950
15 x 12 cm
****
$300-400

5194
Girl with pram
Hanne Varming
16 cm
In production 1981
***
$100-150

5195
Girl with teddy
Hanne Varming
12 cm
In production 1981
***
$100-150

5196
Boy with rocking horse
Hanne Varming
12.5 cm
In production 1981
$100-150

5207
Girl with teddy
Karin Jonzen
***
$125-225

5245
H C Andersen
Hanne Varming
19 cm
In production 1981
***
$200-350

5268
Ballet dancer
Sterett Kelsey
10 cm
In production 1981
***
$150-200

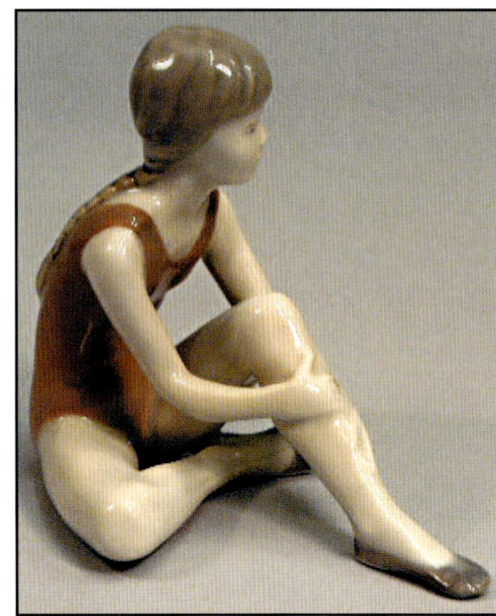

5269
Ballet dancer
Sterett Kelsey
6 cm
In production 1981
***
$150-225

5271
Ballet dancer
Sterett Kelsey
13.5 cm
In production 1981
$150-225

5273
Girl with crown
Sterett Kelsey
22 cm
***
$150-250

5284
Girl with flute
Hanne Varming
15 cm
In production 1981
***
$100-150

5298
Giant Panda
William Timyn
10 cm
In production 1981
****
$500-650

5401
Racoon
William Timyn
11 x 18 cm
In production 1981
***
$300-450

5402
Koala
William Timyn
17.5 cm
In production 1981
***
$300-450

5423
Llasa Apso dog
Jeanne Grut
post 1950
14 cm
In production 1981
***
$250-350

5456
Leaping Salmon

5460
'See no evil'
Hanne Varming
9 cm
In production 1981
***
$100-150

5461
'Hear no evil'
Hanne Varming
13 cm
In production 1981
***
$100-150

5462
'Speak no evil'
Hanne Varming
9 cm
In production 1981
***
$100-150

5598
Girl with deer
Georg Thylstrup
In production 1981
***
$250-350

5599
Kneeling girl
Georg Thylstrup
In production 1981
***
$150-200

5605
'Lucy'
Sterett Kelsey
21 cm
In production 1981
***
$150-200

5651
Boy on rocking horse
Sterett Kelsey
11 cm
***
$150-200

5652
Boy with teddy
Sterett Kelsey
11 cm
***
$150-200

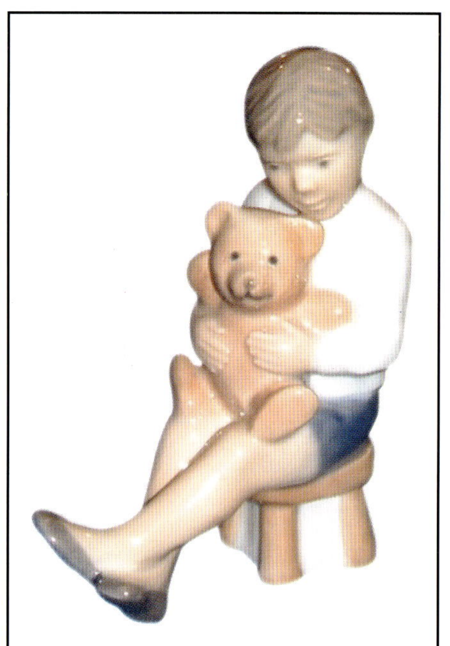

5653
Girl with rabbit
Sterett Kelsey
16 cm
***
$150-200

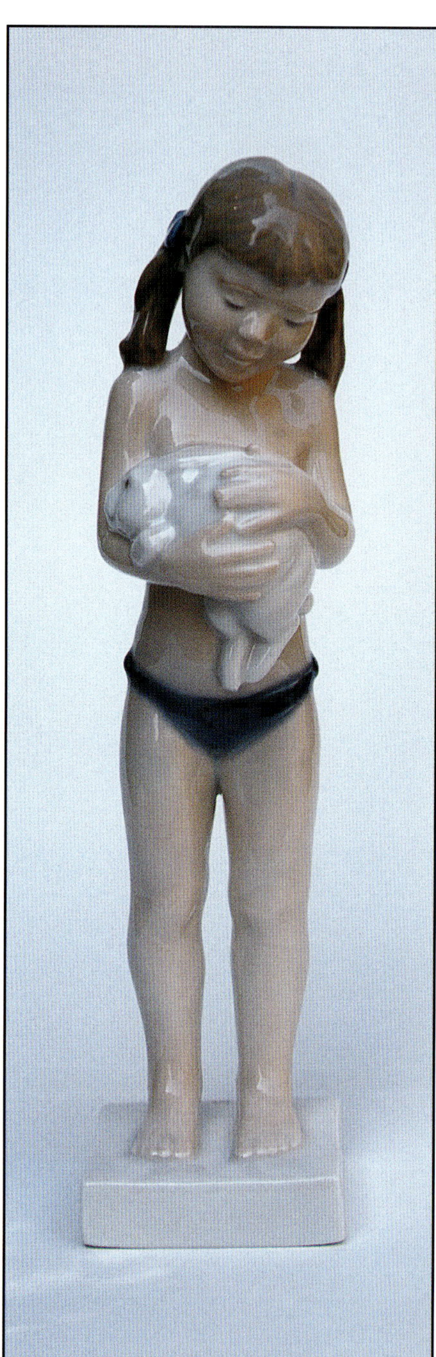

5654
Girl praying
Sterett Kelsey
11 cm
***
$150-200

5655
Girl with teddy
Sterett Kelsey
15 cm
***
$150-200

5656
Girl with snowball
Sterett Kelsey
12 cm
***
$150-200

5657
Footballer
Sterett Kelsey
12 cm
***
$150-200

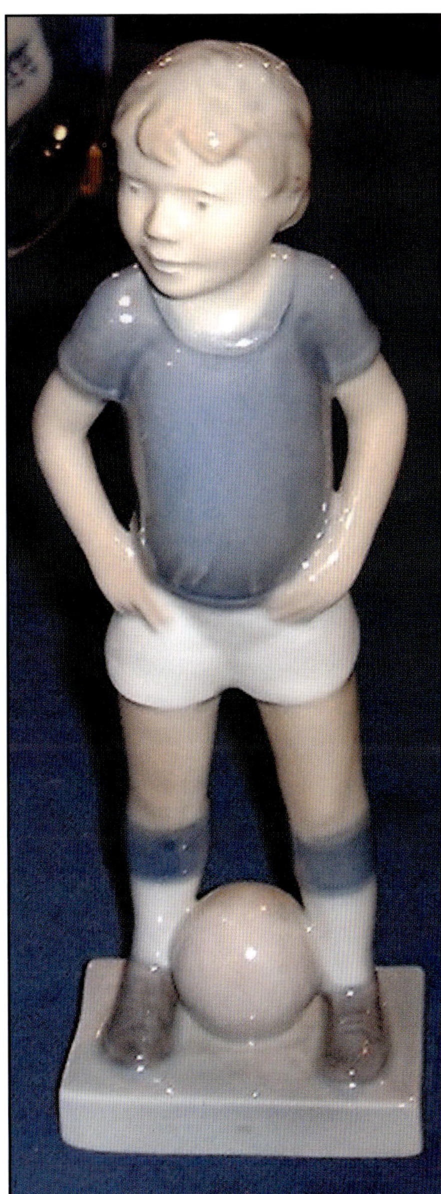

5658
Snowman
Sterett Kelsey
1980
12 cm
In production 2000
*
$50-165

5659
Girl on toboggan
Sterett Kelsey
10 cm
***
$150-200

5660
Boy with dog
Sterett Kelsey
6 x 12 cm
***
$150-200

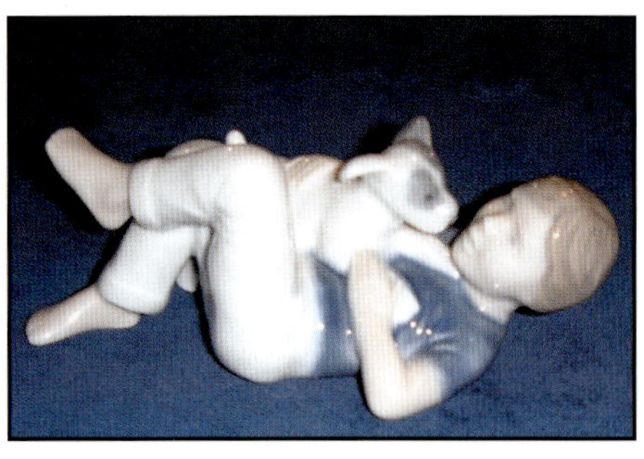

5689
'The Little Mermaid'
Edvard Eriksen
12 cm
In production 2000
*
$125-350

5690
Mare
Jeanne Grut
post 1950
***

5691
Foal
Jeanne Grut
post 1950
8 x 10 cm
***
$150-200

Overglaze and Blanc de Chine

Overglaze painter's color sampler.

12100
Amager Man's Church-going costume
Carl Martin-Hansen
1906
34 cm
Overglaze

12101
Amager Woman's Church-going costume
Carl Martin-Hansen
1906
34 cm
Overglaze

12102
Amager Woman's Market costume
Carl Martin-Hansen
1906
31 cm
Overglaze

12103
Amager Man's Market costume
Carl Martin-Hansen
1906
31 cm
Overglaze

12104
Amager Cook's costume
Carl Martin-Hansen
1906
30 cm
Overglaze

12105
Amager Boy's & Girl's Costume
Carl Martin-Hansen
1907
22 cm
Overglaze

12106
Amager Boy's & Girl's Costume
Carl Martin-Hansen
1907
22 cm
Overglaze

12107
Amager Woman's Mourning Costume
Carl Martin-Hansen
1907
30 cm
Overglaze

12110
'Asia'
1780
32 cm
Reproduction of 18C piece

12114
'America'
1780
28 cm
Reproduction of 18C piece

12118
'Africa'
1780
28 cm
Reproduction of 18C piece

12127
Lady at a table
1780
17.5 cm
Reproduction of 18C piece

12130
'Europe'
1780
27 cm
Reproduction of 18C piece

12134
'Autumn'
1780
21 cm
Reproduction of 18C piece

12136
Flute-Player
1780
17 cm
Reproduction of 18C piece

12138
Blavandshuk
Carl Martin-Hansen
1908
31 cm
Overglaze

12141
'Spring'
1780
19.5 cm
Reproduction of 18C piece

12145
Sea Horse (red sash)
Reproduction of 18C piece

12146
Sea Horse
Reproduction of 18C piece

12151
Hunter group
Overglaze

12159
Mother with children
Overglaze

12162
Hacdrup
Carl Martin-Hansen
1914
30 cm
Overglaze

12163
Hedebo
Carl Martin-Hansen
1909
31 cm
Overglaze

12164
Iceland
Carl Martin-Hansen
1909
32 cm
Overglaze

12165
Laesoe
Carl Martin-Hansen
1909
31 cm
Overglaze

12166
Refsnaes
Carl Martin-Hansen
1909
31 cm
Overglaze

12167
Woman beating baby
35 cm
Reproduction of 18C piece

12171
Skovshoved, Woman
Carl Martin-Hansen
1909
31 cm
Overglaze

12172
Skovshoved, Man & Woman
Carl Martin-Hansen
pre-1910
31 cm
Overglaze

12176
'Summer'
1780
20 cm
Reproduction of 18C piece

12189
'Winter'
1780
19 cm
Reproduction of 18C piece

12208
Man & woman
12 x 14 cm
Reproduction of 18C piece

12210
Ringe
Carl Martin-Hansen
1914
32 cm
Overglaze

12211
Ringkobing
Carl Martin-Hansen
1913
31 cm
Overglaze

12213
Roemoe
Carl Martin-Hansen
1921
33 cm
Overglaze

12214
The Skaw
Carl Martin-Hansen
1921
34 cm
Overglaze

12215
Langeland
Carl Martin-Hansen
1921
32 cm
Overglaze

12216
Falster
Carl Martin-Hansen
1922
32 cm
Overglaze

12217
Bornholm
Carl Martin-Hansen
1922
32 cm
Overglaze

12218
Fanoe
Carl Martin-Hansen
1922
34 cm
Overglaze

12219
Samsoe
Carl Martin-Hansen
1922
32 cm
Overglaze

12220
Als
Carl Martin-Hansen
1922
31 cm
Overglaze

12221
Faroe Islands Woman
Carl Martin-Hansen
1922
31 cm
Overglaze

12222
Faroe Islands Man
Carl Martin-Hansen
1923
32 cm
Overglaze

12223
North Slesvig
Carl Martin-Hansen
1923
32 cm
Overglaze

12224
Greenland Woman
Carl Martin-Hansen
1924
34 cm
Overglaze

12225
Greenland Man
Carl Martin-Hansen
1924
32 cm
Overglaze

12226
Denmark, Jutland, Funen, Sealand
Carl Martin-Hansen
1924
34 cm
Overglaze

12227
Frederiksborg
Carl Martin-Hansen
1925
33 cm
Overglaze

12228
Randers
Carl Martin-Hansen
1925
34 cm
Overglaze

12229
Lolland
Carl Martin-Hansen
1925
33 cm
Overglaze

12230
Horne
Carl Martin-Hansen
1925
33 cm
Overglaze

12231
Mors
Carl Martin-Hansen
1925
33 cm
Overglaze

12237
Cherub with wings
Arno Malinowski
Overglaze/Blanc de Chine

12238
Bali dancer
Arno Malinowski
1924
29 cm
Overglaze/Blanc de Chine

12242
'Girl with the Horn of Gold'
Holger Christensen
1941
22 cm
Overglaze

12406
Stand for 10 overglaze children
Carl Martin-Hansen
Overglaze

12412
Amager Girl
Carl Martin-Hansen
1922
14 cm
Overglaze

12413
Fanoe Girl
Carl Martin-Hansen
1922
14 cm
Overglaze

12414
Amager boy
Carl Martin-Hansen
1922
15 cm
Overglaze

12415
Greenland Girl
Carl Martin-Hansen
1922
14 cm
Overglaze

12416
Faroe Islands Girl
Carl Martin-Hansen
1922
10 cm
Overglaze

12417
Slesvig Girl
Carl Martin-Hansen
1923
10 cm
Overglaze

12418
Sealand Girl
Carl Martin-Hansen
1923
10 cm
Overglaze

12419
Greenland Boy
Carl Martin-Hansen
1923
9 cm
Overglaze

12420
Funen Girl
Carl Martin-Hansen
1923
9 cm
Overglaze

12421
Jutland Girl
Carl Martin-Hansen
1923
9 cm
Overglaze

12428
Crucifix
Arno Malinowski
1923
25 cm
Overglaze/Blanc de Chine

12454
Susanna
Arno Malinowski
1924
27.5 cm
Overglaze/Blanc de Chine

12456
'Market Girl'
Arno Malinowski
Overglaze/Blanc de Chine

12458
Child arms raised ? Buddha
Arno Malinowski
Overglaze/Blanc de Chine

12459
Mermaid
Arno Malinowski
1926
26 cm
Overglaze/Blanc de Chine

12460
Flora
Arno Malinowski
1926
30 cm
Overglaze

12461
Huguenot Girl
Arno Malinowski
1927
20 cm
Overglaze/Blanc de Chine

12463
Iceland
Arno Malinowski
1927
15.5 cm
Overglaze/Blanc de Chine

12466
'Diana'
Arno Malinowski
1928
42 cm
Overglaze

12469
Woman sitting on dog
Arno Malinowski
Overglaze/Blanc de Chine

12470
Bowl
Arno Malinowski
Overglaze

12471
Man kneeling with jackal cape
Arno Malinowski
Overglaze

12473
Vase
Arno Malinowski
1928
80 cm
Overglaze

12475
'Seventeen Years'
Arno Malinowski
1930
14 cm
Overglaze/Blanc de Chine

12477
Cupid on scooter
Arno Malinowski
1931
15.5 cm
Overglaze/Blanc de Chine

12480
Girl sitting
Arno Malinowski
1931
13 cm
Overglaze/Blanc de Chine

12481
Dish - mermaid
Arno Malinowski
10 x 12 cm
Blanc de Chine
***
$200-300

12484
Dish
Blanc de Chine

12485
'Europe'
Arno Malinowski
23 cm
Blanc de Chine
*****
$250-400

12486
'Asia'
Arno Malinowski
Blanc de Chine
*****
$250-400

12487
'Africa'
Arno Malinowski
Blanc de Chine
*****
$250-400

12488
'Australasia'
Arno Malinowski
23 cm
Blanc de Chine
*****
$250-400

12489
'America'
Arno Malinowski
Blanc de Chine
*****
$250-400

12756
Woman with piglets
Arno Malinowski
20 cm
Overglaze/Blanc de Chine

Stoneware

20138
Mammoth
8 cm

20140
Bear standing

20155
Bear

20179
Bear roaring

20182
Hippo

20183
Fawn

20187
Ape

20188
Ape

20193
Bear with cub

20206
Bear sitting

20207
Mammoth
8 cm

20217
Monkey
7 cm

20220
Elephant
Knud Kyhn

02/861

20223
Monkey
7 cm

20225
Elephants

20230
Faun
40 cm

20231
Westies playing
6 cm

20239
Hippopotamus

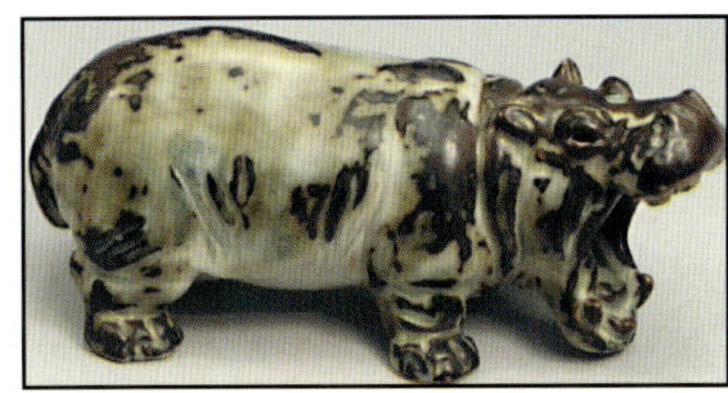

20240
Bears - pair

20242
Bears fighting

20244
Child with cat

20262
Girl with cat

20271
Bear lying on back

20283
Panther

20325
Mammoth

20497
Vase
Blanc de Chine

20498
Flask
Blanc de Chine

20502
Man on horse
Blanc de Chine

20507
Stag
25 cm

20542
Pot - figurines on lid
Blanc de Chine

20569
Vase
Blanc de Chine

20570
Vase
Blanc de Chine

21152
Bear standing

21400
Wild Cat

21406
Bear with cub

21407
Falcon

21410
Duck

21427
Woman in blue dress
Johannes Hedegaard
30 cm

21432
Bear
Knud Kyhn

21433
Bear sitting
Knud Kyhn

21434
Bear
Knud Kyhn

21435
Bear
Knud Kyhn

21436
Bear

21449
Deer - pair

21454
Bear

21516
Horse

21519
Bear standing
Knud Kyhn

21520
Bear lying
Knud Kyhn

21645
Bear standing

21675
Bear sitting

21737
Bear

21818
Bear on back
9.9 cm
In production 2000
*
$50-70

21819
Sparrows - pair
7 cm
In production 1991

21940
Bear lying

22607
Fawn

22653
Rabbit
Jeanne Grut
post 1950

22663
Swan
10 cm

22685
Rabbit
Jeanne Grut
post 1950

22690
Rabbit
Jeanne Grut
post 1950

22692
Rabbit

22693
Rabbit

22714
Elephant
10 cm

22740
Elephant
Jeanne Grut
post 1950

22741
Elephant
Jeanne Grut
post 1950

22745
Bear
Knud Kyhn

22746
Bear
Knud Kyhn

22747
Bear
Knud Kyhn

22748
Bear
Knud Kyhn

22750
Badger

22752
Fox

Chapter 3.
Vases and Other Items

Vases

It will be seen from the main list of the factory production that with about 460 vases, many of which were the earliest underglaze pieces produced, these items formed an important element of design and production. The piece numbers reflect only the shape of each vase and many were produced with several decorative schemes and thus no estimate can be made of the number available.

It will be noted that some numbers have a suffix of a, b, c, etc., and this indicates that the same shape was produced in several different sizes.

We have not attempted to price vases; however, the factors involved in determining vase prices are size, shape, age, and decoration. Many collectors prefer unusual subjects such as bats, mice, insects, and fish to landscapes, flowers, etc.

The most sought after vases are those with a crystalline finish (see numbers 768 and 1215). These can command prices 10 times that of similar underglaze decorated vases.

29, Vase, Arnold Krog, 1887, 18 cms.

29, Vase, Arnold Krog, 1887, 18 cms.

42a, Vase, Arnold Krog, 1887, 5.7 x 7.7 cms.

70, Vase, Arnold Krog, 1892, 38 x 25 cms.

100, Vase, Arnold Krog, 1894, 18.5 x 3.1 x 6.6 cms.

113, Vase, Arnold Krog, 1894, 15.5 x 10 cms.

115, Vase, J. Jacobsen, 1894, 11 x 2.1 x 5 cms.

140, Vase, pre-1910, 22 cms.

162, Vase, 1897, 12 cms.

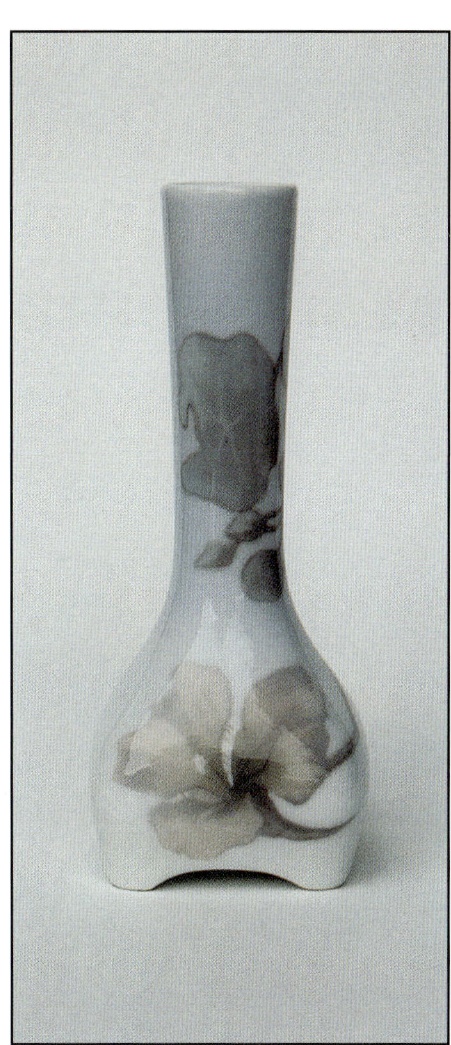

164, Vase, 11 cms.

176, Vase - snake around rim, J. A. Heuch, 1898, 14 cms.

185, Vase, Arnold Krog, 1898, 36 x 10 cms.

209, Vase, Arnold Krog?, pre-1929, 10 x 8.5 x 4 cms.

224, Vase, pre-1910, 10 cms.

257, Vase, pre-1910, 14 cms.

209, Vase, Arnold Krog?, pre-1929, 10 x 8.5 x 4 cms.

225, Vase, pre-1910, 8 cms.

303, Vase – place setting, 4 cms.

328, Vase - butterfly wings, pre-1910, 10 cms.

743, Vase

768 – Crystalline vase by V Engelhardt, developer of the technique.

Crystalline mark for 1910

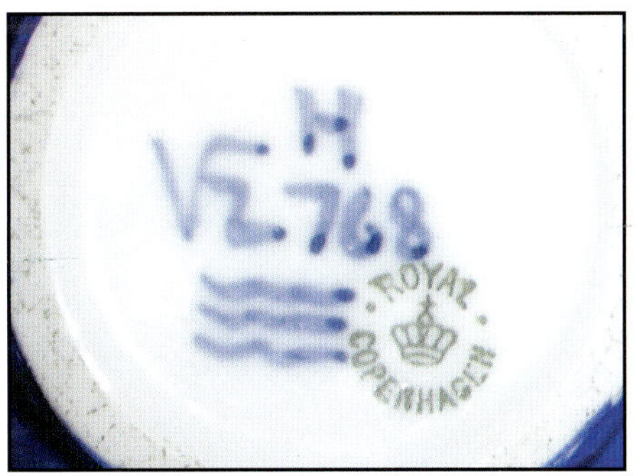

1215, Vase, pre-1929, 27 cms.

2130, Vase, 38 cms.

2490, Vase – crackle

3207, Vase

4426, Vase with stopper

2584, Vase, 19 cms.

3300, Vase

Vase - celadon

Other items

During research sessions, we came across a number of other items produced by the factory. These are of interest, showing the diversity of the factory's output. There are also a few items which either have no number or cannot in any way be identified at present. The factory produced a wide range of advertising materials which are also in demand by serious collectors.

The factory also produced Christmas plates annually since 1908. For the first few years, these plates were in a variety of languages. In addition, there are many commemorative plates and huge numbers of individually produced chargers.

Dealer Sign

Dealer Sign

Dealer Sign

Dealer Sign

Dealer Sign

Flora Danica Dealer Sign

Overglaze Dealer Sign

Dealer Ashtray

54, Lampshade, 10 cms.

1166, Lampshade, 12 cms.

1117, Plate

Wall plate – 1895

260, Bowl – bear

Dish – frog (Celadon)

Fish plaque

Cat – Aluminia

1158, King –Aluminia

1159, Queen – Aluminia

1271, Boy with hat – Aluminia

3280, Budgie – Aluminia

Commemorative faience plate

1775-1975 Mug

10, Dish with lid, Pre-1910, 6 x 14 cms.

310, Dish with lid

2760, Dish – triangular celadon, Jais Nielsen

4505, Dish with lid – snake handles, Arnold Krog?

Teapot with dragonfly handle, Arnold Krog

486a, Inkwell, Part of a garniture of 11 pieces

486d, Garniture – shell, Part of a set of 11

Painted plaque in porcelain frame.

Flora Danica Brooch

Pepper Pot 1900 Paris Exhibition

Woman & Crocodile Blanc de Chine, Number unknown

Girl Kneeling, Number unknown

Coelacanth, Jeanne Grut, 1963, 1143 cms. wide
Largest piece in production. 2 versions – curved or straight.
*
$5000-9400

Bibliography

Bing, Harald. *Bing & Grondahls Porcelaensfabrik 1853 – 1928* Copenhagen: 1928.

Bing & Grondahls Porcellainfabrik Kjobenhavn 1890. Copenhagen: 1890.

Brohan-Museum. *Porzellan Kunst und Design 1889 bis 1939.* Berlin: 1993.

Fredstrup, S B. *Figurer og Andre Plastiske Arbejder* Copenhagen: Gyddendalske Boghandel Nordisk Forlag, 1939.

Grandjean, Bredo L. *Kongelig dansk Porcelain 1884-1980.* Denmark: 1983.

Haydn, Arthur. *Royal Copenhagen Porcelain.* London: T. Fisher Unwin, 1911.

Haydn, Arthur. *Chats on Royal Copenhagen Porcelain.* London: T. Fisher Unwin, 1918.

Heritage, Robert J. *Royal Copenhagen Porcelain Animals and Figurines.* Atglen, Pennsylvania: Schiffer Publishing Ltd., 1997.

Hecht, Robin. *Scandinavian Art Pottery Denmark and Sweden.* Atglen, Pennsylvania: Schiffer Publishing Ltd., 2000.

Lassen, Erik. *En Kobenhavnsk porcelaensfabriks historie.* Denmark: Nyt Nordisk Forlag Arnold Busck A/S 1978.

Museum fur Angewandte Kunst – Koln. *Kopenhagener Porzellan und Steinzeug.* Cologne: 1991.

Rostock, Xenius. *The Royal Copenhagen Porcelain Manufactory and the Faience Manufactory Aluminia past and present.* Copenhagen: 1939.

Royal Copenhagen Porcelain 1775-2000. Copenhagen: Nyt Nordisk Forlag Arnold Busck A/S and the authors, 2000.

Royal Copenhagen Japan Ltd. *Flora Danica 1790 –1990.* Japan: Shigehiko Koshiba, 1989.

Royal Copenhagen Porcelain Manufactory. *The Royal Copenhagen Porcelain Manufactory 1775-1975.* Copenhagen: 1975.

Winstone, H.V.F. *Royal Copenhagen.* London: Stacey International, 1984.

Zachariae, F. *For og nu.* Copenhagen: Alfred G Hassings Forlag, 1920.

Appendix

The first column gives the original Royal Copenhagen number followed by the current number.

RC#	Modern #
259	51
263	52
320	53
321	54
340	55
402	56
422	57
422	57
453	58
473	59
502	60
507	61
510	62
511	63
516	64
518	65
527	66
528	67
532	68
694	69
707	70
727	71
729	72
772	74
779	75
827	76
834	77
856	78
905	79
1019	80
1040	81
1072	82
1081	83
1087	84
1107	85
1108	86
1126	87
1132	88
1137	89
1189	90
1190	91
1192	92
1251	93
1309	95
1311	96
1314	97
1316	98
1317	99
1395	100
1400	101
1407	103
1408	102
1468	104
1518	106
1519	107
1661	109
1691	111
1739	112
1741	113
1769	114
1803	115
1829	116
1858	117
1924	118
1933	119
1934	120
1938	121
1941	122
2033	123
2215	124
2238	125
2257	126
2266	127
2313	129
2374	130
2444	135
2676	136
2769	137
3002	138
3003	139
3140	140
3250	141
3281	142
3468	144
3476	145
3539	146
3556	147
3647	148
4431	150
4502	151
4507	156
4535	152
4539	153
4705	154
4882	174
5658	158
5689	159
7550	073

The original Bing & Grondahl number used before amalgamation in 1987 now has an equivalent Royal Copenhagen number, as shown below.

RC#	B&G#
400	1526
401	1552
402	1567
403	1568
404	1574
405	1582
406	1614
407	1619
408	1624
409	1629
410	1633
411	1635
412	1636
413	1642
414	1656
415	1670
416	1684
417	1692
418	1713
419	1728
420	1744
421	1745
422	1747
423	1770
424	1779
425	1785
427	1790
428	1808
429	1809
430	1810
431	1821
432	1826
433	1857
434	1875
435	1876
436	1885
437	1902
438	1909
439	1926
440	1951
441	1953
442	1954
443	2017
444	2026
445	2037
446	2161
447	2162
448	2168
449	2169
450	2172
451	2179
452	2181
453	2206
454	2207
455	2208
456	2209
457	2210
458	2217
459	2218
460	2225
465	2233
466	2246
467	2247
468	2262
473	2298
474	2310
477	2316
478	2324
479	2329
481	2481
482	2482
483	2483
484	2484
485	2485
486	2353
487	2354
488	2355
489	2370
490	2372
491	2379
492	2385
493	2425
494	2426
495	2435
499	2453
500	2454
502	2366
503	2235
504	2504
505	2505
506	2506
507	2507
508	2508
509	2509
510	2510
511	2511
514	2514
515	2515
516	2516
517	2517
525	2525
527	2527
530	2530
532	2532
533	2533
535	2535
536	2536
537	2537
538	2538
539	2539
540	2540
541	2468
542	2471
543	2472
544	2544
546	2546
547	2547
548	2548
549	2549
558	2558
560	2560
561	1721
562	2562
564	2564
565	2565
573	2573
575	2575
576	2576

Index

I

J

K

L

M

N

O

P

R

S

T

V

W